Oxford Studies in Social Mobility

Working Papers 1

THE ANALYSIS OF
SOCIAL MOBILITY
METHODS AND APPROACHES

EDITED BY

KEITH HOPE

CLARENDON PRESS · OXFORD

1972

Oxford University Press, Ely House, London W. 1

GLASGOW NEW YORK TORONTO MELBOURNE WELLINGTON
CAPE TOWN IBADAN NAIROBI DAR ES SALAAM LUSAKA ADDIS ABABA
DELHI BOMBAY CALCUTTA MADRAS KARACHI LAHORE DACCA
KUALA LUMPUR SINGAPORE HONG KONG TOKYO

PRINTED IN GREAT BRITAIN
AT THE UNIVERSITY PRESS, OXFORD
BY VIVIAN RIDLER
PRINTER TO THE UNIVERSITY

ACKNOWLEDGEMENTS

This collection of papers is the firstfruits of an extensive and continuing piece of collaborative research by a group* of Oxford sociologists. Although, like the other contributors to the collection, he takes full responsibility for the views he presents, the editor would like to express his gratitude to his colleagues for the illumination and stimulation which he has received from them in formal and informal discussions. In addition to the authors whose work appears in this volume he would like to mention his debt to Mrs. Jean Floud and Dr. A.H. Halsey for the clarity with which they have elucidated the concepts, theories and problems of social stratification and social mobility. If he has failed to profit from the expositions or to imitate the lucidity of his colleagues the fault rests with him.

Every member of the Oxford group joins with the editor in taking this opportunity of recording their indebtedness to Professor O. Dudley Duncan, whose six-month stay with them in Oxford, and whose continuing interest, encouragement and criticism have done so much to further work whose initial impetus was in good measure derived from his outstanding contribution to the study of the phenomena of social mobility.

We wish also to thank the Warden and Fellows of Nuffield College for initially sponsoring the work and providing it with a physical base, and the Social Science Research Council which has provided the bulk of the finance.

* In the period during which these working papers were being written the members of the group were Mr. P. Duncan-Jones, Mrs. J.E. Floud, Mr. J.H. Goldthorpe, Dr. A.H. Halsey, Dr. K. Hope, Mr. K.I. Macdonald, and Mr. J.M. Ridge.

CONTENTS

TAKING THE METAPHOR SERIOUSLY

The members of the Oxford Group for the study of Social Mobility have set themselves initially a twofold task: the detection of trends in intergenerational social mobility within the society of England and Wales, and the comparison of the processes of occupational achievement in British and in American society. In its first aspect our task is to repeat the enquiry reported by Professor David Glass and his colleagues in *Social mobility in Britain,* and in its second aspect our task is to replicate the enquiry reported by Professor Peter Blau and Professor Dudley Duncan in *The American occupational structure.*

In seeking to achieve the highest possible degree of empirical comparability with these two important enquiries, we have set ourselves the problem of relating the rather different sociological assumptions which underly the two sets of data. The English study was undertaken twenty years ago in a society in which it was still possible to undertake an analysis on the assumption that a man belongs to a discriminable so-called 'social class' or status group, membership of which tends to be life-long and to have implications for his life-chances, his values and norms, his style of life, his deference behaviour and his social perceptions. The American study emanates from a society which appears to require a different assumption, namely that the desirable things in life can be conceived to be distributed in proportion to men's degree of success in running an economic and social race, albeit one in which the starting positions are not equal. Though their relative usefulness may change in time and space, the two approaches are not incompatible; both employ occupation as the key to status or achievement. By deploying them both in a single study we hope to cast light on the relations between them and on their relative strengths and weaknesses for the exploration of social processes.

This volume of working papers, whose primary concern is to explore and, if possible, advance the state of the technical apparatus for the study of mobility, attempts to relate the two kinds of technique appropriate to the two approaches. The substantive enquiry upon which we are about to embark will, it is hoped, shed light on the sociological implications and relative value of the two approaches in the study of British society in the 'seventies. The papers, all of which have been written before the main enquiry has begun, contain the first tentative attacks on various issues which have emerged from our reading of the work of our precursors in this field. If the contents at times seem to be unduly technical and the sociological conclusions meagre, we can only emphasize the preparatory nature of these studies and point to the fact that often we have been developing and applying fairly powerful techniques to data which have been presented by previous workers in ways

1

which are less than ideal for our purposes.* It is evident that, if technique is to be an adequate servant of sociology, then the needs of the various analytical methods must be clearly recognised and allowed for in the collection and organisation of data. And as a salutary illustration of this view we may cite the impressive exploration of the method of path analysis which preceded the successful deployment of that technique in *The American occupational structure*.

In the first of the following papers the authors engage the problem of what people are doing when they rank occupations according to social standing. The attack is mounted on two fronts: first we make a conceptual analysis of the notion of prestige, and secondly we apply a powerful analytical technique to a small body of purely illustrative data, which was not collected for the purpose of deriving quantitative results, but as a vehicle for the elaboration of a set of concepts, systematically related to one another, which adequately map the field of occupational status.

This opening paper, 'Occupational grading and occupational prestige', is an example of how, in principle, we would like to marry techniques to sociology. Often a technique will serve simply as a means of answering a problem posed, quite independently, by the student of social mobility. Examples of the employment of analytical methods in this way occur in the paper. However, in order to overcome the ever-present danger that technical limitations will set bounds to the substantive questions which we might pose and, further, in order to exploit the power of analytical processes to sharpen and clarify our theorizing, we have sought to bend the analytical methods to our purposes and to use them as a resource for elaborating and systematizing our thinking about social stratification.

Halting analytical methods have, in the past, hindered the progress of social enquiry. Today it might be supposed that the danger is of technical over-elaboration, and a glance through some of the following contributions may lead the cursory reader to believe that they belong to the dry-as-dust school of 'methodology' for its own sake. This is a charge which we would repudiate, since our criterion of a useful method is that it makes sociological sense, if possible producing new sociological questions (and the conceptual framework within which they may be answered) which are statable in plain prose, but which are unlikely to have been clearly formulated and systematically tackled in the absence of the technical scaffolding.

Metaphor into model

As some of the following papers show, we have been exploring

* It is hoped that a second volume of working papers, containing analyses and re-analyses of more directly sociological interest, will be prepared and published at a later date.

uses of multivariate analysis in the description of social mobility, the plotting of the space in which it occurs, the determination of the channels through which it flows, and the constraints upon, and facilities for movement which may be inferred.

The remaining sections of this introduction are devoted to a conceptualization of the problem of social mobility in terms of 'stratification space'. It is not suggested that this conceptualization is the only one possible, nor is it implied that we shall make no attempt in our future investigations to construct and apply others. Nevertheless it is a formulation which arises out of figures of speech universally employed by sociologists when they discuss social mobility, and it can be shown to be capable of comprehensive and fruitful development. In fact, it lays claim to the status of a model but it makes no claim to be *the* model. It would, indeed, at this stage of our work, be premature to assert that this model is in some sense prior to or more basic than others, or that it provides a necessary framework within which more limited models can be deployed for the exploration of local phenomena.

The conceptualization should not be regarded as a collective statement by members of the Oxford group for the study of social mobility, but rather as an attempt by one of its members, with the encouragement of others, to integrate and render systematic definitions, propositions and problems involved in the study of mobility. This attempt is made in the following sections which show how a collection of images may be systematized into a coherent framework, which can then be schematized as a full-blown model or set of models.

Stratification space

The idea that individuals or social collectivities exist in a 'stratification space' in which they lie at certain 'social distances' from one another is not new. It is, however, possible, using multivariate methods, to expand an idea which has up to the present been little more than a series of literary images, into a coherent framework for empirical facts which has the advantage that it is relatively theory-neutral and so allows the student to stand back and judge the extent of fit between fact and theory.

A stratification space may be conceived of as a space of up to k dimensions spanned by k correlated axes. Basically, one may conceive of a 'class' space which represents the material circumstances of individuals or families by plots of their economic positions. In addition, one may envisage what might be termed a 'subcultural' space, within which may be plotted manifestations of individuals' values and norms as they are expressed, within economic constraints, in particular styles of life.

The appropriate axes of both spaces will, of course, vary according to the society studied. Choice of axes is a matter for observation, sociological theorizing, and empirical trial. In a western urban industrial society obvious axes of the class or economic space are wealth, education and qualifications, income, authority and responsibility at work, and political power and influence. These purport to measure an individual's relative power and advantage in the context of his market and work situations in terms of the contributions he can bring to the economy and the monetary and other rewards which are vouchsafed to him. It may well prove desirable to multiply the number of axes, distinguishing, for example, between different forms of property, between current income and income expectations, between authority and autonomy in work-roles, and so on.

In the case of subcultural space the choice of axes is likely to present considerable operational difficulties; but, theoretically, what is required is the specification of a set of dimensions spanning the range of attitudinal and behavioural variation in terms of which life styles are usually conceived—for example, patterns of consumption, of use of leisure time, conjugal, parent-child and wider kinship relations; modes of participation in political and 'public' life generally, and so on. The existence of clusters in the subcultural space would indicate the existence of discrete life-styles and quasi status-groups (i.e. social collectivities whose members might associate on a basis of social equality) which might be supposed to be the carriers of differing sets of norms and values.

Clearly, multivariate methods are required to handle spatial conceptions of the kind in question, even in the limited and mutilated form which may be the best we can achieve in research practice. In the sense of the term to which we wish to adhere, *social* mobility can be said to occur only if (a) the movement of an individual (or other unit) in class space is paralleled by a movement of some kind in subcultural space, and (b) the movement is from one identifiable collectivity—or stratum—to another, and (c) the movement involves some degree of change in the subcultural position of associates (the acquisition of associates in new positions, a decline in the relational importance of old associates, or the simultaneous subcultural movement of old associates).* These characteristics of social mobility follow from our conception of a social class as a collectivity with associational

---

* In other words, social mobility is to be seen as entailing some degree of subcultural discontinuity and also relational discontinuity (the spatial representation of social association is discussed in a later section of this introduction).

It is possible, of course, that discontinuity would be actually experienced by individuals at a local rather than societal level—that is, in the context of a particular employment situation or a structure of status groups or networks of limited extent. As one's concern moves from the distributive to the relational aspects of stratification, a corresponding shift from a macro- to a micro-sociological perspective is for many purposes necessary.

properties formed by concomitant clustering in the economic and sub-cultural spaces. The nature of the concomitance is, indeed, not speci-fied, and it is conceivable that differing relations between the dual elements of the spatial representation might form a basis for a typology of collectivities.

From the point of view of the model presented here, a necessary (but not sufficient) condition for the existence of strata is the exist-ence of a certain kind of distribution of points (each point representing an individual or group such as a family): namely that they tend to ag-gregate into clusters separated by relatively empty space. These clusters need not necessarily be ordered in a straightforward linear fashion, one on top of the other; the relative extent of inequality and diversity among them may be measured by the ratio of vertical disper-sion to all other dispersion, where the vertical axis is simply the mean or general factor of the correlated stratification axes. If such a distri-bution were to be found in the class space, it would then be an empiri-cal matter, though a difficult one, to determine the relations between the clusters in this space and the distribution of their constituent individuals in the analogously conceived subcultural space.*

Studies of the dimension of occupational 'prestige', or as we would prefer to call them, studies of the general desirability or 'goodness' of occupations (see the paper by Goldthorpe and Hope which follows this introduction) indicate that, when persons are projected on to this di-mension the result is a fairly smooth, unimodal distribution. The same is true of the axis representing income. It is not, however, legitimate to argue from the nature of the distribution along axes to the nature of the joint distribution in the space as a whole. This point deserves to be laboured because it appears not to have been adequately appreciated by many theorists of stratification. The angle between any two axes may be adjusted so that its cosine is equal to the product-moment cor-relation between the variables which the axes represent. Thus if two variables are uncorrelated the axes representing them will make an angle of 90° (cosine = 0), if they correlate 0·71 the angle will be 45° (cosine = 0·7071), and so on. So long as the axes of a simple two-dimensional space are not identical it is possible for two or more dis-crete clusters of points to exist in the space as a whole even though, when the individual points are projected on to either axis they form a continuous unimodal distribution.†

* The use of the term 'class' in its Weberian sense appears to imply the existence of clusters with distinguishable relations to the sources of power, wealth and income, and the use of 'subcultural' appears to imply the existence of clusters with distinguishable modes of expression of values. The employment of the two adjectives to qualify 'space' is intended to imply only that, *if such clusters exist*, they will manifest themselves in the respective spaces.

† This is true whatever the shape of the clusters. If the axes are very highly correlated the scope for the occurrence of this apparent paradox is reduced.

In our re-analyses we have not been able to tackle the prior problem of the distribution of individuals in a stratification space simply for want of data. In the first paper, however, we provide an illustrative analysis of data at one remove from the real world, when we construct a typology of *perceptions* of the standing of *occupations* on various dimensions by means of numerical taxonomy.

Another question which we have not dealt with is the adequacy of occupation as an index of social-class position.* But in this area too taxonomic analysis has been used to furnish indirect evidence of the relevance of occupation to class. The paper 'Quantifying constraints on social mobility' contains a taxonomic analysis of the mobility-relations of census occupational categories which suggests a modification of an earlier interpretation of the American social structure. It would be desirable, however, in the first instance, to investigate the relations between occupation and social class independently of mobility patterns.

One of the failures of the sociology of stratification has been its refusal to push its imagery to its logical conclusion. Sorokin, for example, makes considerable play with images of social distance, and the height, gradation and profile of occupational stratification.† Writing his first edition of *Social mobility* half a century ago he may be forgiven for not realising the analytical potential of his analogies. It is now time to take them quite literally and to clarify the problems, if not plan the collection of data, by geometrical explication. The clarification will be fruitful if it can do no more than indicate the sort of questions which theorists can and ought to ask about a changing society.

Social mobility and social change

It is sometimes suggested that the picture which has been drawn, of individuals crowded into clusters or strata, is one which may have portrayed British society before, say, the first world war but not one which applies today. It is also supposed that one of the many factors leading to the presumed loosening of clusters is a presumed increase in the extent of lifetime or intergenerational movement of individuals about the stratification space. If such an increase has in fact occurred since the first world war, there is good reason to suppose that it has continued since the second and, in particular, since Professor Glass and his co-workers collected their data in 1949. One of our major aims, therefore, is to assess the degree to which social mobility has changed, whether in frequency of occurrence, distances travelled, or paths

* For the importance of this question see Floud J.E. (1952). Social stratification in Denmark (review article). *Brit. J. Sociol.*, 3, 173–7.

† See the chapter headings in Sorokin, P.A. (1927). *Social mobility*. Harper, New York.

traversed; and the papers 'Quantifying constraints on social mobility' and 'MDSCAL and distances between socio-economic groups' concern themselves with techniques for assessing the observed relations among categories in the extent and nature of movement.

The emphasis which this introduction has so far placed on social mobility or movement between strata rather than on individual achievement in an occupational structure may seem old-fashioned and out-of-place in a study which seeks comparability with the work of Blau and Duncan on achievement, measured in terms of occupational 'prestige' and, to some extent, the level of personal income reached. In particular it may be argued that factors in modern society are tending to change and, perhaps, to simplify the stratification space. It may be said that one cannot meaningfully speak of changes in social mobility because the nature of the mobility itself is changing from social to occupational even as the amount of mobility increases. Underlying this suggestion is the supposition that occupation is increasingly becoming a key to all other economic factors, which are themselves becoming more tightly associated with one another.

An outstanding advantage of the geometrical model of stratification is that each kind of social change has its analogue in the model. One may distinguish, for example, changes in the degree of stratum-differentiation (modelled by the individuation of clusters, i.e. the clearness of their separation and their compactness) from changes in the amount of movement of individuals between strata. One may also distinguish between rigidity or intergenerational occupational inheritance in the sense of absence of movement, and intergenerational transmission of status in the sense that some paths between clusters are trodden more frequently than others (this distinction is discussed in some detail in the paper on the quantification of constraints on mobility). One may further consider a set of clusters as a system of exchange which may be in bilateral or multilateral equilibrium in the senses, respectively, that movements between any two clusters A and B are in balance or that movements into and out of any and every cluster are in balance.

It is not only not necessary, but it may for some purposes be undesirable, to *define* extent of stratification in terms of degrees of movement of individuals. The model allows us to hold the two concepts apart and to manipulate either one of them alone or both together.

There are in fact many kinds of change which the stratification system can undergo and the model allows, indeed compels, us to examine them systematically. It is a matter for empirical sociological investigation how far one kind of change tends to accompany another, while theory and the descriptive investigation of symbolic significance may reveal the extent to which concomitance indicates causal relationship. While a person's position in the economic space could scarcely fail to place constraints upon his subcultural position the model leaves open the question of how far his economic position is a consequence of his values or life-style.

If we begin by considering a society in which clusters of individuals do in fact occur we can envisage low or high degrees of movement between clusters, whether intergenerationally or intragenerationally. The clusters may be quite stable whatever the degree of movement, provided that individual mobile persons conform to the conditions of the aggregate in which they find themselves. Clusters may shrink or expand, come into being or disappear, as for instance did numerous trades with distinct modes of relation to industrial society during the English industrial revolution, without greatly altering the overall appearance of the stratification space. The waxing and waning of a cluster, in the sense of variation in its relative or absolute membership over time, must be distinguished from its spatial expansion or shrinkage.*

The question may be posed of whether the elements of the stratification space are positions or incumbents. The answer to this question is equivocal, and quite deliberately so. If the space were simply the manifold (multidimensional continuum) of all possible positions then the axes would, for ease of reference, be drawn at right angles to one another. What has been suggested, however, is that the actual distribution of incumbents should determine the angles between axes, so that the space is transformed as the distribution varies. This is a useful device for signalling the difference between changes within a constant structure and changes of the structure itself. Both the conservative and the radical are interested in the point at which the structure begins to change and in the causes and nature of such change. The model is useful in considering the question of how far rigidity and fluidity within a structure promote or retard changes in the structure.

The extent and patterns of mobility may differ in different parts of the space: the paper 'Quantifying constraints on social mobility' shows how differential mobility may be measured and patterns compared. In a highly mobile society an individual may have kin and affines in a number of widely separated collectivities and the additive or interactive effects of the two factors, mobility and social heterogeneity of family, provide a rich field for speculation.

The paper 'Social mobility and fertility' provides some evidence for an 'effect' of mobility as such on the number of children a man has.

---

* In reading this introduction John Goldthorpe commented that the *embourgeoisement* thesis may be represented as an upward enlargement of the higher working class strata with a concomitant movement in the subcultural space. This exemplifies a point which I make below in the general discussion of what constitutes an effective model, namely that it should fit comfortably in the hands of research workers other than its author. Among other useful comments John Goldthorpe has also raised the question of the nature of a stratification space which is dealt with in the following paragraph of the text.

It may be noted in passing that we make a clear distinction between
mobility and 'status inconsistency', whether the inconsistency takes
the form of a lack of equilibration among the various aspects of a man's
status or whether it refers to heterogeneity of status among members of
an extended family. Mobility always implies comparison of different
moments in time while inconsistency refers to concurrent measurement
of different aspects of status. The model distinguishes the two concepts
with complete perspicuity. Mobility means movement of a point.
Inconsistency means the degree of displacement of a point from the
vertical axis. Lenski has correctly indicated that complete status
crystallization may be defined as being right on this axis.*

The subcultural space may be regarded as a kind of sociological
schematization of the class space. In so far as distinct clusters of
individuals or families within the latter are empirically associated with
distinct styles of life, they can be regarded as social collectivities
within which status groups or networks are likely to be constituted, at
least at a local level. The paper 'Marriage markets in the stratification
system' applies to the field of marriage the same processes of quantification as have been applied to intergenerational mobility and it reveals
a remarkably similar pattern of status relationships. The appendix to
the paper 'MDSCAL and distances between socio-economic groups'
indicates the desirability of simulating these social processes by generating tables from distributions with specified properties. We have as yet
done very little work in this potentially fruitful area.

Two important ingredients of life styles are child-rearing practice
and probable mode of secondary socialization. In so far as individuals
tend to remain stationary in the economic class space, one would
expect distinctive modes of socialization to reinforce the individuation
of strata. But an increase in the amount and extent of movement in the
class space will, we may surmise, have the effect of diffusing the
various value systems (in so far as these are instilled early and not
modified by subsequent life history) about the society. As well as
reducing the predictability of social behaviour by increasing its heterogeneity within social classes, this may react upon individuals' economic
position by modifying the kinds of choice which they make among the
components of material well-being. At the same time rising real incomes and the existence of a mass-market make the formation and
maintenance of socially distinctive (as opposed to idiosyncratic) life
styles more difficult, and so would-be status groups are frustrated in
their endeavours at producing peculiar life-styles. The model is
invaluable as a framework within which the course of these complex
feedback processes may be traced.

* Lenski, G.E. (1954). 'Status crystallization: a non-vertical dimension of social status'.
Amer. Sociol. Rev. 19, 405-13.

A society need not be uniformly ordered into collectivities. It is conceivable, for example, that in a society in transition the higher clusters—that is, social strata—will begin to disintegrate before the lower, perhaps because there is net upward mobility with consequent diffusion of values, perhaps because possession of greater resources enables individuals to assert their independence of general norms, perhaps because at the higher levels there is greater scope for a trade-off between the various aspects of stratification enabling individuals to achieve quite idiosyncratic balances of prestige, income, autonomy, etc. In general, one might expect economically constituted classes which have high inflows from diverse cultural backgrounds to show the greatest tendency to disintegration in socio-cultural terms.

If we consider now a society where strata as defined by our spatial model do not exist, or exist only residually for the old, the disabled, the unemployed and perhaps the very wealthy, it is easy to see how two societies might differ in the overall distribution of points, and how the nature of the distribution might change in a single society over time. The processes of individual achievement are readily modelled as the movements of individual points. To take an example which employs one axis of the class or economic space and one axis of subcultural space: one can conceive of a person whose occupational career starts in the lower half of the distribution and whose occupational prestige (in the strict sense, as defined by relationships of derogation, acceptance and deference) is consistently greater than his income as he ascends vertically until, in mid-career, he switches to the opposite displacement, moving more swiftly up the income axis while remaining stationary on the prestige axis. Finally, an accident, redundancy or retirement brings him down into the lower half of the distribution with prestige even lower than his income. Any number of such lifetime occupational profiles might be constructed and it may be found that there is a tendency for some profiles to occur frequently and others only rarely. Different typical patterns of movement may also be associated with different starting points, and all this within a distribution of points which is cross-sectionally uniform over time.

It is easy to fall into the habit of thinking of social mobility and lifetime occupational profile as a fairly clear-cut progression from 'origins' to 'destinations', whether the movement is monotonic in one direction, or a parabolic return to base, or describes any other simple curve. But, in fact, it is reasonable to suppose that there is a considerable amount of change of level in the short term which requires us to speak of the overall pattern at any one time as a cross-sectional resultant rather than as a distribution of destinations. In other words, from the individual point of view, considerable short-term instability may exist. The practical difficulty which faces us when we try to quantify this instability is the prblem of separating errors of measurement in recording stratification position from actual shifts in position. And following upon this is the further problem of distinguishing between changes which are, from the point of view of mobility research, random and those which are systematic.

One might hazard a guess that a well-conducted enquiry can achieve a reliability of perhaps 0·9 in the assessment of stratification position on a single axis. It may be that the 'test-retest' correlation of position over a period of, say, two to three years is of the order of 0·75 or 0·8. Correcting this guess for our estimated unreliability gives us a true correlation of 0·8 to 0·9, which would imply that about 25 per cent of the variance of position two or three years hence connot be predicted from knowledge of present status. But knowledge of present status is itself only a cross-sectional snapshot and does not take account of the systematic or dynamic elements which transform a series of movements into a career. Unless evidence is made available which disconfirms the above guesses and shows that stability is higher than they suppose, it seems advisable to assume that there is a good deal of movement in the stratification space over the short term. How much of this is random, and whether the proportion of random to systematic movement varies from level to level, are questions which we are certainly not in a position to answer.

Axes of the subcultural space.

The difficulties of measuring life-styles may be such that many proposed axes of the subcultural space have to be represented by sets of two-valued 'dummy variables'. The paper 'Social mobility, canonical scoring and occupational classification' discusses a method of handling such a situation.

Although the technical difficulties are surmountable any empirical research in this area runs the risk of trivializing the choice of subcultural variables. It is tempting to ignore difficult questions of categorizing and assessing, say, child-rearing, and to employ relatively simple check-lists of consumer goods and possessions. Since much of the interest of the subcultural space lies in its character as a mirror of values and norms it is as well to consider whether a rather unreliable measure of a more central cultural characteristic should not be preferred to many 'hard' data on peripheral and transient consumption behaviour. Within the field of consumption it is arguable that choices among alternatives, all of which are inexpensive by almost any standards, may be better and more enduring discriminators among life-styles than choices which imply considerable expenditure and seem to the consumer to have more status-relevance.

It seems probable that, whatever axes are employed, the modes of life mapped in the subcultural space will bear only loose and changing relations to the values which they express, and that material circumstances impose constraints upon the symbolic expression of values. Thus a movement in the subcultural space may reflect not so much a change of values as a change in the degree or nature of the constraints on possible ways of expressing those values. One can imagine a particular value system manifesting itself in the subcultural space not as a discrete cluster of persons but as a set or range of clusters whose position varies with the material basis of the life-style. In so far as a style of life is pursued as distinctive from or conforming to others, changes in the reference group may lead to changes in that style.

Structural change and structural comparisons

Having looked at movements between collectivities, changes in the collectivities themselves, and changes in overall distribution and movements of individuals, we may now relax the implicit assumption of consistency of variances and covariances among the various axes. In fact two societies, such as Britain and the United States, may differ in the extent of correlation between any two axes, in the variance of any particular axis, and in the relative variances of two axes. Variance is a particularly difficult concept to handle in stratification studies because it is not clear how the axes should be scaled. It may be argued for example that, measured in terms of a 'just-acceptable increment', the subjectively appropriate scaling for income is logarithmic. This is one of the basic problems which must be faced if the geometrical model is to be employed in empirical research. But the practical difficulties of applying the framework to sociological facts should not be allowed to deter us from attempting to exploit the possibilities of this powerful and elegant conceptual tool.

Some sociologists, particularly in the United States, tend to suppose that the stratification space is simplifying in the sense that the correlations among the axes are increasing. The inference is that the variances of some dimensions of the space are diminishing and one or two may virtually disappear, implying that one or more axes are denotatively, if not connotatively, identical with some other axis or combination of axes. Writing elsewhere* John Goldthorpe has cited evidence which runs counter to this view. In addition there is a technical reason for suggesting that some correlations may actually be declining.

For example, if we accept as tenable the proposition that income is becoming more symmetrically distributed[†] with the growth of middle-

---

* Goldthorpe, J.H. (1964) 'Social stratification in industrial society' In *The development of industrial societies* (ed. P. Halmos). *Sociol. Rev. Monogr.* No. 8. Reprinted in *Class status and power* (2nd edn.) (ed. R. Bendix and S.M. Lipset). Free Press of Glencoe, New York, 1966.

[†] This does not imply (nor does it contraindicate) any increase in equality.

range occupations, and if we accept likewise that the distribution of authority has been and remains more skewed than that of income, with many people being in positions of little or no authority and only relatively few holding positions of command, then the maximum possible degree of correlation between the two variables will actually have declined.

The general proposition which underlies this inference deserves to be expressed as clearly as possible because it is almost universally neglected in spite of its obvious importance. Two distributions can display perfect correlation only if they are identical in shape (irrespective of whether they are skewed or symmetrical) and as the shapes of two distributions diverge so does the maximum possible correlation between them decline. (An interpretative problem which this technical fact poses is discussed in detail in the paper 'Quantifying constraints on social mobility'.)

Comparable problems arise in the interpretation of path analyses. A path analysis does not make any assumptions about the separate or joint distributions of the variables anterior to a particular posterior variable, but differential skew in the variables can lead to difficulties in the interpretation of path coefficients. For example, the variable 'father's terminal age of education' and the variable 'son's terminal age of education' which, in Britain, have high and similar degrees of skew tend, for that reason alone, to have a higher correlation with one another than either has with other variables. It could be misleading to perform, let us say, a path analysis on British data including these two variables, and compare it with the analogous American path analysis where education would be more symmetrically distributed and so would have a higher limit to the correlation with other symmetrical (or opposite-skewed) variables. In our own work on social mobility we propose to take the precaution of computing maximum product-moment correlations for given marginal distributions of variables. General problems arising in the interpretation of path analyses are discussed in the paper 'Path analysis: supplementary procedures'.

It is not suggested that path analysis cannot be applied to social mobility data. On the contrary, deployed on a basis of reasonable sociological assumptions, as it is in *The American occupational structure*, it provides valuable, quantified insights into the channels and determinants of mobility. As a *comparative* technique, however, it is limited both by the problems of skew already mentioned (and these problems are not merely technical, since they reflect real differences in, say, the structure and processes of educational opportunity) and by the differential extent to which linearity may hold in the societies compared. The extent of non-linearity of British intergenerational mobility which is demonstrated in 'Quantifying constraints on social mobility' would not persuade us to rule out a path analysis of British data on the Blau–Duncan model, but we would eschew mechanical comparison of the co-efficients of the British and American analyses. Some of the difficulties of comparative work are discussed in the paper 'Social mobility, canonical scoring and occupational classification'.

It has been claimed that the geometrical model is, to a considerable degree, theory-neutral, and that in particular it provides an empirical framework within which various of the theories of students of stratific-ation and mobility may be tested. However, when we come to the re-analysis of existing data we are usually not in a position to decide how correct are the presuppositions about the stratification space implicit in the collection and presentation of the data. Indeed, in the case of the 1949 British enquiry the nature of the presupposition is not unequivo-cal. It is not clear whether the occupational categories are to be treated as representing collectivities which are at least quasi status-groups or simply as bands of the economic pyramid. On the whole the former seems to be the preferable interpretation of the manner in which they were compiled. One must ask, therefore, whether it is in fact likely that social collectivities, as these are characterized by our model, existed in England and Wales in 1949.* There is very little substantively to be said about this question except that we do not know the answer. How-ever, even a speculative attempt to fit a set of facts into the *a priori* framework of a model can suggest the kind of considerations which must be borne in mind when the model is applied in practice.

We suppose that one of the features of English society which dis-tinguished, and distinguishes, between collectivities, if these exist, is wealth, and that this is an axis on which the top one or two strata have high variance, and the remainder of society has low variance because it has relatively little wealth *in toto*. Although wealth is likely to be correlated with income, the correlation may be quite moderate because there will be relatively greater variance for income in the bulk of society than there is for wealth. When we look, however, at authority or autonomy, somehow defined, we may find that the point of greatest differentiation lies somewhat lower down the scale in that, for instance, many foremen and supervisors are, or were in 1949, in a position which combined a high degree of autonomy with considerable authority and indeed more general power over the lives of a significant number of people. The idea of authority within a military or bureaucratic chain of command is difficult to operationalize; nevertheless, an impressionistic consideration of the diffusion of power in 1949 might lead us to expect only a moderate degree of correlation between authority and the other two axes, since the possession of wealth or high income is not the only

---

* Although Professor Glass and his co-workers collected data on Scotland the analysis of them which they present is very brief.

source of authority nor is it always a source of authority of a wide-ranging kind.

It is indeed quite possible that, by an explicit or implicit use of this sort of argument, the earlier workers arrived at a truly representative list of collectivities and assigned individuals to them with reasonable accuracy on the basis of occupations. But it cannot be denied that a proferred taxonomy would gain credibility if it were based on an explicit empirical investigation of the stratification space, or at least on a degree of inter-subjective agreement between observers working independently.

Theory and the model

Although the geometrical model is basically theory-independent, any particular application of it, like an application of, say, path analysis, involves theoretical assumptions. Obviously the subdivision of the stratification space into two spaces, the class or economic space and the subcultural space, already presupposes a theoretical position. Again, the assignment of occupational prestige, in the sociological sense of deference-entitlement, to the subcultural space runs counter to the practice of American workers who tend to use prestige as a surrogate for income, education and other components of the desirability or goodness of a job which have here been assigned to the material space. In fact, of course, it is quite reasonable to use prestige as commonly assessed as a surrogate for economic position since the rated 'prestige' or 'social standing' of occupations is quite highly correlated with the median income and length of education of their incumbents.

Another presupposition built into the application of the model presented here is the assumption that other characteristics of an occupation besides income and hours can be regarded as coordinate with more specifically market factors. Power, for example, is not considered as operating only, or primarily, through the market. It is true that pure market strength, in the sense of capacity to withhold one's labour or one's product from the market, may be a source of power. But power—in the form, say, of bureaucratic authority—and autonomy may be implicit in the functions of an occupational role, and their enjoyment, which is not an exercise of market power, may be part of the rewards of that role. Indeed, the case is more complicated than this formulation might suggest because the functions of a job, and the manner in which they are exercised, may be defined in part by the incumbent. Autonomy is often a rent paid by an employer for the inelastic natural resource of ability; and authority is a dividend which accrues to the human investment of education or training. So far from being entirely functionally determined, the degree of authority and self-determination can be the subject of implicit or explicit bargaining in the miniature market within the job. The concept of the labour market has, therefore, been extended beyond the practice of hiring labourers annually on lady-day, and beyond the world of newspaper advertisements and agencies, to the shifting and uncertain processes of role-definition as the basis for input of natural endowments, educational capital, and labour, and the receipt of components of job-satisfaction which are non-symbolic but also not overtly monetary.

Association

So far in this introduction we have dealt with the economic and the normative aspects of social class but have made only passing reference to the relational or associational aspects. The model, however, is quite capable of representing patterns of association by the very simple device of locating a particular person (ego) in the economic and sub-cultural spaces and similarly locating his associates. It is an easy matter to define measures of dispersion of the points representing associates around the point representing ego, and to define measures of displacement of the mean associate from ego in a particular dimension (e.g. vertically). In computing such measures it might, for some purposes, be desirable to weight an associate by the frequency of ego's contact with him, or by ego's subjective assessment of his associational importance.

The model

Sociologists are by now as accustomed to reading about 'models' as they are to reading about 'theories', and frequently with as little justification for the use of the term in the one case as in the other. A proferred model often enough boils down to no more than a proposition or analogy or image which says what it says with more or less precision and has no further implications or ramifications. If the term 'model' has any distinct meaning it denotes an analogical device which persons other than the inventor can confidently wield to express the propositions and hypotheses which they seek to confirm or refute. A model should simplify the process of simultaneously considering a number of aspects of a field of study, and changes in those aspects. It should be a means by which the tyro can acquire something of the overall conspectus of the field which the master has attained only after long and difficult labours. It should be a prophylactic against the confusion of distinct concepts, especially concepts (such as stratification and inequality) which are at different logical levels. And above all, it should spring on its inventor and its users definitions, questions, and relations of contrariety and subcontrariety which are more or less novel though not necessarily arcane.

With luck, a good model will prove fruitful even when the theoretical elements which are analogised by its parts are taken away and replaced by quite different elements of a different theory, or by elements of a different field of study. In favourable circumstances a model will not only express questions and pose them, it will also provide a framework for the organisation of enquiry and analysis within which their answers may be sought. Reviving an old distinction, we may say that, to its hermeneutic function—the adequate expression of propositions—a good model will add an exegetic function—giving practical direction to its user's work.

Models do not contradict one another, they are not true or false; they are more or less compendious, more or less distorting, more or less fruitful and more or less consonant with a particular cast of mind. A model need not be exclusive; a general model, in so far as it is adequate, will tend to subsume less general models, but the latter will remain in currency if they have local virtues which the broader model cannot match.

Euclidean geometrical models, because they relate to the powerful information-processing capacity of our sense of sight, and because they are amenable to powerful mathematical treatment, tend to be general, easily comprehended, readily manipulated, and fertile. The model of social stratification which has been described here promises to have all of these characteristics in some measure. Questions which it throws up are at the root of the technical investigations described in some of the following papers. It would be surprising and disappointing if it could not be pressed into further service in our future enquiries.

K. Hope

OCCUPATIONAL GRADING AND OCCUPATIONAL PRESTIGE

by JOHN H. GOLDTHORPE and K. HOPE

Summary. The first part of the paper contains a review and criticism of the interplay of definitions and empirical methods in research on occupational prestige. The second part reports the results of a small pilot experiment and analysis which were designed to introduce conceptual clarity and quantitative precision into the field.

This paper was read to the International Workshop on Career Mobility, Konstanz, April 1971.

Introduction

A cursory glance at the form and content of this paper would suggest that the first part contains a sociological analysis of the concept of occupational prestige and its uses, which generates certain propositions amenable to empirical test, and the second part consists of a small-scale sketch of methods of testing those propositions. However, while such a sequence does occur, it is at the same time important for the reader to recognise that *both* parts of the paper are intended as conceptual analyses of the field of occupational grading; the one being linguistic in form, based on a reading of previous empirical work, while the other seeks conceptual clarification by imposing a design on possible data. The emphasis of Part I is on the nature of the components of occupational grading. Part II takes certain components as given and shows how one can define a set of quantifiable concepts covering all aspects of the employment of those components. This set is in an important sense complete, in that it exhausts all possible sources of variance.

In the first part of the paper we begin with an attempt to explicate the concept of prestige in what seems to us to be the sociologically most meaningful sense, and that generally found in the classical literature on social stratification. Specifically, we suggest that prestige should be understood as a particular form of social power and advantage that is of a symbolic rather than of an economic or political character, and which gives rise to structured relationships of deference, acceptance and derogation. We then consider whether such a concept of prestige has been that usually adopted in conventional studies of the prestige of occupations. We conclude that in fact the theoretical basis of these studies has been often confused, and that the occupational gradings they produce cannot be safely regarded as a valid indicator of a prestige order in the sense previously established. Rather, we argue, conventional occupational 'prestige' ratings are better interpreted as representing popular evaluations of the general 'goodness' (in the broad sense of 'desirability') of occupations. This interpretation is consistent both with respondents' accounts of the considerations they actually have in mind when performing conventional occupational grading tasks and with the pattern of individual and group variation that the results of such grading exercises typically reveal. Finally, on the basis of this interpretation, we examine critically the appropriateness of the uses to which occupational 'prestige' ratings have been put in both theory and research. As regards the former, we question whether these ratings can offer any firm empirical support for a functionalist theory of social stratification. As regards the latter, we conclude that occupational classifications or scores derived from 'prestige' ratings are likely to provide a sounder basis for studies of specifically occupational mobility than for studies concerned with social mobility in any wider sense.

Although the burden of the research reviewed in Part I is that in conventional occupational prestige studies a strong 'general factor' in the grading of occupations is present, the research design expounded in Part II starts from the position that there may still be discriminable strands in the grading activity. Some of these, admittedly, may be idiosyncratic in the sense that they are not shared by all persons, and the design allows for the estimation of such effects; but it also seeks out other effects, where there is agreement among respondents but distinctions are made between different aspects or dimensions of grading. A pilot analysis of data obtained from a small number of respondents provides some tenuous evidence that both these factors are at work, but we do not wish to ascribe substantive significance to the analysis of these data—the reader is asked to consider the numbers employed as simply there to give content to the quantitative conceptual analysis which is the real substance of Part II.

In addition we show how the method of analysis proposed may provide a basis for the representation of cognitive maps of the occupational structure, and we briefly indicate how, with adequate data, it might be possible to investigate the social determinants, or at least concomitants, of aspects of the perception of occupations.

The preliminary nature of the analysis is further emphasized by the inclusion of an Appendix describing the findings of an identical analysis of results from a different set of respondents. The reports of these pilot studies are in fact prolegomena to another study, now under way, in which a moderate-sized random sample of the electors of Oxford is being asked to undertake a slightly different version of the task performed by our pilot respondents. The purpose of the study is to illustrate what it is that people are doing when they assess the standing of occupations, and to tease out some of the social determinants or correlates of aspects of this activity. Having cast some light on the processes of occupational perception and discrimination, we hope, if the technical difficulties are not too great, to undertake yet one more study, in which we shall provide a means of assigning a grade or score to any occupation.

PART I.   OCCUPATIONAL PRESTIGE—USES AND ABUSES

Introduction

Over the last forty years or so, there has accumulated in the literature of sociology and social psychology a relatively large number
(probably several score) of studies in which respondents have been required to grade a selection of occupations in some hierarchical fashion.
It has become customary to refer to such studies as being ones of
'occupational prestige.' Indeed, when the matter of occupational prestige is now considered, it is almost invariably in terms of studies of the
kind in question. Furthermore, the data provided by these enquiries
have come to play an important part both in theoretical discussion and
in the conduct of empirical investigation in the general problem-area of
social stratification and mobility. Yet, oddly enough, 'occupational
prestige' studies have rarely been subjected to critical examination
other than from a technical point of view.

In this paper, therefore, we begin in Part I with some critical observations which are chiefly concerned with theoretical matters. They lead
on, however, to a number of issues of a kind amenable to empirical research. We proceed, then, in Part II to report an investigation which
we designed and carried out as a 'pilot' for more extensive and refined
studies relevant to these issues.

The meaning of prestige

An appropriate starting point for a more radical appraisal of 'occupational prestige' studies than seems hitherto to have been made is
with the concept of 'prestige' itself. In a sociological context, we
would suggest, prestige can be most usefully understood as referring
to a particular form of social advantage and power, associated with the
incumbency of a role or membership of a collectivity: specifically, to
advantage and power which are of a *symbolic*, rather than of an economic or political nature. That is to say, such advantage and power
imply the ability of an actor to exploit—in the pursuit of his goals—
meanings and *values*, rather than superior material resources or positions of authority or of *force majeure*.

From this conception it follows that a hierarchy of prestige is constituted by intersubjective communication among actors, and must therefore be characterized in attitudinal and relational terms. It cannot be
characterized—other than misleadingly—as a distribution in which units
have differing amounts of some particular substance or quality. As a
provisional statement, a prestige hierarchy might be one in which
actors

(i) *defer to* their superiors—that is, acknowledge by speech or other action their own social inferiority—and seek, or at least appreciate, association with superiors;

(ii) *accept* their equals as partners, associates etc. in intimate social interaction—entertainment, friendship, courtship, marriage, etc.;

(iii) *derogate** their inferiors, if only by accepting their deference and avoiding association with them other than where their own superiority is confirmed.

The attributes of roles or collectivities which differentiate actors in respect of their prestige are various. What they have in common is some symbolic significance—some generally recognised meaning—which, in conjunction with prevailing values, constitutes a claim to social superiority or, conversely, some stigma of inferiority. For example, having the role of doctor and working in a hospital or clinic implies having knowledge of, control over and close involvement with matters which are generally regarded as ones of ultimate concern—matters of life and death. Belonging to an aristocratic family and owning a landed estate signifies descent from illustrious forebears and participation in an historically-rooted, distinctive and exclusive way of life. Working as a clerk in a bank evokes such generally valued characteristics as honesty, trustworthiness, discretion and dependability, and again in relation to 'important'—in this case, financial—matters. In all of these cases, then, 'deference-entitlements' (Shils, 1968) exist, and are likely to be honoured at least by some actors in some contexts. In contrast, being, say, a gypsy scrap-metal dealer or a West Indian refuse-collector is likely to mean relatively frequent exposure to derogation, on account both of the symbolic significance of the ethnic memberships in question and of the implied occupational contact with what is spoiled, discarded and dirty.† In other words, prestige positions do not derive directly from the attributes of a role or collectivity 'objectively' considered, but rather from the way in which certain of these attributes are perceived and evaluated in some culturally determined fashion.

The particular modes in which prestige is manifest as a form of advantage and power in social relationships are ones conditioned by its symbolic character. The following are perhaps the most obvious:

(i) by creating favourable presumptions: e.g. that an aristocrat will be an honourable man, that a bank clerk will be credit-worthy;

(ii) by providing a basis for exerting influence: a high prestige actor is in a position to offer his (prestige-giving) association and

---

* We use 'derogate' in this context following Shils (1968). Were it not that its usual connotations go beyond its strict meaning, 'disparage'—literally 'to make unequal'—might be a preferable term.

† On 'stigma symbols' as the obverse of 'prestige symbols', see Goffman (1963).

support to those who are prepared to be guided by him, accept his 'advice', think as he thinks, etc.;

(iii) by giving the ability to determine standards, tastes and styles—in the arts, manners, leisure pursuits, dress, speech etc.: the high valuation set on some symbolic aspect of a social role or collectivity tends to 'spill over' and lead to emulation of the total life-style thought to be characteristic of the incumbents of the role or members of the collectivity.

It is not difficult to envisage how, through modes of expression such as the above, prestige can be 'converted' into advantage and power of an economic or a political kind—just as the latter may of course in turn be utilized in order to gain increased prestige. However, it is still important to recognise that advantage and power in the form of prestige remain distinctive in that they *entirely depend upon* the existence of some shared universe of meaning and value among the actors concerned. One cannot have an objective or 'factual' hierarchy of prestige *in the same sense* as one can a hierarchy of, say, wealth or bureaucratic authority: one, that is, which can exist and maintain its force independently to some important degree of the subjective dispositions of the individuals involved in it, at any one point in time. If the symbolic significance of roles and collectivities is not recognised, or if what is symbolized is subject to divergent evaluations, then no consistent basis for deference, differential social acceptance or derogation is present. While one may talk of an actor pursuing his ends through the exercise of 'sheer money power' or 'naked force', it would be meaningless to speak of 'naked' prestige. Wherever and however ego expresses his prestige in a social relationship, the 'complicity' of alter is always entailed. In other words, a prestige hierarchy is part of 'socially constructed' reality. It is as it is because the actors implicated in it make it that way through their own actions—although not necessarily, of course, in a fully conscious or intended manner*.

Recognition that prestige hierarchies are analytically distinct from economic or political hierarchies and are, moreover, not merely epiphenomena of the latter is in fact widely revealed in the 'classical' literature of social stratification (Pareto, Weber, Michels etc.). It is evident, for example, in discussions of 'old aristocracies', or of the situation of

---

* That prestige is a phenomenon of the kind in question can be elucidated by considering the way in which in interpersonal relations its force may be annulled by that of esteem. Following Davis (1945) one may regard esteem as deriving not from attributes of a role or collectivity but from what an individual actually does and achieves as an incumbent or member. Among persons having close knowledge of each other's performances, therefore, esteem is also a possible basis for deference etc. And where performances are recognised as incongruent with the expectations associated with roles or memberships (the aristocrat is a boor and a cheat; the bank clerk an embezzler) prestige structures tend to collapse. Persons are seen 'for what they are'. It is not entirely misleading to keep in mind the etymological connections between 'prestige' and 'illusions' (*prae-stigiae*) or the act of blindfolding or dazzling (*praestringere oculos*).

nouveaux riches or *parvenus,* or of the emergence of 'new men of power' such as political bosses or trade union officials. In all these cases, the focus of interest is on the discrepancy that exists between the position of certain groups within a prevailing prestige hierarchy and their position in terms of economic or political power and advantage. By what means does an aristocracy maintain its superior prestige once it has lost its economic and political dominance? What are the consequences of the non-acceptance of newly-risen entrepreneurs or other 'men of talent' by established status groups? Can popular leaders who achieve political pre-eminence resist *embourgeoisement* and the embrace of the existing prestige order?—and so on. Obviously, the very posing of such questions implies a conception of prestige similar to that we have proposed (though some other term—e.g. 'honour' or 'respect'—may be used) in which the relation of prestige to other forms of social advantage and power is taken as problematic.

In more recent sociological writing, it should be added, this perspective has often been blurred, or lost, as a result of one or other of two tendencies: first, the tendency to think (for theoretical—or ideological—convenience) of stratification as comprising no more than an 'evaluative' hierarchy of prestige or status groups, and thus to leave out of account the sheer 'facticity' of inequalities in life-chances; and secondly, the tendency to think (for methodological convenience) of stratification as being unidimensional and to construct scales of 'socio-economic status' in which prestige is amalgamated with other components that are deemed to be relevant. However, both of these tendencies are open to, and have met with, strong objections on empirical and analytical grounds alike. Although aimed at simplification, conveniences of the kind in question often in fact lead to greater rather than less difficulty in comprehending stratification phenomena. Indeed, it would seem that if prestige is not to be understood in something approximating the way we have suggested, then certain fairly obvious and intrusive problems—of the kind illustrated in the classical literature—cannot even be raised, let alone investigated.

Occupational prestige

Assuming, on the other hand, that a conception of prestige consistent with classical analyses *is* adopted, then the reference of 'occupational prestige' follows from it directly: it is to the chances of deference, acceptance and derogation associated with the incumbency of occupational roles and membership in occupational collectivities. Such prestige will be related to the 'objective' attributes of occupations—their rewards, requisite qualifications, work-tasks, work environments etc.— but only indirectly: only, that is, in so far as these attributes carry symbolic significance of a kind that is likely to be interpreted as indicative of social superiority or inferiority, with corresponding interactional consequences.

We may, therefore, now go on to ask such questions as: (i) whether such a conception of occupational prestige has been that generally held by the authors of conventional occupational prestige studies; (ii) whether the results of such studies provide valid indicators of prestige in the sense in question; (iii) whether the uses to which results have been put have been appropriate ones.

The conception of occupational prestige in conventional studies

The two investigations which have undoubtedly had greatest influence in setting the pattern for occupational prestige studies generally in the period after the second world war are those of NORC in the US (1947) and of Hall and Jones in the UK (1950). The findings of both of these investigations have, moreover, been subject to further detailed analyses and review subsequent to their initial presentation (Reiss, 1961; Moser and Hall, 1954). It will therefore be convenient, and not seriously misleading, to concentrate chiefly on these two studies in considering questions (i) and (ii).

Whether or not the conception of prestige which guided the authors of these studies is similar to that we have previously discussed is an issue which cannot easily be settled on account of some lack of clarity in the research reports in question. In both studies alike there is certainly recognition of the fact that 'prestige' may well be used in different senses; but there is no sustained attempt at specifying these senses and at making clear which is being employed at any one time. Some considerable confusion results.

For example, Hall and Jones state that their classification 'aims at distinguishing between occupations according to their social prestige' (p. 33) and go on to suggest that the prestige of an occupation is chiefly indicated by 'the class of people with whom the person so occupied would normally associate, whether at leisure or at work.' (p. 36). This would seem to imply something close to the 'classical' idea of prestige as being manifest in relational terms through participation in status groups. However, in the later presentation of the Hall–Jones scale by Hall and Moser this viewpoint is not consistently maintained. Although sometimes 'social prestige' and 'social status' are apparently treated as synonymous, social status is also used as some kind of generic term to refer to the 'overall' position of a social unit within a total stratification structure: as, for instance, when it is argued (p. 46) that social status involves 'associated, prestige and allied matters' *and not simply* objective characteristics such as income, working conditions, responsibility, educational standards etc. Moreover, it becomes evident that

'occupational prestige' is in fact most frequently interpreted as 'occupational social status' in this last-mentioned, broad sense of social
status, and that consequently it is as an indicator of the *latter* that the
Hall—Jones scale is effectively intended. This is perhaps most clearly
revealed when, in discussing occupations such as 'Nonconformist
Minister' on which respondents showed considerable disagreement,
Hall and Moser write: 'they are occupations for which material rewards
and traditional social prestige are at variance' (p. 40). Obviously, *if*
the Hall—Jones scale were seriously meant as a measure of prestige in
the 'classical' sense—as something distinct from economic position
(and always in some degree 'traditional')—then a suggestion of this
kind would imply that the scale was of very dubious validity, and it
would not do merely to observe that 'the spread in ranking in such
cases indicates that different rankers may employ different criteria as
a basis for their judgment'. (*ibid.*)

    In the case of the NORC study, it is recognised, at least by Reiss
in his re-presentation of the enquiry, that 'The term "prestige"... is
perhaps used more loosely in this monograph than would be consistent
with the definition of it in theories of social stratification.' (p. 1)
This recognition is a wise one, and what is surprising, in view of data
later discussed, is that it is not made far more emphatically. After they
had rated ninety occupations in terms of their 'general standing', respondents in the NORC study were immediately asked: 'When you say
that certain jobs have excellent standing, what do you think is the *one
main* thing about such jobs that gives them this standing?' In the outcome, the answers given were quite varied, and, most notably, only 14%
of responses were classified as referring to 'social prestige'—as
against 40% referring to potential occupational rewards and 32% to job
or occupational requirements. For the most part, then, as Reiss concludes, respondents 'do not appear to have made their evaluations in
terms of a conscious awareness of the social prestige attached to the
occupation. They are more likely in fact, to emphasise the relevance of
indicators sociologists use to measure socioeconomic status...'* However, despite this significant result, the fact that Reiss continues to
speak of the NORC ratings as ones of occupational 'prestige' leads to
a number of quite unwarranted shifts back to the use of this term in a
stricter sense. For instance, Reiss spends some time (pp. 75—7) on the
question of why, 'contrary to conventional views on the prestige of
white-collar work', the occupational group of sales, clerical and kindred
workers has a score below that of craftsmen, foremen and kindred
workers. But since it appears that most respondents in the NORC study

* Taft (1953) and Tiryakian (1958) also investigated the criteria used by respondents
in 'occupational prestige' ratings, and in these cases a greater variety of criteria were
reported than in the NORC study; also, it was found that respondents used different
criteria at different ranges in the scale. However, the NORC findings were confirmed
in that only a small minority reported using specifically 'prestige' criteria.

were rating on the basis *not* of social prestige, but rather of occupational rewards or requirements, there is in fact no particular problem
here, or at least not of the kind that Reiss raises.

We may then conclude that in the two studies of 'occupational
prestige' in question—on which nearly all subsequent work has been
modelled—underlying theoretical conceptions were, to say the least,
uncertain; and further, that whatever interpretation of 'prestige' their
authors had in mind, it seems most unlikely that the occupational gradings that were produced do in fact measure the relative prestige of
occupations in what we would regard as the most sociologically useful
sense.

The validation of occupational prestige ratings

In this last connection, some few remarks specifically on the
matter of validation might appropriately be added, since the issue of
the relationship between concept and empirical indicator is thus, of
course, directly posed.

In the British enquiry, it is noteworthy that the validity of the
Hall—Jones scale as a measure of prestige is never explicitly considered. This further confirms the view that it is intended to serve as
some kind of 'composite' social status measure rather than as, say, an
indicator of the probability of differential association as initially implied. Assuming this is so, it might be argued that the only validation
required is sufficient consensus among respondents to make possible
the claim that a publicly recognised hierarchy of 'occupational prestige'
does exist. Such an argument is in fact advanced by Reiss in regard to
the NORC scale: '... the validation of a construct like "general standing" or "prestige-status structure" rests upon the convergence of evaluations apart from any general agreement upon the criteria for making
the evaluations. The high correlations among the ratings for occupations by individuals with ostensibly different evaluative criteria
stongly suggests the existence of an underlying and agreed upon structure of occupational prestige.' (p. 195).*

Consideration of this position will be deferred until later: for the
moment, it may be said simply that it appears to be that adopted, implicitly or explicity, in most other 'occupational prestige' studies. The
one exception which deserves to be mentioned occurs in the work of
Svalastoga (1959). Svalastoga clearly wishes to work with a conception
of prestige which approximates the 'classical' notion, and in a section

---

* This follows Duncan and Artis (1951): 'The validation of a construct like general
standing, prestige structure or community reputation is not to be found in the uniform
conceptualization of a social system by its members, but in the convergence (if it exists)
of their several schemes of evaluation upon the same individuals. The problem is not
one of a consensus in the realm of values, but of the inter-correlations of the several
dimensions of stratification.' (p. 21)

of his book specifically devoted to the question of the validity of
ratings of occupational prestige gained through conventional methods,
he writes (p. 120): 'Occupational prestige ratings may be considered
valid to the extent, that they correlated with verbal or non-verbal defer-
ential behaviour, shown towards persons having the rated occupations.'
The problem then is, of course, that of finding some reliable direct
measure of such behaviour, by reference to which validation may be
attempted. The approach that Svalastoga adopts, *faute de mieux*, is to
examine those occupations included in his study which are embraced
by major social organisations such as the civil service, the church, the
military, etc. Since positions within these organisations have a formally recognised rank order, prestige ratings may be considered as invalid if they are in contradiction with this order—if, for example, they
result in a lower-grade civil servant being rated above a higher-grade
one, a dean above a bishop, a captain above a colonel, etc. On the
basis of such a test—involving paired comparisons among 13 of his 75
occupations falling into five formal hierarchies—Svalastoga arrives at
a best estimate of 'the average invalidity of all occupational prestige
ratings, reported in this study' of 6% (p. 120). However, while applaud-
ing the way in which Svalastoga faces up to the real issue, one must
be highly sceptical about whether he has come at all close to resolving
it. First, the occupations to which Svalastoga can apply his test, by
virtue of their being incorporated within some formal hierarchy, may
well be *ipso facto* less likely to give rise to invalid ratings than other
occupations. Secondly, and again because of the principle by which
the occupations have to be selected, the test can in any case provide
only negative results: the fact that the occupations in question are
generally rated according to their position in a formal rank order cannot constitute a positive indication that prestige is the basis of the
rating, rather than, say, occupational rewards or requirements; for
within a bureaucratic organisation *all* these attributes will tend, of
course, to be very closely intercorrelated. In other words, Svalastoga's
test provides no good grounds for rejecting the view formed on other
evidence that conventional 'occupational prestige' studies do not
specifically tap a distinctive prestige dimension of stratification.

Accepting this conclusion, then, the question which obviously
follows is: how should the results of such studies be interpreted?
Some answer must be formulated before our third issue, concerning
the appropriateness of the uses of these results, can be broached.

The interpretation of occupational prestige ratings

It has been regularly remarked that in occupational prestige ratings,
as conventionally carried out, both cognitive and evaluative processes
are involved. However, precisely what are supposed to be the objects

of these processes has rarely been made clear. For example, if it really were occupational prestige in the sense we would favour which was being assessed, then what would have to be cognized (or, rather, recognized) and evaluated would be the symbolic significance of certain features of an occupation with regard to the chances of those engaged in the occupation meeting with deference, acceptance or derogation in their relations with others. If, for instance, the occupational 'stimulus' given were that of 'coal miner', a possible response might be on the lines of

'dirty, degrading   ⟶   'rough, uncultivated   ⟶   'likely to be looked down
work'   men'   on by most groups'

or, alternatively perhaps

'difficult, dangerous   ⟶   'able, courageous   ⟶   'likely to be respected
work'   men'   by many groups'

But is this in fact the kind of thing that usually happens? As we have seen, there is little reason to believe so, at least if we are guided by respondents' own accounts of what chiefly influenced their ratings. Rather, we would suggest, the operation that most respondents have tended to perform (perhaps in accordance with the principle of least effort) is a far more obvious and simple one: namely, that of rating the occupations on the basis of what they know, or think they know, about a number of objective characteristics, evaluated in terms of what they contribute to the general 'goodness' of a job. In other words—and consistently with their own accounts—respondents in occupational prestige studies have not typically been acting within a distinctively 'prestige' frame of reference at all. The sensitivity to symbolic indications of social superiority and inferiority which this would imply has not usually been evoked by the task of grading set them. Rather, this task has led them to assess occupations only in some far less specific fashion, according to a composite judgment on an assortment of their attributes which might be thought of as more or less desirable.*

Such an interpretation of what 'occupational prestige' ratings are actually about would seem, moreover, to fit far better with what is known of the pattern of variation in such ratings than would the idea that they relate to prestige *stricto sensu*. The basic feature of this pattern is that while some considerable amount of disagreement in rating occurs as between *individuals*, differences between the mean ratings of age, sex, regional, occupational and other collectivities are

*   As regards the NORC study, it is worth recalling what is usually forgotten: that this enquiry, at least in the view of those who devised it, was in fact specifically aimed at finding out what people thought were the best jobs, in the sense of the most desirable. Where 'prestige' and 'standing' are referred to in the initial report on the study, they are obviously equated with desirability. See NORC (1947).

never very great. If one assumes that in making their judgments, respondents more or less consciously (i) consider a number of different occupational attributes which they take as determining how 'good' a job is;
(ii) attach some subjective 'weight' to each of these; (iii) for each
occupation presented apply their rating 'formula' to what they know
about the occupation, and thus (iv) come to some overall assessment of
it—then one might well anticipate some appreciable degree of variation
in ratings at the individual level. Individuals are likely to differ in their
familiarity with particular jobs and in their priorities as regards what
makes a job 'good'. However, one would not expect—other than in somewhat special and limited cases*—that such differences would be socially
structured in any very striking way. Knowledge about the more general
characteristics of other than rather esoteric occupations is relatively
'open'; and, again in general terms, the kinds of thing thought of as
'good' in a job are unlikely to give rise to systematic differences in
ratings, especially since there is, in any case, a clear tendency for
such advantages to go together. To take a particular example—from the
NORC data—it is not surprising, given an interpretation of the kind we
have proposed, that individuals should quite often disagree about the
ratings of 'building contractor' vis-à-vis 'welfare-worker'—nor that, at
the same time, in the case of age, sex, regional, occupational or other
categories, the former job should invariably have the higher mean rating.
(See Reiss 1961, pp. 55–6, 225–8). †

On the other hand, if we were to suppose that 'occupational prestige' scores did give a valid indication of a structure of prestige relations, then the degree of consensus that is shown among different social
groups would indeed be remarkable, at least in those societies where
other research has indicated some notable diversity in value systems
and in particular between members of different social strata. For in this
case it would not be a matter of evaluative consensus simply on what
attributes make a job 'good', but rather on certain symbolic criteria of
generalized superiority and inferiority, with all their attitudinal and
behavioural implications. As Shils has observed, the conditions necessary for an entirely, or even a largely, 'integrated' prestige order to

---

* e.g. where respondents are rating occupations within their own status or situs areas,
c.f. Gerstl and Cohen (1964).

† Our interpretation of the meaning of 'occupational prestige' ratings is also consistent
with the fact that certain variations in the task set to respondents appear to make little
difference to the results achieved: e.g. whether respondents are asked to rate occupations according to their 'social prestige', 'social standing,' 'social status', 'general
desirability' etc: or whether they are asked for their own opinions or what they believe
are generally prevailing opinions. It seems reasonable to suppose that if respondents
are required to grade occupations according to any one criterion which, while rather
imprecise, implies a 'better-worse' dimension, they will produce results of the kind in
question; and further, that the level of consensus in this respect is such that the
distinction between personal and general opinion is of little consequence—provided that
there is no suggestion of a normative, judgment being required; that is, one in terms of
which jobs ought to be the best.

exist are in fact demanding ones. It would seem, therefore, the safest assumption to make that, within modern industrial societies, such conditions will prevail only locally, transiently or imperfectly, and thus that social relations expressive of a prestige order will occur only in an intermittent or discontinuous fashion. On the basis of available empirical data, one might suggest that while derogation is still quite widely manifest—as, for example, in the form of differential association or status-group exclusivity— the claim to superiority thus made by one group is not necessarily, or even usually, acknowledged by those regarded as inferior; that is to say, the latter are often not inclined to display deference.* This refusal may be revealed passively—by disregard for the claim to superiority, in that no particular 'respect' is shown, and little concern to reduce social distance from the 'superior' group; or, perhaps, some direct challenge to the claim may be made where real interests are felt to be threatened by it—as, say, by 'exclusivity' in housing areas, use of amenities, etc.

In the light of the foregoing we may now move on to consider the third issue that we raised in regard to occupational prestige studies— that of how far the uses of their results in stratification theory and research have been appropriate ones.

The uses of 'occupational prestige' ratings

One notable use of the data in question results from the fact that over the last two decades occupational prestige studies have been carried out in a steadily increasing number of countries at different levels of economic development. The opportunity has therefore arisen of making cross-national comparisons which, it has been supposed, can throw light on the relationship between value systems and social structural characteristics and are thus relevant to the thesis of the 'convergent' development of societies as industrialism advances. For example, Inkeles and Rossi (1956), comparing occupational prestige ratings in studies from six industrial societies, showed that a high degree of similarity prevailed. On this basis, they concluded that common structural features of these societies were of greater influence on the evaluation of occupations than were differences in cultural traditions. Subsequently, however, occupational prestige ratings from several countries as yet little industrialized have *also* been shown to be broadly in line with the hierarchy found in economically advanced societies—in so far, that is, as comparisons can be made. This result has then led to the modified argument (Hodge, Treiman and Rossi, 1966) that what is chiefly reflected in prestige ratings is the set of structural features shared by national societies of *any* degree of complexity—'specialized

* cf. for example, Goldthorpe, Lockwood, Bechhofer and Platt (1969) chapters 4 and 5.

institutions to carry out political, religious, and economic functions, and to provide for the health, education and welfare of the population ...'. Occupations at the top of these institutional structures, it is suggested, are highly regarded because of their functional importance and also because they are those which require the most training and ability and those to which the highest rewards accrue. Thus, 'any major prestige inversion would produce a great deal of inconsistency in the stratification system.' (p. 310).

In this way, therefore, it is clearly indicated how occupational prestige data may further be employed in support of a general theory of social stratification of a structural-functional type. Such an application has in fact been made quite explicitly in the work of Barber (1957). Following a Parsonian approach, Barber takes the results of the Inkeles—Rossi study as the main empirical foundation for the view that the factual order of stratification in modern societies tends in the main to be consistent with the dominant normative order. Inequality in social rewards and relationships, it is held, is structured in accordance with functional 'needs', and this arrangement is then seen as receiving general moral support: 'functionally important roles are congruent with or partly determine a system of values'. (p. 6).

Clearly, for occupational prestige data to be used in the ways in question, it is necessary to assume that such data reflect prevailing values and norms *of a particular kind*: ones pertaining to the 'goodness' —in the sense of the 'fairness' or 'justice'—of the existing distribution of social power and advantage. However, in view of our previous discussion, it is difficult to regard such an assumption as a valid one or indeed to understand why it ever should have been made. Even if it were to be supposed that data on publicly recognized occupational hierarchies do indicate a prestige order in something approximating the classical conception, it still then would not follow that they can provide evidence that the objective reality of stratification is morally legitimated. For while prestige relations do depend upon a certain range of shared understandings, consensus on principles of distributive justice is not necessarily involved.* Moreover, as we have argued, by far the most plausible interpretation is that occupational prestige ratings reflect prevailing ideas at a much lower level of abstraction: that is, ideas of what is 'good' in the sense simply of what is generally found desirable in an occupation. And if *this* is the case, then the consensus

---

* In fact, one might suggest the hypothesis that societies of the kind in which an integrated and stable prestige order is to be found will tend to be ones in which the factual order of stratification is not commonly appraised in terms of distributive justice, or indeed envisaged as capable of being in any way substantially different from what it is.
   The distinction between the recognition of prestige and the attribution of justice is foreshadowed—as are several other points in the above paragraph—by Gusfield and Schwartz (1963) in a paper that has been curiously neglected by subsequent American writers on occupational grading.

that exists is obviously of no very great moral or legitimatory significance at all. Apart from quite unsurprising agreement on such matters as,
for example, that high pay is preferable to low pay, more security to
less, qualifications to lack of qualifications, etc., the consensus that
is implied is of a cognitive and perceptual kind, not an evaluative one.
The fact that, on average, all groups and strata agree that certain occupations should be rated higher than others tells one nothing at all about
whether the occupational hierarchy that is thus represented is regarded
as that which *ought* to exist. And in so far as the publicly recognized
hierarchy corresponds to that proposed by structural-functional theorists,
this would seem to indicate no more than that broadly similar sets of
rating criteria are being applied: i.e. occupational rewards and occupational requirements.*

Thus, as regards the utilization of occupational prestige data in the
advancement of stratification theory, our view must be that this has been
fundamentally misguided. What, now, of their application in research?
Primarily, of course, occupational prestige ratings have been used in
studies of social mobility, in which they have constituted the hierarchy—
scalar or categorical— in the context of which mobility has been
assessed. Assumptions about what prestige ratings rate are thus necessarily involved in the interpretation of mobility patterns, and the crucial
issues that arise are once more ones of 'validity'.

Concerning the question: What, in mobility studies, may occupational
prestige ratings be taken to indicate? —three main positions can be
distinguished. These can be usefully considered in turn, together with
their implications and problems.

(i) Ratings may be taken—as, for example, by Svalastoga— as
indicative of the position of an occupation within a prestige order; that
is, as indicative of the chances of those holding that occupation en-
countering deference, acceptance or derogation in their social lives. In
this case, therefore, mobility between different occupational levels,
other than of a marginal kind, may be interpreted as involving the probability of subcultural and relational discontinuity. While such a perspective does not necessarily mean that society is seen as divided up
into more or less discrete strata, it does imply that social mobility, as
measured, is not just a matter of individuals gaining more qualifications,
more income, more interesting work etc., but further of their experiencing
changes in their life-styles and patterns of association. The difficulty

---

* It is a well-known problem of the structural-functional theory of stratification that
other usable criteria of the functional importance of occupational roles are hard to find:
employing the two criteria in question does, of course, introduce a serious degree of
circularity into the argument.

is, however, as already remarked, that the validity of occupational prestige ratings construed in this way has never been established, and that
there are indeed strong grounds for doubting their validity. In other
words, we are simply not in a position to infer, with any acceptable
degree of precision and certitude, what are the typical consequences of
mobility, as measured via occupational prestige ratings, for the actual
social experience of those deemed to be mobile.

(ii) Prestige ratings may be taken as indicative of the status of
occupations in the generic sense earlier distinguished—that is, as
being in effect comparable with composite measures of 'socio-economic'
status, derived from data on income, education, housing, possessions
etc. Justification for this position is twofold: first, to repeat the observation of Reiss, respondents in prestige-rating studies appear 'to emphasize the relevance of indicators sociologists use to measure socio-
economic status ...'; secondly, as shown by Duncan (1961), it is possible, at least in the American case, to predict prestige ratings fairly
accurately from census data on occupational income and education. If
then, 'occupational prestige' is understood in the way in question, some
reasonable basis may be claimed for interpreting occupationally-
measured mobility in terms of movement between grades of occupation
differentiated chiefly by their levels of rewards and requirements. At
the same time, though, it must be emphasized that in this case no good
grounds exist for any interpretation in terms of prestige *stricto sensu*,
and, of course, no basis at all for any consideration of how far mobility
may be incongruent from one form of stratification to another. Precisely
because of the inevitably 'synthetic' nature (Ossowski, 1963) of socio-
economic status, as indicated by prestige scores, the analysis of
mobility must be strictly unidimensional. These limitations would lead
one to suggest, therefore, that if it is accepted that occupational prestige ratings are not valid indicators of a prestige order but are being
used simply to stand proxy for socio-economic status, then it would be
preferable, where possible, to seek to measure the latter more directly—
and without any concern to combine components so that a good 'fit' with
prestige scores may be obtained. To discard the notion of prestige altogether would, in this case, mean losing nothing but the possibility of
terminological confusion; and developing separate indices of occupational income, education etc., as well as some composite measure, would
permit the analysis of mobility in a multi-dimensional manner. In short,
there seems no good argument for basing mobility research on occupational prestige ratings, interpreted as socio-economic status scores,
other than where a lack of data on the socio-economic attributes of
occupations makes this procedure an unavoidable *pis aller*.

(iii) Prestige ratings may be taken as indicating popular evaluations
of the relative 'goodness' of occupations in terms of the entire range of

prevailing criteria. In this case, related mobility data are open to interpretation as showing, basically, the chances of individuals entering more or less desirable grades of occupation, given certain grades of origin. While an interpretation of the data on these lines has rarely, if ever, been pursued consistently throughout a mobility study, it is that which, on grounds of validity, could best be defended. First, as we have already argued, grading occupations according to notions of their general 'goodness' is what respondents in occupational prestige studies appear, in the main, to be doing. Secondly, it is in regard to *this* understanding of prestige scores that it would seem most relevant to claim, following Duncan and Artis and Reiss, that their validity lies in the degree of consensus which emerges, despite the use of quite various criteria of evaluation. The argument that this consensus points to 'the existence of an underlying and agreed upon structure of occupational prestige' is difficult to sustain once it is recognized just what consensus on a prestige order entails. But the idea of a broadly agreed upon ordering of occupations in terms of 'goodness' does, on the evidence in question, receive some clear—and not very surprising—support. Furthermore, if prestige ratings are taken as indicative of an occupational hierarchy of this kind, then the fact that they represent synthetic judgments and cannot be 'disaggregated' is no longer a problem in the analysis of mobility patterns. For if mobility is being interpreted as being simply between grades of occupation of differing desirability in some overall sense, a unidimensional approach would appear the appropriate one. However, it must be added that what would then be a dubious and potentially dangerous step would be to shift from such an interpretation of specifically occupational mobility to one in which conclusions were drawn regarding the stability of status groups, income classes, or social strata in any sense whatsoever; that is, conclusions regarding *social* mobility as generally understood. In effect, of course, a shift of this nature has been made in most large-scale mobility studies carried out in the recent past. But while it might reasonably be held that such a manoeuvre is unlikely to be very misleading so far as the 'gross' patterns of social mobility are concerned, the difficulty is (apart from the limitation of unidimensionality) that we have no way of knowing at just *what* point and in *what* ways it might turn out to be quite deceptive. Yet again, the problem of validity recurs.

The general—and rather pessimistic—conclusion to which one is led is, therefore, the following: that to the extent that the meaning of occupational prestige ratings is correctly construed, the less useful they appear to be as a basis for mobility studies which pursue the 'classical' sociological interests of mobility research.

Empirical questions which arise

The discussion of the foregoing paragraphs has to a large extent been concerned with conceptual and methodological issues. However, it is possible to think of a number of questions which are relevant to the arguments we have deployed, which could be determined—or at least explored—empirically, and which remain so far unanswered. It is to *some* of these questions that we now turn,

To begin with, it would obviously be of value to know more on the matter of just how individuals do grade—or are capable of grading—occupations when occupational titles are in some way presented to them. We have argued that occupational prestige ratings, as collected via conventional methods, should be interpreted as indicating popular conceptions of the general 'goodness' of occupations. But is this the only kind of grading that can be reliably elicited? If our view is correct, then the possibility should exist, in principle at least, of obtaining gradings on various more specific criteria, which would differ systematically, even if not perhaps substantially, from conventional occupational prestige ratings—as well, of course, as from each other. And of particular interest here would be to investigate whether such discrimination can be achieved on criteria relating to dimensions of stratification which, in the classical literature and subsequently, it has been found theoretically important to distinguish—including, perhaps, that of prestige in the classical sense.*

Furthermore, our interpretation of conventional occupational prestige ratings is specifically opposed to the idea that these ratings are evaluative in the sense that they imply moral approval of the occupational hierarchy which they serve to constitute. For example, we would hold that this hierarchy cannot be taken—as it is by structural-functional theorists—as indicating how occupations are seen as receiving legitimately differentiated rewards in accordance with their relative importance in meeting societal needs. If, then, our argument is sound, it should be possible for us to show that there exists some significant degree of discrepancy between ratings of the kind in question and those that result when respondents' specifically normative assessments *are* obtained.

Further still, if we assume that individuals *do* in general have the ability to grade occupations on different dimensions in some meaningful fashion, then another whole set of questions can usefully be posed. One can ask not only how far particular occupations or groups of occupations are 'in line' or discrepant when 'normative' and 'non-normative' assessments are compared, but also about discrepancies in their ratings on different non-normative dimensions. In other words, one could, in principle, investigate the *perceived* degree of 'status crystallization'

---

* Assuming, that is (which may well be doubtful) that in modern societies a recognizable prestige order actually exists to be 'tapped' in this way.

throughout the occupational structure. From this, it is not a long step to thinking in terms of typologies of occupations based on their differing 'profiles' across the dimensions considered. Such typologies, if they could be established, could then be taken as reflecting 'cognitive maps' of the occupational structure which popularly prevail, and could obviously be used in the analysis of occupational mobility data to investigate the advantages of working on a multidimensional basis, rather that with the unidimensional notion of occupational 'goodness'.

Finally, exploring issues of the kind in question must in turn re-open the whole matter of consensus. We have previously used our interpretation of the meaning of conventional occupational prestige ratings to suggest an explanation of the pattern of consensus (and dissensus) which these ratings display. Specifically, we have claimed that the consensus which is in evidence at the level of groups and strata has far more a cognitive than an evaluative character. If a primarily normative assessment of the occupational hierarchy could in some way be obtained, then, following our arguments and in the light of existing data on subcultural differences, we would expect far more structured (as well as individual) disagreement to be revealed. Moreover, even with the ostensibly non-normative grading of occupations, one might anticipate some increase in dissensus of this kind where respondents were required to make their ratings multidimensionally. For one thing, there would then of course exist the possibility of disagreement not only about the rating of occupations on any one dimension but also about the shape of their profiles across a number of them. And, in addition, socially patterned differences in values could conceivably show more influence on judgments relating to fairly specific criteria than on ones of a more comprehensive kind, where possibilities for 'cancelling out' would be the greater.

The conception of a pilot study

Chiefly to investigate how empirical issues such as those raised above might best be approached, we planned a pilot study in multidimensional occupational grading on the following lines:

(i) Forty occupational titles were selected. These included 28 out of the 30 titles used in the Hall–Jones study, for which there exists a known ordering on the basis of a conventional prestige-rating task. The two titles omitted were both ones which had become rather archaic: coal hewer and carter. The remaining 12 titles were chosen mainly so as to compensate for the under-representation in the Hall–Jones list of manual factory jobs or because they seemed ones very likely to provide instances of 'discrepant' ratings (e.g. psychiatrist, ballet dancer).

(ii) Four rating criteria were selected. Three were chosen with the familiar distinction among the 'economic', the 'prestige' and the 'power' aspects of stratification in mind. They were: 'Standard of Living' 'Prestige in the Community' and 'Power and Influence over other people'. As the fourth criterion, we sought one which would induce respondents to make primarily normative assessments, rather than ones which might be supposed to be largely descriptive. Previous investigations have suggested that if respondents are asked directly to rate occupations according to what *should* be their 'general standing' etc., they tend to experience some difficulty in maintaining a normative stance throughout the exercise (Turner, 1958). We decided, therefore, to adopt a rather different approach and to ask respondents to rate occupations according to their 'Value to Society'. In this case, we believed, it could be argued that, regardless of how respondents themselves construed what they were doing, the judgments they made must be determined primarily by values which they held rather than directly by their perception of some aspects of social fact. Notions of the Standard of Living, Prestige in the Community and Power and Influence over other people which attach to occupations are ones with some generally accepted empirical referents (although arguably in differing degree). This is not so with Value to Society: one could not, for example, 'refute' ratings on this criterion by recourse simply to logic and evidence. Thus, in this case, it is difficult to see how the makings of relatively 'pure' value judgments can actually be avoided.*

(iii) Ten respondents were selected. Because we thought it premature at this stage to tackle questions of variation in ratings between different groups, strata etc., we did not aim for a large number of respondents nor to have a sample of any particular population. Rather, we chose individuals from among our relatives, friends and acquaintances of both sexes so as to have as socially heterogeneous a group as could be arranged.†

(iv) It was decided that respondents should perform the same rating task on two different occasions, separated by an interval of a week. In this way we would have some opportunity for checking on how far the occupational gradings produced by our respondents did appear to reflect their actual perceptions, evaluations etc., rather than being the result of operations more or less arbitrarily performed simply in order to satisfy the investigators.

---

* This is not to claim, of course, that one will necessarily or even probably get respondents' considered, personal judgments, rather than some more or less 'stock' cultural or subcultural response. But the *form* of the response will be an evaluative one.

† The Appendix describes a subsequent study of ratings by ten persons drawn from the electoral register of Oxford. An enquiry based on a larger sample is under way at the time of writing.

TABLE 1.

The forty occupational titles ranked by the respondents

1. Agricultural Labourer
2. Ambassador to a foreign country
3. Ballet Dancer
4. Barman
5. Bricklayer
6. Bus Driver
7. Business Manager
8. Car Worker
9. Carpenter
10. Chartered Accountant

11. Chef
12. Civil Servant (Executive)
13. Commercial Traveller
14. Company Director
15. Country Solicitor
16. Dock Labourer
17. Farmer (over 100 acres)
18. Fireman
19. Fitter
20. Foreman in a Factory

21. Insurance Agent
22. Jobbing Master Builder
23. Medical Officer
24. News Reporter
25. Newsagent & Tobacconist
26. Nonconformist Minister
27. Policeman
28. Primary School Teacher
29. Psychiatrist
30. Quarry Worker

31. Railway Porter
32. Road Sweeper
33. Routine Clerk
34. Sheet Metal Worker
35. Shop Assistant
36. Social Worker
37. State Registered Nurse.
38. Tractor Driver
39. TV Announcer
40. Works Manager

In Part II of this report, the methods and results of the pilot study are presented in detail. The potential relevance of the type of data and the analytical technique to the issues set out above should be evident. This potential will, it is hoped, be realized when more adequate data have been collected.

PART II.   RESULTS FROM A PILOT EXPERIMENT

Method

Each occupational title in Table 1 was typed on a $5'' \times 1\frac{1}{2}''$ piece of card, and the corresponding number from the table was written on the back of the card. Each respondent was asked to rank all occupations on each of four dimensions. In some cases the respondent rated Standard of Living before Prestige in the Community. Other respondents took these two dimensions in the opposite order (see Table 2; the order for for a particular subject was randomly determined). These were always

TABLE 2

Characteristics of the ten respondents.

S *indicates that the respondent rated 'Standard of Living' first*
P *indicates that the respondent rated 'Prestige in the Community'*
first.

Respondent	Sex	R.G.'s social class 1966	Order of presentation
A	M	I Nm	S
B	F	I Nm	P
C	M	I Nm	S
D	F	I Nm	P
E	M	III Nm	S
F	F	III Nm	S
G	M	III M	S
H	M	IV Nm	P
I	F	V M	P
J	F	V M	P

the first two dimensions to be employed. In every case Power and Influence over other people came third and Value to Society came last.

The respondent was seated at a large table. The experimenter shuffled the cards and handed two or three to the respondent saying:

'Here you have forty cards. On each is the name of an occupation.
I'm going to ask you to rate these forty occupations in a number of
different respects. The first of these is *standard of living.** I would
like you to arrange the cards in a column, so that the occupation
which you think carries *the highest standard of living* is at the top,
with the rest following in order until you have the occupation carrying *the lowest standard of living* at the very bottom. If you think that
any two or more occupations have the same *standard of living*, just
put their cards side by side in the column. You can put as many cards
side by side as you like. Try to think of the occupations generally,
and *not* of particular people in them. Take as much time as you need
and change your mind as much as you want as you go along. Have
you any questions? Shall I repeat that?'

The cards were spread out on the table and the respondent was left to
sort them at his leisure. He was occasionally reminded of the name of
the dimension he was employing. When he had finished, the experimenter
recorded the results on a schedule. Starting from the top of the column,
he picked up the cards in order, recording a 1 against the occupational
title(s) in the top rank, a 2 against the title(s) in the second rank, and
so on. The highest number recorded was the number of separate ranks
employed by the respondent.

The cards were shuffled and the subject was asked to rank the titles
on the second dimension (Prestige in the Community or Standard of
Living); then again on Power and Influence over other people; then again
on Value to Society.

During the course of the experiment a respondent was sometimes
asked what he had in mind as he ranked the occupations on a particular
dimension and his observations were recorded. At the end of the session
it was arranged that he would attend again one week later 'to discuss
results'. At the second session the task was repeated exactly as on the
first occasion. The respondent was asked not to think back to how he
rated the occupations on the previous occasion but to rate them as he
felt now. The order of presentation of Standard of Living and Prestige
in the Community was the same on both occasions for each individual.

Distribution of ranks

On each dimension a respondent could utilize up to forty ranks or
grades. In fact, on the first occasion of testing, this number was used
in only two out of forty sets of rankings. The mean number of grades
employed by the ten respondents was 27·9 for Prestige, 24·2 for
Standard of Living, 21·8 for Power and Influence, and 17·9 for Value to
Society. On the second occasion the corresponding means were, respectively, 20·5, 20·3, 18·4 and 16·5. Ties were more frequent in the

---

* *Prestige in the community* for some respondents.

ascription of value than they were in the assessment of the other three characteristics. The nature of the ties was explored further by calculating, separately for each set of rankings, the correlation (tau$_h$*) between the grade to which an occupation or occupations were assigned and the number of occupations assigned to that grade. In so far as ties tend to occur in the upper levels of the occupational distribution tau is positive, and in so far as ties occur among the low-ranking occupations tau is negative. The nearer the ties congregate towards one extreme the higher is the absolute value of tau.

The mean of all eighty values of tau is -0.28, and the mean of the eight values for a respondent is negative for each of the ten respondents. We conclude, therefore, that tying tends to occur among the occupations which the respondent assigns to the lower end of a dimension. It must, however, be remembered that the tenor of the instructions encouraged respondents to begin their ranking task at the top end of the scale.

A mean tau was computed for each of the four dimensions. There is some evidence here that Power and Influence (mean tau -0.44) shows greater skew than the other three dimensions (for which the means lie between -0.21 and -0.25). There was very little difference between mean taus for the two occasions.

---

* tau$_h$ (Hope, 1968, p. 278) is a rank correlation coefficient which always has attainable limits of ±1. It has as its numerator Kendall's (1962) S. Its denominator is the maximum value S can take subject to the constraint that the marginal totals of the contingency table from which S_{max} is calculated are identical with those of the observed table.

The application of tau$_h$ in the text is rather unusual and may be illustrated by an example in which a respondent, grading occupations on a certain dimension, groups the forty cards into only seven rows or ranks. The frequency distribution might then be

Rank	Number of occupations
1	9
2	6
3	6
4	7
5	3
6	5
7	4
	40

This distribution may be laid out in the form of a contingency table as follows:

		Frequency					
		9	7	6	5	4	3
	1	9	0	0	0	0	0
	2	0	0	6	0	0	0
	3	0	0	6	0	0	0
Rank	4	0	7	0	0	0	0
	5	0	0	0	0	0	3
	6	0	0	0	5	0	0
	7	0	0	0	0	4	0

Kendall's S and tau$_h$ are then computed from the elements of the table in the usual way. In this example they are clearly positive in sign.

Isolating the elements of occupational status*

The preceding analysis has explicitly taken into account differences among respondents and among dimensions in the shape and scatter of the frequency distributions. The analysis to which we now come deliberately irons out all such differences, so far as this is possible. The ten respondents, each employing four dimensions on two occasions, supplied eighty columns of ratings, each column containing rankings of forty occupational titles. In the following analysis the rank assigned to an occupation is treated as a score, and a mean and standard deviation are calculated for each of the eighty columns of scores. Each score is then centred and standardized by, firstly, expressing it as a deviation from its colmn mean and, secondly, dividing this deviation by the column standard deviation. The standard deviations were calculated with $40 - 1 = 39$ degrees of freedom. The resulting 40×80 matrix of centred and standardized scores has a sum of squares of $39 \times 80 = 3120$.

The justification for these preparatory procedures is implicit in the design of the experiment. The collection of the data was planned in such a way that they conform to the pattern of a completely-crossed four-factor design in the analysis of variance. The virtue of the analysis of variance in a rating experiment is that it enables the research worker to identify a number of possible elements or sources of variance and to uniquely ascribe a quantity to each source which is an indication of its relative importance. This quantification of importance is possible so long as the experimenter is able to specify a model which may be supposed to generate the data.

The terms and procedures of the analysis of variance are not, of course, primarily designed for data-reduction in rating experiments, and it is not pretended that the model which is adopted can be defended in the same terms as in the analysis of a more typical experimental design, where independent errors may be supposed to be generated by a truly random process. Nevertheless, at several points in the analysis the results of the application of the model are examined to see whether or not the data are behaving as if they conformed to the canons of analysis of variance. The fact that no noticeable malfunctioning of the model is detected is at least negative evidence for its appropriateness and may stimulate theoretical workers to elaborate a rationale for this kind of application.

The design to which the data conform is a four-factor Occupations $\times$ Respondents $\times$ Occasions $\times$ Dimensions ($40 \times 10 \times 2 \times 4$) design. Because the data have been centred for all factors except the first the variance of the remaining three terms, and the variance of all possible interactions among the three, is necessarily zero. The justification of

---

* Throughout the second part of this paper 'status' is used in the purely locational sense of position on an axis.

this brutal elimination of so many possible effects is simply that the mean of a column of ranks is an artefact, and comparison among such means would be comparison of artefacts. The justification for standardizing every column of ranks is that, although differences in column variances are of interest, we do not wish to give greater weight to a particular column simply because it has a high variance. By equating the variances we equate the contribution of each column to the analysis.

Factors involved in the ascription of status

The sums of squares and mean squares of the effects which have not been eliminated are shown in Table 3. It will be seen that the analysis accounts for the total sum of squares of the 40×80 matrix of scores. In order to estimate the relative importance of the terms we must specify a model which indicates the components of variance which, when weighted and linearly combined, constitute the mean squares. The model we have employed is of the kind which is known as mixed because it comprises effects of two different sorts: random effects and fixed effects. We propose to regard Occupations*, Respondents and Occasions as random effects. It must be admitted that the occupational titles and the respondents were not, in fact, chosen randomly from a population of titles and persons, but they were chosen with an eye to their representativeness. We are not simply interested in conclusions about these particular occupations and these particular persons, rather we wish to use the evidence of the study for which this is a pilot as a means of gaining information about general attitudes to the whole range of occupations. If we are mistaken in treating the occupations and respondents as if they were random samples from wider populations the data may belie us by throwing up negative estimates of variance. In the event we shall see that no negative variance of any size does, in fact, occur in our pilot analysis, and this is encouraging, though it is not a sufficient proof of the adequacy of our model. Dimensions differs from the other three factors in that we are interested in drawing conclusions about these specific axes of stratification, so we regard Dimensions as a fixed effect. (In fact, the estimates of variance would be very little altered if Dimensions too was treated as random.)

In this analysis there is no estimate of random error other than the third-order interaction term, that is the interaction of all four main terms. In a mixed model it is necessary to distinguish these two components because it is not the case, as it is with a completely random model,

---

* The nature of the Occupations terms is disputable. However, it is not in fact necessary to specify whether Occupations is fixed or random since, in their present application, the equations of the model are identical whichever view we take.

TABLE 3

Analysis of variance and estimates of components of variance. 'Occupations', 'Respondents' and 'Occasions' are assumed to be random and 'Dimensions' is assumed to be fixed.

Source	d.f.	Sum of squares	Mean square	Variance component
Occupations	39	1868·2842	47·9047	0·5853
Occupations × Respondents	351	380·8301	1·0850	0·1164
Occupations × Occasions	39	5·9333	0·1521	-0·0000
Occupations × Dimensions	117	318·2015	2·7197	0·1195
Occupations × Respondents × Occasions	351	53·9829	0·1538	0·0088
Occupations × Respondents × Dimensions	1053	355·0089	0·3371	0·1093
Occupations × Occasions × Dimensions	117	13·0362	0·1114	-0·0007
Error	1053	124·7228	0·1184	0·1184
Sum	3120	3119·9999	—	1·0570

that both contribute to the mean square of every other term. In carrying through the analysis it has been assumed that the third-order interaction variance is zero and the whole of the mean square for this effect is attributable to error.*

Having specified the model it is a simple matter to write the equations using Schultz's (1955) rules of thumb, and to estimate the component of variance attributable to each term in the analysis (Table 3). It can be seen that two of the estimates are negative. If these quantities had been large we should have had reason to doubt the appropriateness of the model; the fact that they are practically zero is reassuring.

The structure of the social status of occupations

Examination of the components reveals a fairly simple hierarchy of three levels of importance:

a) Occupations, which accounts for over half the total variance
b) Occupations × Respondents, Occupations × Dimensions, and Occupations × Respondents × Dimensions, each of which accounts for about ten percent of the variance
c) the remaining three terms (apart from Error) which have practically zero importance. †

As a shorthand means of referring to the terms of the analysis let us assign the letters J (for 'Jobs'), R, O and D respectively to the factors Occupations, Respondents, Occasions and Dimensions. Then a combination of letters will refer to the interaction of the factors signified.

The terms which have negligible variance indicate: (JO) that, taking the sample of ten persons as a whole, there is no systematic tendency for some occupations to rise in status between first and second testing while others fall; (JRO) that neither is there any such tendency in the ratings of the individual respondents; nor (JOD) is there any such tendency for the sample as a whole when dimensions are looked at individually. We cannot ask whether there is systematic change in the ratings of individual occupations by individual respondents on individual dimensions because we have set the variance of the third-order interaction term to zero by assumption. The fact that the reliability of the individual element of our 40×80 score matrix is $(1 - 0\cdot1184)/1\cdot0570 = 0\cdot89$ is an indication that further scope for the reduction of error is limited.

*   Stanley (1961) writes 'Probably we are well advised to design fuller studies, in which each rater rates each ratee [occupation] at least twice on each trait [dimension]. Then there will be a third-order interaction mean square whose mathematical expectation more nearly approaches pure measurement error than does the expected mean square for the second-order interaction.' The examination of the third-order term which we carry out below tends to bear out Stanley's advice.

†   The sum of the variance components in Table 3 is 1·0570. If we had assumed a completely random model then the sum would have been unity.

The lesson of the preceding paragraph is that there is no systematic change of mind be tween the two occasions of testing. In future work retesting of respondents may well prove unnecessary, unless for the purpose of estimating random error.

The three terms which each contribute about ten percent to the total variance of an individual score indicate (JR) that different persons do have different ideas about the relative ranking of occupations, considered as an average over the four dimensions, and that these idiosyncrasies persist from one occasion to the next; (JD) that the sample as a whole, in the sense of the average respondent, discriminates in its use of the three dimensions, in other words that the four dimensions are not treated as synonymous; (JRD) that individual respondents make idiosyncratic differentiations among the dimensions, over and above those made, on average, by the sample.

Although these effects have been shown to exist and they merit discussion, their quantitative importance should not be exaggerated. The size of the variance attributable to Occupations indicates that the most important single effect is simply the mean of an occupational title over all ten respondents, both occasions, and all four dimensions. This effect is a vector of forty terms, each being a mean for an occupation over the eighty columns of the centred and standardized data matrix. These occupational means are reported in Table 4, in the column headed 'Four dimensions'. They have been themselves standardized so as to have a mean of 100 and a standard deviation of 15. This is, in fact, the 'general f actor' of our four dimensions of social standing. In crude terms its proportionate sum of squares is 1868/3120 or 60 per cent of the total sum of squares (Table 3). The refinements introduced by the model assign to it a contribution of 55 per cent to the total variance.*

The term 'general' is here used in a double sense, since it signifies variance shared by respondents and by dimensions. The factors which we have called idiosyncratic are also general in that they represent variance common to the four dimensions, but they are specific to respondents. Since psychologists have arrogated the term 'general' to variance common to several tests or dimensions we propose to refer to the variance of occupations as 'common-general' variance, that is,

---

* These assessments of its importance differ from that which would be made by a factor analysis in two respects. In the first place the general factor of our analysis is an unweighted sum or mean of the four dimensions. The introduction of differential weighting, as by a principal component analysis, would increase its importance somewhat (though experience with the two kinds of analysis in circumstances similar to the present suggests that the increase would not be great). And in the second place the employment of a model takes account of the fact that the sum of squares of the general factor is inflated by higher-order terms in the analysis. In these respects our estimate of 55% is a double deflation of the comparable figure which would be derived from a principal component analysis. Nevertheless, it remains high and is in fact very similar to the value which a psychologist would expect to find for 'general ability' in the analysis of variance of a battery of cognitive tests (cf. Mahmoud, 1955).

TABLE 4.

*Mean ratings of each occupation. The means have a mean of 100
and a standard deviation of 15.*

	Occupation	Four dimensions (SPIV)	Three dimensions (SPI)	Difference
1.	Agricultural Labourer	82	78	+ 4
2.	Ambassador to a foreign country	130	131	− 1
3.	Ballet Dancer	96	99	− 3
4.	Barman	80	84	− 4
5.	Bricklayer	86	86	0
6.	Bus Driver	87	85	+ 2
7.	Business Manager	117	119	− 2
8.	Car Worker	92	93	− 1
9.	Carpenter	87	87	0
10.	Chartered Accountant	116	118	− 2
11.	Chef	92	93	− 1
12.	Civil Servant (Executive)	119	119	0
13.	Commercial Traveller	94	97	− 3
14.	Company Director	126	129	− 3
15.	Country Solicitor	118	119	− 1
16.	Dock Labourer	90	88	+ 2
17.	Farmer (over 100 acres)	105	103	+ 2
18.	Fireman	100	95	+ 5
19.	Fitter	87	87	0
20.	Foreman in a Factory	102	102	0
21.	Insurance Agent	97	99	− 2
22.	Jobbing Master Builder	101	102	− 1
23.	Medical Officer	123	119	+ 4
24.	News Reporter	113	113	0
25.	Newsagent & Tobacconist	89	91	− 2
26.	Nonconformist Minister	106	107	− 1
27.	Policeman	112	107	+ 5
28.	Primary School Teacher	111	106	+ 5
29.	Psychiatrist	121	119	+ 2
30.	Quarry Worker	82	83	− 1
31.	Railway Porter	79	80	− 1
32.	Road Sweeper	76	75	+ 1
33.	Routine Clerk	82	84	− 2
34.	Sheet Metal Worker	90	91	− 1
35.	Shop Assistant	84	85	− 1
36.	Social Worker	109	106	+ 3
37.	State Registered Nurse	110	105	+ 5
38.	Tractor Driver	82	82	0
39.	TV Announcer	117	121	− 4
40.	Works Manager	110	111	− 1

variance which is common to all persons and general over all dimensions. We may then refer to the idiosyncratic variance (the term JR) as 'personal-general' variance. The term 'personal' should not be taken to imply 'unshared', since two or more persons may deviate from the common-general assessment of status in very similar ways. To sum up: 'general' implies average status over a number of dimensions, 'common' implies average status over all persons, and 'personal' implies aspects of status which are not common (i.e. universal) but may be shared.

Stability of the structure of occupational gradings

It has been shown that the variance components are of considerable interest in themselves. They may, however, be put to further use in the construction of a number of coefficients which estimate the stability of the structure which the analysis has uncovered. Coefficients of this nature are an elaboration of Fisher's (1958) intraclass correlation coefficient.* Previous work has thrown up two basic types of coefficient. These are Mahmoud's (1955) coefficient of person stability and Hope's (1964) coefficient of pattern stability. The title appropriate to either coefficient varies according to the context in which it is employed. We shall here use Mahmoud's coefficient as a measure of the reliability or 'function stability' of the status of occupations. It should be noted that the reference of this coefficient is to the stability of the status of occupations rather than to measurement of that status. Hope's coefficient likewise is an index of stability of the effect measured, irrespective of errors in the means of measuring it.

We shall refer to Mahmoud's coefficient as a coefficient of stability of the status or rank of occupations and to Hope's coefficient as a coefficient of stability of status profiles of occupations. Sociologists are accustomed to think of the status of a person or an occupation as more or less 'crystallized' (Lenski, 1954). The profile stability coefficient tells us how far we may regard the pattern of departure from crystallization as a constant feature of the occupations. Naturally, we should be surprised to find any ponderable inconstancy over the space of one week.

Earlier factorial studies employing these coefficients (Mahmoud, 1955; Hope, 1964; Pilliner, 1965; Hope and Caine, 1968; Hope, 1969a) have been less complex than the four-factor design of the present investigation. The complications of this analysis imply that we must distinguish two forms of each of the coefficients, one which is common in that it refers to averages over all the respondents, and the other which

---

* The groundwork of this elaboration is largely due to Sir Cyril Burt and it is accessible in Burt (1955) and Mahmoud (1955).

is personal in that it refers to the individual respondents. Let us write lower-case j, r, o and d, and combinations of these letters, for the estimated components of variance in Table 3.

Then the coefficient

$$\frac{j}{j + jo} = \frac{0 \cdot 5853}{0 \cdot 5853 + (-0 \cdot 0000)} = 1 \cdot 00$$

is an index of the stability of the social ranks of occupations (in so far as our respondents form a representative sample of society) over the short interval of one week. We freely concede that this value serves more as a test of our method and our model than as a source of information about society, but we commend the coefficient for future research into status stability over longer periods.

The second version of Mahmoud's coefficient is

$$\frac{jr}{jr + jro} = 0 \cdot 93$$

which is an index of the stability of an individual's assessment of occupations in so far as that assessment differs from the sample average. It must be allowed that, since this is a measure of idiosyncratic or personal-general deviations from a collective norm of occupational assessment (as represented by the scores averaged over all the respondents), the coefficient is higher than might have been expected. But it would be unwise to place much weight on a ratio of estimates computed for our miscellaneous collection of respondents over a short time interval.

The following two coefficients are, respectively, the common and the personal version of the coefficient introduced by Hope (1964), and they indicate the stability of pattern of ratings over the four dimensions. For example, an occupation with a mean of 120 over the four dimensions (on the standardized scale of Table 4) might have values on the individual dimensions of 125, 115, 110 and 130. Its pattern or profile may be represented in terms of deviations about its mean as +5, –5, –10 and +10. The question which the coefficients of profile or pattern stability seek to answer is, how far do patterns such as this reproduce themselves from occasion to occasion (leaving out of account random measurement error)?

First, we calculate

$$\frac{jd}{jd + jod} = 1 \cdot 01$$

which is slightly in excess of unity because jod is slightly on the wrong side of zero. This is an estimate of the constancy of the differentiation among the four dimensions which is made by the average respondent. Again, computed for a truly representative sample over a longer time interval it would serve to indicate the degree of change within the 'stratification space' of the society which is not simply vertical movement up or down the common-general factor of social standing.* So far as the evidence for our respondents goes, stability is complete.

The second version of the profile stability coefficient is conceptually obvious but practically incalculable. It is

$$\frac{jrd}{jrd + jrod}$$

The reason why it is incalculable is that we have explicitly assumed that the third-order interaction term is zero and assigned all its variance to error. Thus, so long as jrd is positive we have, as it were, defined the value of this coefficient as unity.

It would, of course, be useful to be able to assess these coefficients in the light of their standard errors. However, little is known of the standard errors of estimates of components of variance, and still less is known of the properties of ratios of such estimates. In the absence of theory, the sociologist must rely on experience and replication. The three levels of variance components (0 per cent, 11 per cent and 55 per cent) are so clearly differentiated in these data that we are inclined to give credence to the coefficients derived from them.

Dimensions of occupational grading

So far the analysis has been of the four specified dimensions, with each contributing equally to the general factor of the social assessment of occupations. However, in choosing these dimensions we considered that the fourth—Value to Society (V)—and possibly also the third—Power and Influence over other people (I)—would behave more eccentrically than the first two—Standard of Living (S) and Prestige in the Community (P). The present analysis has not yet taken account of this possibility. In calculating a mean for an occupational title by averaging over all four dimensions we are implicitly assuming that the four dimensions are symmetrically related to the mean. In fact, the correlations between the four dimensions (each being averaged over all ten respondents and both occasions) and the grand means (averaged over all eighty columns of the data matrix) are (S) 0·91 (P) 0·98 (I) 0·97 and (V) 0·82. †

---

* The concept of a stratification space which is elaborated in the editorial Introduction has been found to be most helpful in distinguishing the sorts of ways in which a society may change over time. The statement in the text refers to movements of occupations within the space defined by a set of stratification axes which do not themselves move in relation to one another. It should be noted that in this paper 'dimension' is used to mean the same as 'axis' in the Introduction.

† The lower correlation for V must in part be due to the difference in distribution between V and the other three dimensions.

TABLE 5.

Correlations among the four dimensions and their correlations with the grand means over all respondents, occasions and dimensions (Table 4)

	S	P	I	V
Standard of living (S)	1·0000			
Prestige (P)	0·9324	1·0000		
Power and influence (I)	0·8614	0·9484	1·0000	
Value to society (V)	0·5458	0·7401	0·7842	1·0000
Grand mean	0·9144	0·9842	0·9747	0·8166

These correlations, and the correlation of each pair of dimensions, are shown in Table 5. When the grand mean is partialled out S retains 16 per cent of its variance, P retains 3 per cent, I retains 5 per cent and V retains 33 per cent. This suggests that we are correct in supposing that value to society is rather different from the other three dimensions. When V is omitted and the grand means are calculated from the remaining three dimensions (second column of Table 4) S retains 8 per cent of its variance, P retains 2 per cent and I retains 7 per cent.

It will be recalled that twenty-eight of our forty occupations were taken from the list of occupations employed by Hall and Jones (1950). For each of these twenty-eight we converted average rating on each dimension into a rank and we similarly recorded the rank of each occupation in the Hall—Jones study. Both sets of ranks run from 1 to 28; there are no ties. Each of our dimensions was then correlated with the Hall—Jones ranking. The product-moment correlations (with the corresponding value of Kendall's tau in brackets) are: (S) 0·94 (0·81), (P) 0·96 (0·87), (I) 0·85 (0·70), and (V) 0·70 (0·52). We conclude that our non-normative dimensions, particularly Prestige and Standard of Living, approximate closely to the dimension which our predecessors measured twenty years ago, but that our normative dimension stands somewhat apart from the non-normative dimensions.

The analysis of variance was repeated for the three dimensions S, P and I (Table 6). Examination of the variance components reveals a distinct increase in the variance due to the common-general factor for occupations, and a corresponding decrease in two of the three middle-ranking variance components. The error component also falls to about 8 per cent. The net effect of the changes is to leave the stability of the common-general factor unchanged at 1·00, to reduce the stability of the personal-general factors from 0·93 to 0·88, and to reduce the estimated stability of the status profiles of the occupations from 1·01 to 0·95.

In fact, all possible combinations of two, three and four dimensions were analysed (Table 7). Negative variance components occur in, and only in, analyses which include Value to Society. But in none is a

TABLE 6

Repeat of the analysis reported in Table 3 with one of the dimensions omitted

Source	d.f.	Sum of squares	Mean square	Variance component
Occupations	39	1677·1405	43·0036	0·7032
Occupations × Respondents	351	276·4568	0·7876	0·1103
Occupations × Occasions	39	5·9327	0·1521	0·0009
Occupations × Dimensions	78	102·1371	1·3095	0·0522
Occupations × Respondents × Occasions	351	44·1437	0·1258	0·0144
Occupations × Respondents × Dimensions	702	167·8402	0·2391	0·0783
Occupations × Occasions × Dimensions	78	8·4425	0·1082	0·0026
Error	702	57·9065	0·0825	0·0825
Sum	2340	2340·0000	—	1·0444

TABLE 7

Items drawn from each of the analyses of all possible combinations of four dimensions

Dimensions	Variance Components				Coefficients		
	Largest negative	Occupations	Error	Sum	$\dfrac{j}{j+jo}$	$\dfrac{jr}{jr+jro}$	$\dfrac{jd}{jd+jod}$
SPIV	−0·0007	0·5853	0·1184	1·0507	1·00	0·93	1·01
SPI	—	0·7032	0·0825	1·0444	1·00	0·88	0·95
SPV	−0·0033	0·5464	0·1297	1·0928	1·00	0·99	1·02
SIV	−0·0008	0·5465	0·1250	1·0955	1·00	0·91	1·00
PIV	−0·0019	0·5848	0·1365	1·0715	1·00	0·95	1·02
SP	—	0·7135	0·0831	1·0529	1·00	0·97	0·98
SI	—	0·6975	0·0763	1·0928	1·00	0·84	0·95
PI	—	0·7246	0·0880	1·0539	1·00	0·87	0·92
SV	−0·0040	0·4739	0·1416	1·2168	1·00	0·96	1·01
PV	−0·0077	0·5302	0·1644	1·1478	1·00	1·05	1·04
IV	−0·0029	0·5512	0·1572	1·1201	1·01	0·94	1·01

negative component as large as 1 per cent of the total variance. In every case the constancy of the shared-general assessment of the social standing of occupations is 1·00 or 1·01. The personal assessments have stabilities ranging from 0·84 to 1·05, and the status profiles have stabilities ranging from 0·92 to 1·04. Analyses which include Value to Society have variance components for the common-general factor which range between 0·47 and 0·59. Those which do not include this dimension have components ranging between 0·70 and 0·73. The implication of Table 7 is that the first three dimensions form a cluster or sheaf while Value to Society lies somewhat apart. This is not, of course, to say that S, P and I are indistinguishable. On the contrary, although they are highly correlated (Table 5*), the analyses of variance have shown that respondents agree with one another, and with themselves over time, in the differential ranking of occupations along the dimensions.

The choice of Value to Society as one of the four dimensions was made in the explicit expectation that there would be less inter-respondent, and perhaps less intra-respondent, agreement on this dimension than on the other three. The findings of this section are consistent with either or both of these suppositions, but it is possible, by analysis of the dimensions severally, to make a direct test of our expectation. A three-factor, Occupations × Respondents × Occasions, analysis of variance was carried out on each of the dimensions. The results for the first three dimensions are remarkably uniform, with the second-order interaction variance component being (S) 0·0800, (P) 0·0950 and (I) 0·1157 and the Occupations component being (S) 0·7391, (P) 0·7280, and (I) 0·7468. But in the analysis of Value to Society the second-order interaction component is 0·2184 and the Occupations component is only 0·4856. (These values of the components represent proportions of total variance because the data have been standardized and because each of the three factors of the analysis is random.) The relative extent of evaluative dissensus is indicated by the Occupations × Respondents component of 0·3061 for Value to Society compared with not more than 0·18 for any of the other three dimensions. All four Occupations × Occasions components are virtually zero.

We conclude, therefore, that the lower degree of consensus (49 per cent compared with 74 per cent) on Value to Society is partly explained by a greater degree of intra-respondent disagreement (22 per cent as against about 10 per cent) and partly by a higher degree of dissensus (31 per cent as against 13—18 per cent). The second-order interaction variance of 22 per cent indicates a greater amount of intra-respondent

---

* The correlations in Table 5 are for the dimensions averaged over the sample. Their size, therefore, dissembles the personal-general components in the assessment of occupational status.

disagreement on the normative dimension, but it is not possible to say whether this is entirely random or whether it includes an element of systematic changes of mind by individual raters.

A surrogate for mean status

One of the purposes of this enquiry was to throw light on the practical problem of assessing occupational status. Two main kinds of relations among the various possible dimensions of such status may be envisaged. In their idealized forms these two possible situations may be represented as follows. On the one hand, we may have a set of dimensions all of which are equidistant from a central dimension, like the ribs of a partly-opened umbrella round its stock, or like the feathers of a fan, one of which is at the centre of the arc. On the other hand, we may have a situation in which no one dimension is central to all the others. If a central dimension exists it is important to find it, because it may be supposed to represent a general measure of the status of occupations. If no central dimension exists then status can be measured without bias only by a careful choice of dimensions which are symmetrically arranged with respect to their centroid.

The problem of finding the central dimension or centroid of status is not an easy one. A full empirical solution might be said to involve the specification of all possible dimensions of status and the measurement of each with the same degree of reliability. But dimensions are, operationally, only forms of words. And a new dimension may be produced from an old one by a very slight alteration in wording. Even the theoretical specification of possible dimensions of status is fraught with conceptual difficulties, and these are of two kinds: those which arise on the borders of the stratification space and those which arise within that space. If we think of a conical space, bounded by axes like the ribs of a partially-opened umbrella, we can always, in imagination, insert an axis which lies at a slightly greater angle to the umbrella stock than do the ribs. So long as it is not at right angles to the stock this axis will be a correlate, and, therefore, to some extent a measure, of status. And, secondly, if we imagine our space as traversed by axes having no symmetrical relation to one another we may suppose that in our choice of dimensions we inadvertently introduce a bunched axis-set which, in the determination of the position of the central axis of the space, gives undue weight to the part of the space through which it passes. The search for *the* measure of status is not unlike the corollary of universal symmetry which posed such a problem for Newton's cosmology.

The shot-gun method of inventing as many dimensions as possible and getting respondents to rate them is probably impracticable. It may

TABLE 8

*Percentages of variance remaining to each dimension after partialling
out the grand mean in every possible combination of the dimensions.*

Dimensions	S	P	I	V
SPIV	16	3	5	33
SPI	8	2	7	—
SPV	15	3	—	33
SIV	19	—	5	30
PIV	—	8	5	22
SP	3	3	—	—
SI	7	—	7	—
PI	—	3	3	—
SV	19	—	—	27
PV	—	11	—	15
IV	—	—	9	13

also be theoretically undesirable in that local bunching* may occur, and
the effect of this bunching may be exaggerated by differential reliability
of the ratings of the various dimensions.

The alternative approach is to choose a few theoretically significant
dimensions as carefully as possible with the aim of spanning the space
in a regular fashion. Whether we have succeeded in our attempt to ac-
complish this we cannot know until other possible sets have been tried.
What we can say is that, of the three dimensions S, P and I, the second,
Prestige in the Community, comes very close to being the central axis
of the space of all three. This emerges from a repetition for all possible
dimension-sets of the correlational procedure which was described in the
preceding section for two dimension-sets. Table 8 shows that, over the
four analyses from which Value to Society has been omitted, Prestige
in the Community comes closer to the grand means than do its two
rivals. †

In the light of the discussion of the first part of this paper, the interpretation of this finding calls for some comment. We had entertained
hopes that by asking about prestige 'in the community'—and in the context of a multidimensional grading task—we might achieve more obvious

* Some kinds of bunching would be worse than others. There is always the possibility
that the bunches may be symmetrically arranged with respect to the general factor of
status. Furthermore, distortions are less serious if the angles between the most dis-
similar axes are of only moderate size, that is if the dimensions are highly correlated.

† It is unlikely that this is a position-effect since P sometimes preceded and sometimes followed S in the administration of the task. A more adequate elimination of such
possible effects would involve balanced ordering of all the dimensions which are
intended to span the stratification-space.

success than in conventional enquiries in inducing respondents to grade occupations within a distinctively 'prestige' frame of reference. However, given the results produced, we are doubtful if we made any significant advance in this respect.* The very high correlation between ratings on Prestige in the Community and the grand means strongly suggests to us that again 'prestige' was being usually construed as generalized 'goodness' or 'desirability' in a process something like that indicated on page 32. It is in this manner, that is to say, that we would interpret its 'central' position. For if some central dimension of occupational status can be shown to exist, it seems to us far more plausible that it should be a general 'goodness' or 'desirability' one, rather than one relating to prestige in the classic sociological sense. Thus, what one would ideally like to be able to show is that one can pick out a number of theoretically relevant dimensions on which the status of occupations is not especially highly correlated but across which *mean* ratings of occupations are produced that correlate very highly indeed with those resulting from conventional 'prestige' rating tasks.

The status indeterminacy of occupations

In the following part of the analysis we omit the dimension Value to Society, we take the common-general factor of occupational status (defined by the analysis of the three dimensions, S, P and I) as given, and we look at the contribution of individual occupations to various kinds of deviation from their grand mean status.

Table 9 lists the occupations in order of their common-general status as recorded in the second column of Table 4. It also lists the contribution of each occupation to each of four sums of squares, followed by the sum of the contributions to all sums of squares except that for Occupations. The first four sums of squares columns add up, apart from rounding errors, to the equivalent sums of squares in Table 6, and the last column adds up to 2340 – 1677 where 2340 is the total sum of squares and 1677 is the sum of squares for Occupations.

In previous sections of this report we have defined the terms 'general', 'common', 'personal' and 'profile' by reference to certain features of assessments of occupational status. Now we are going to consider these same features as sources of uncertainty or heterogeneity in the determination of status. We shall, therefore, assign an appropriate name to each feature which indicates the sort of indeterminacy which it reflects, and we shall refer to the features collectively as sources of *status indeterminacy* of occupations.

---

*   We would again make the point that it may well be that in modern societies no sufficiently integrated and stable ordering of prestige relationships exists to make the prestige rating of occupations (or other roles or positions) at all a feasible proposition.

TABLE 9

Contribution of each occupation to certain sums of squares in the analysis of the three dimensions S, P *and* I (*Table* 6)

	Occupation	Mean status	Sums of squares				
			JR	JD	JRD	JROD	All except J
2	Ambassador to a foreign country	131	2	0	6	1	11
14	Company Director	129	1	1	2	1	6
39	TV Announcer	121	4	5	7	1	18
7	Business Manager	119	6	1	3	2	11
15	Country Solicitor	119	5	1	4	3	14
12	Civil Servant (Executive)	119	16	1	5	3	26
29	Psychiatrist	119	3	0	5	1	10
23	Medical Officer	119	10	0	3	1	16
10	Chartered Accountant	118	11	2	5	1	21
24	News Reporter	113	13	2	3	2	22
40	Works Manager	111	11	0	3	2	18
26	Nonconformist Minister	107	9	2	9	2	25
27	Policeman	107	5	21	3	2	32
28	Primary School Teacher	106	3	7	6	1	20
36	Social Worker	106	3	7	2	1	16
37	State Registered Nurse	105	5	6	9	2	24
17	Farmer (over 100 acres)	103	21	6	6	2	39
22	Jobbing Master Builder	102	10	1	6	2	20
20	Foreman in a Factory	102	4	2	8	1	17
21	Insurance Agent	99	7	0	5	2	16
3	Ballet Dancer	99	13	11	13	2	42
13	Commercial Traveller	97	8	2	8	0	20
18	Fireman	95	7	3	5	2	18
11	Chef	93	7	1	3	3	16
8	Car Worker	93	12	5	4	1	25
25	Newsagent & Tobacconist	91	8	1	3	2	15
34	Sheet Metal Worker	91	4	2	2	1	10
16	Dock Labourer	88	12	3	9	1	29
9	Carpenter	87	4	1	2	1	8
19	Fitter	87	3	1	2	2	8
5	Bricklayer	86	6	1	3	1	11
6	Bus Driver	85	2	0	1	1	5
35	Shop Assistant	85	4	1	4	2	11
33	Routine Clerk	84	4	0	2	1	8
4	Barman	84	9	0	1	1	12
30	Quarry Worker	83	9	0	1	1	11
38	Tractor Driver	82	2	0	1	2	8
31	Railway Porter	80	3	1	1	1	6
1	Agricultural Labourer	78	5	1	2	1	12
32	Road Sweeper	75	3	0	1	1	7
Sum		—	274	99	168	60	664

The first of the four features is the term JROD which is an indicator of *random measurement error*. Looking at the JROD column of Table 9 we see that the sums of squares are pretty uniform from occupation to occupation, which gives us no cause to retract our assumption that the variance of this term is largely error.

Each of the remaining three sources of status indeterminacy is related to a sum of squares in Table 9, but the relationship is not straightforward. It will be recalled that the model to which we are working assumes that higher-order terms in the analysis enter into lower-order terms and inflate their mean squares and sums of squares. The equations of the model specify which higher-order terms contribute to which lower-order terms and with what weighting. We propose to define each species of status indeterminacy for an occupation in terms of the contribution of that occupation to the appropriate variance component in Table 6. We write s_k for a sum of squares of term K (and s_{kl} for the sum of squares of the interaction of K and L, and so on) in Table 9, and n_j, n_r, n_o and n_d for the number of levels of each of the factors (40, 10, 2 and 3 respectively). We append the subscript i to our variance components to indicate that we are now calculating the contribution to a variance component of a specific occupation i.

Then, taking the personal-general component jr we define our measure of *status disagreement* as

$$jr_i = \frac{s_{jr} - s_{jro}}{(n_j - 1)(n_r - 1) n_o n_d}$$

Taking the common-profile component jd we define a measure of *status discrepancy* as

$$jd_i = \frac{(n_r - 1)(s_{jd} - s_{jod}) + s_{jrod} - s_{jrd}}{(n_j - 1)(n_d - 1) n_r n_o}$$

Thirdly, taking the personal-profile component jrd we define a measure of a new concept, for which we propose the name *status profile disagreement*

$$jrd_i = \frac{s_{jrd} - s_{jrod}}{(n_j - 1)(n_r - 1)(n_d - 1) n_o}$$

The measure of random error may be brought into line with the other measures of status indeterminacy by defining

$$e_i = \frac{s_{jrod}}{(n_j - 1)(n_r - 1)(n_d - 1)}$$

It should be noted that these definitions have simplified slightly because Occasions has only one degree of freedom.

Table 10 contains the indices of status indeterminacy. Each index

has been multiplied by one thousand, and so the columns sum to one
thousand times the appropriate variance component in Table 6. The
last column, which is headed 'Status Indeterminacy' is a sum, not
merely of the four indices which have been explicitly defined and which
form the first four columns of the table, but also of similar indices
which may be defined for the remaining interaction terms in Table 6.
Thus the sum of the status indeterminacy column is one thousand times
$(1\cdot0444 - 0\cdot7032)$, which is the variance not accounted for by the
common-general factor. The table may be read both horizontally and
vertically, that is, we may compare different types of indeterminacy for
the same occupation, or we may compare occupations on a given measure
of indeterminacy.

It will be appreciated that no standard errors of these indices are
available and that the caveats which apply to the estimates of components of variance apply with even greater force to these partitions
of those estimates. Nevertheless, we are encouraged by the negligible
number and size of negative indices. In the absence of statistical theory
the sociologist's recourse must be to replication. In future work with
this design it will be desirable to employ a sample of respondents which
is large enough to be split into several sub-samples, each of which may
be analysed separately.

The status indeterminacy column of Table 10 indicates the extent
to which ratings of an occupation vary about the grand mean. It can be
seen that occupations with the highest status indeterminacy tend to lie
toward the middle of the status range. An exception to this tendency is
civil servant (executive), about which respondents evinced much uncertainty, most of them not being familiar with civil service grades. We
suspect that the high mean status of this occupation is a consequence
of the confusion of executive with administrative functions. The occupations with the highest indeterminacy are ballet dancer, farmer (over
100 acres) and policeman. Dock labourer also has high indeterminacy.
A remark by one of our respondents suggested that there is uncertainty
about this occupation because its apparently low-status work contrasts
with reiterated assertions of its national importance when a stoppage is
threatened. Another respondent thought that dock labourers and car
workers have the income to support a high standard of living but that
they do not spend their money wisely. The implied contrast between two
senses of 'standard of living' could contribute to indeterminacy. Nonconformist minister, SRN, and car worker also have high indeterminacy.

The error column of Table 10 is proportional to the JROD column of
Table 9 and so yields no new information when read vertically.

Occupations about whose status there is much disagreement are
farmer (over 100 acres), civil servant (executive), news reporter and
ballet dancer. It would in principle be desirable at this point to explore

TABLE 10

Indices of *status indeterminacy* for each of the *occupations* (× 1000).

Occupation	Status disagreement	Status discrepancy	Status profile disagreement	Error	Status indeterminacy
2 Ambassador to a foreign country	0·70	−0·48	3·32	1·62	5·81
14 Company Director	0·08	0·45	1·14	1·13	3·05
39 TV Announcer	1·38	2·20	4·29	1·60	10·26
7 Business Manager	2·59	0·19	1·26	2·26	5·60
15 Country Solicitor	1·51	0·39	0·96	3·79	6·33
12 Civil Servant (Executive)	6·68	0·68	1·38	3·84	12·30
29 Psychiatrist	1·40	−0·12	3·07	1·12	5·57
23 Medical Officer	4·09	−0·00	1·05	1·83	7·85
10 Chartered Accountant	4·97	1·12	2·26	1·99	10·42
24 News Reporter	6·15	1·20	0·95	2·43	10·70
40 Works Manager	4·62	0·08	0·80	2·89	8·36
26 Nonconformist Minister	3·67	0·69	5·13	2·98	13·26
27 Policeman	2·20	13·41	0·98	2·66	18·81
28 Primary School Teacher	1·08	4·39	3·46	1·89	11·07
36 Social Worker	0·61	4·44	0·47	1·64	8·43
37 State Registered Nurse	1·84	3·04	4·98	2·54	13·07
17 Farmer (over 100 acres)	9·06	2·60	2·82	2·49	19·70
22 Jobbing Master Builder	4·14	0·36	2·48	2·93	10·18
20 Foreman in a Factory	0·82	0·88	4·59	1·63	9·26
21 Insurance Agent	2·74	0·03	1·95	2·98	8·12

3 Ballet Dancer	·5·50	5·77	7·77	3·40	23·36
13 Commercial Traveller	3·02	0·95	5·63	0·49	11·01
18 Fireman	2·85	1·52	2·58	2·23	9·62
11 Chef	3·18	0·45	-0·06	4·08	7·25
8 Car Worker	4·29	3·09	1·94	1·61	12·73
25 Newsagent & Tobacconist	3·72	0·56	0·93	2·23	7·09
34 Sheet Metal Worker	1·67	1·33	0·53	1·49	5·13
16 Dock Labourer	4·08	1·09	5·32	2·00	15·34
9 Carpenter	1·76	0·28	1·09	1·01	4·12
19 Fitter	1·23	0·31	0·16	2·61	3·54
5 Bricklayer	2·43	0·27	1·67	1·18	5·49
6 Bus Driver	0·85	0·13	0·27	1·04	2·39
35 Shop Assistant	1·32	0·01	0·92	3·18	5·23
33 Routine Clerk	1·68	-0·16	0·85	1·12	3·87
4 Barman	4·00	-0·14	0·36	0·89	5·77
30 Quarry Worker	4·20	0·09	0·41	0·80	5·44
38 Tractor Driver	0·54	-0·03	-0·04	2·17	3·68
31 Railway Porter	1·02	0·45	0·08	1·35	2·86
1 Agricultural Labourer	1·39	0·52	0·63	1·41	6·16
32 Road Sweeper	1·24	0·20	-0·05	1·96	3·00
Sum	110·30	52·24	78·33	82·49	341·23

the data further in a search for the determinants of status disagreement. We might, for example, classify the respondents by age, sex and social status and calculate the mean of each category of respondent for each disputed occupation on the JR term of the analysis. Or, taking an alternative approach, and writing **A** for the JR matrix of mean deviation ratings of each occupation by each respondent, we might calculate the pairs of latent vectors $\mathbf{q}_j$ and $\mathbf{u}_j$ such that $\mathbf{q}_j{'}\mathbf{A}\mathbf{u}_j = \lambda_j$ (a latent root), which represent patterns of relations between respondents and occupations.* Similar analyses might be made of each index of status indeterminacy (apart from error). However, the number and method of selection of the respondents in the present study do not justify such detailed explorations.

The indices of status *discrepancy* are more heterogeneous than the indices of status disagreement. The outstanding occupation is that of policeman, whose power is well above his mean status, while his standard of living is well below. For the ballet dancer, by contrast, standard of living and, to some extent, prestige are thought to exceed power and influence. The social worker and the primary teacher are regarded as having a relatively low standard of living and relatively high power and influence. †

Coming now to the index of status *profile disagreement* we must first explain what we mean by the term. The index corresponds to the personal-profile component jrd and it indicates the extent to which people have profiles of the occupation over the four dimensions which differ from the average profile in the sample as a whole. Profile disagreement, therefore, means 'disagreement about discrepancy'. Ballet dancer is again the subject of considerable disagreement. A group of occupations which manifests a fair degree of disagreement consists of: commercial traveller, dock labourer, nonconformist minister, SRN, foreman and TV announcer. These differ from ballet dancer in that none, except possibly nurse, has high discrepancy over the sample as a whole. The low value of the index for policeman indicates that there is little disagreement over the discrepant profile of that occupation.

Seeking the determinants of status indeterminacy

Ballet dancer is the only occupation which has been high on each of the three measures of status indeterminacy. It is, therefore, analysed

---

* An example of the factorization of an interaction matrix is reported in Hope, 1969a.

† One of our respondents, when asked to say what he had in mind in ranking occupations for their 'power and influence over other people' drew a clear distinction between the influence of a psychiatrist or a shop assistant and the power of a trade union leader. This respondent also distinguished between intensive power or influence brought to bear on few people, as by a psychiatrist, and extensive power or influence. Having ranked the occupations on three dimensions and being told that another was to be employed he guessed that it might be 'how their health is affected'.

TABLE 11

Position of 'ballet dancer' in terms of three analyses which represent aspects of status indeterminacy

Respondent	S	Term JRD Dimension P	I	Term JR
A	0·13	0·16	−0·30	−0·11
B	0·04	−0·23	0·19	0·10
C	−1·12	0·23	0·89	0·52
D	−0·27	0·99	−0·72	0·21
E	0·35	−0·17	−0·17	0·02
F	0·03	−0·02	−0·00	0·18
G	1·03	−0·39	−0·63	0·18
H	−0·40	−0·37	0·77	−1·16
I	0·16	−0·06	−0·10	0·52
J	0·05	−0·13	0·08	−0·47
Term JD	0·44	0·13	−0·57	(Term J = −0·06)

in Table 11 for illustrative purposes. The body of the table contains mean ratings of the occupations on each dimension, averaged over the two occasions. The sum of every row and every column is, apart from rounding errors, zero. If each element of the 10×3 matrix is squared and multiplied by the number of occasions the resultant values sum to the sum of squares JRD for ballet dancer in Table 9. Similarly, the eleventh row of the table sums to zero and is the source of the JR sum of squares for ballet dancer. The fourth column sums to zero and is the source of the JD sum of squares. The grand mean (in brackets) is the mean rating of ballet dancer over all eighty columns of the standardized data matrix. It is a non-standardized version of the mean 99 in Table 9.

In Table 11 it is possible to see that respondent H, who has a low opinion of the status of ballet dancers, credits them with about equal power, prestige and standard of living, that is, his profile is roughly equal and opposite to the overall profile given in the bottom row of the table. The two profiles iron one another out. Respondent J, on the other hand, who also has a fairly low assessment of the occupation, follows the sample profile closely, and G, who is a little above average in his overall assessment, displays a much-intensified version of the sample's profile.

Analyses of this sort are of no more than psychological interest so long as we are not in a position to relate them to social characteristics of the respondents. However, with a large sample of respondents, each of whom would be assigned to a position on each member of a set of social variates, we could explore the extent and nature of the social determination of the perception of occupational status. An appropriate analysis would involve a multivariate non-orthogonal design in the analysis of variance supplemented by the extraction of 'explanatory variates' as these are defined in the paper *Quantifying constraints on social mobility*.

The evaluation of occupations

Most of the preceding analysis has been of the three dimensions S, P and I. In this and the following section we look at the relations among all four dimensions, and first we look at the discrepancies between non-normative and normative gradings.

An examination of the difference column of Table 4 shows the effect of introducing Value to Society into the criteria of status. There are no surprises here. Those occupations whose 'value' exceeds their non-normative status are the life-giving (agricultural labourer), life-saving or protecting (fireman, policeman, medical officer, nurse), and life-enhancing (teacher, social-worker) occupations, all of which are associated with central social values. The craft occupations undergo little revaluation. The most disvalued occupations are barman and television announcer, occupations associated with leisure and entertainment. We may surmise that the former suffers because his trade is thought to be noxious whereas the latter is downgraded because his non-evaluated status is thought to be excessive. Occupations which also suffer disvaluation (clerk, company director, insurance agent, newsagent, accountant) are commercial service functions which lack immediate biological or welfare relevance. Foreman and works manager change little.

A typology of occupational profiles

The element of Table 3 which reflects the extent to which the sample as a whole attributes different profiles to the various occupations is the Occupations × Dimensions (JD) term. The sum of squares of this term is derived from a 40 × 4, Occupations by Dimensions, matrix, each of whose elements is a mean over the ten respondents and the two occasions. The JD sum of squares is the sum of squares of this matrix multiplied by 10 × 2 = 20. The matrix, therefore, contains the averaged profiles of the occupations.

An empirical classification of occupations in terms of the extent to which they share a profile, irrespective of their general ranking in the status hierarchy*, may be obtained by treating the columns of the matrix as axes of a space in which each occupation is represented by a point, and examining the clustering of these points. The method used to identify the empirical clustering is that known as Complete Analysis, which incorporates an approximately minimum-variance taxonomic procedure applied to a Euclidean metric (Hope, 1969b).

The variances of the four dimensions in the Occupations × Dimen-

* This is a particular case of taxonomic analysis after the elimination of the 'size' factor, which is discussed in Hope, 1970.

TABLE 12

Latent roots and vectors of the Occupations × Dimensions matrix of means.

Dimension	Component		
	1	2	3
Standard of Living (S)	0·57	−0·52	−0·39
Prestige in the Community (P)	0·20	0·08	−0·84
Power and Influence (I)	0·02	0·78	0·37
Value to Society (V)	−0·79	−0·34	0·07
Latent root	0·31	0·07	0·02
% variance	77·65	16·68	5·67

sions matrix are: (S) 0·12 (P) 0·03 (I) 0·04 and (V) 0·20. The mean of these variances is 0·10. There are three non-zero latent roots accounting respectively, for 78 per cent, 17 per cent and 6 per cent of the variance. The latent vectors are shown in Table 12. The positions of the occupations in the space of the first two components are shown in Figure 1 and the clustering of the occupations in the space of all three components is shown in Figure 2.

If we look at level 0·66 of the dendrogram we see that the taxonomic analysis finds three clusters, whose means have been indicated in Figure 1 by the letters A, B and C. Policeman is not included in this taxonomy, though it joins cluster C at the next level of the dendrogram. The tightness or looseness of a cluster may be indexed by a coefficient of dispersion which is the sum of squared distances of constituent occupations from the mean of their cluster, divided by the number of occupations in a cluster and also by the number of dimensions = 4. (The index of dispersion for all forty occupations considered as a single cluster is 0·10, the mean of the variances of the dimensions.) The dispersion of each cluster is given in Table 13. When A and B unite to form a single cluster at level 0·73 the dispersion of this larger unit is 0·06.

TABLE 13

Relations of three clusters of occupations to the four dimensions in the Occupations × Dimensions matrix. (Note that one occupation does not belong to any of the clusters)

Cluster	n	Index of dispersion	Distance of cluster mean from the origin	Mean of cluster on			
				S	P	I	V
A	15	0·03	0·56	0·27	0·14	0·07	−0·47
B	19	0·03	0·18	0·00	−0·08	−0·07	0·15
C	5	0·02	0·95	−0·62	−0·06	−0·05	0·72

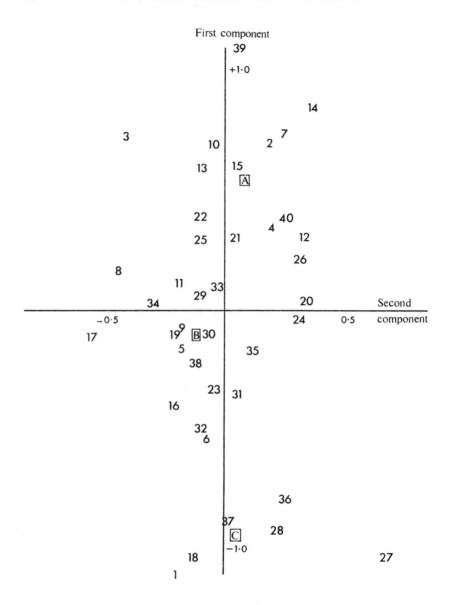

FIG. 1. Plot of forty occupations in a two-dimensional space which contains 94 per cent of the sum of squares of their profiles.

Occupation

Level of the criterion

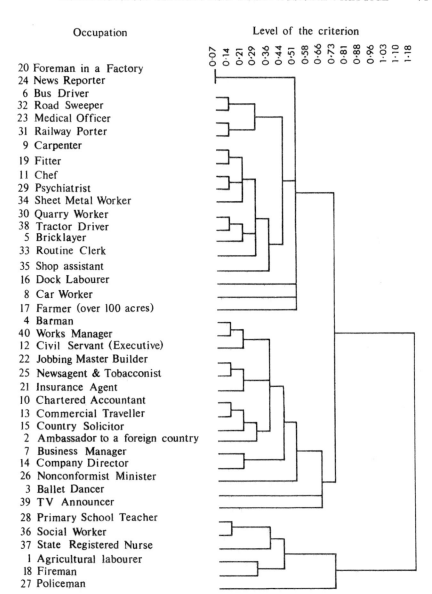

20 Foreman in a Factory
24 News Reporter
 6 Bus Driver
32 Road Sweeper
23 Medical Officer
31 Railway Porter
 9 Carpenter
19 Fitter
11 Chef
29 Psychiatrist
34 Sheet Metal Worker
30 Quarry Worker
38 Tractor Driver
 5 Bricklayer
33 Routine Clerk
35 Shop assistant
16 Dock Labourer
 8 Car Worker
17 Farmer (over 100 acres)
 4 Barman
40 Works Manager
12 Civil Servant (Executive)
22 Jobbing Master Builder
25 Newsagent & Tobacconist
21 Insurance Agent
10 Chartered Accountant
13 Commercial Traveller
15 Country Solicitor
 2 Ambassador to a foreign country
 7 Business Manager
14 Company Director
26 Nonconformist Minister
 3 Ballet Dancer
39 TV Announcer
28 Primary School Teacher
36 Social Worker
37 State Registered Nurse
 1 Agricultural labourer
18 Fireman
27 Policeman

FIG. 2. Dendrogram showing the clustering of occupations according to the
similarity of their profiles across four dimensions of occupational status.

TABLE 14
*Mean of each cluster on each principal component of the Occupations ×
Dimensions matrix.*

		Component		
Cluster	n	1	2	3
A	15	$-0{\cdot}56$	$0{\cdot}08$	$-0{\cdot}02$
B	19	$-0{\cdot}14$	$-0{\cdot}11$	$0{\cdot}05$
C	5	$-0{\cdot}94$	$0{\cdot}04$	$-0{\cdot}16$

The means of the clusters on the original dimensions are given in
Table 13 and their means on the components are given in Table 14. It
can be seen that the taxonomy is effected mainly in terms of the first
component, which contrasts relatively affluent with relatively valued
occupations.

Reliability of the ratings

We have already examined the stability of the functions measured
by the ratings but we have not yet assessed the reliability with which
those functions may be measured. Several types of reliability may be
specified in a design of this nature and these may be introduced by the
device of a pooling square which is a more complex version of that employed by Mahmoud (1955) and Hope (1969a). The elements of the pooling square (Table 15) represent variances and covariances. Two conditions are distinguished for each of three terms of the analysis. For
example, taking the term Respondents, in estimating the covariance of
two sets of ratings we distinguish two cases, one in which both sets

TABLE 15
Pooling square

			R_1				R_2					
Respondents		O_1		O_2		O_1		O_2				
Occasions												
Dimensions	D_1	D_2	D_1	D_2	D_1	D_2	D_1	D_2				
	v_{rod}	c_{ro}	c_{rd}	c_r	c_{od}	c_o	c_d	c	D_1	O_1		R_1
		v_{rod}	c_r	c_{rd}	c_o	c_{od}	c	c_d	D_2			
			v_{rod}	c_{ro}	c_d	c	c_{od}	c_o	D_1	O_2		
				v_{rod}	c	c_d	c_o	c_{od}	D_2			
					v_{rod}	c_{ro}	c_{rd}	c_r	D_1	O_1		R_2
						v_{rod}	c_r	c_{rd}	D_2			
							v_{rod}	c_{ro}	D_1	O_2		
								v_{rod}	D_2			

were obtained from the same respondent and one in which the sets were obtained from different respondents. It is sufficient, therefore, to represent Respondents in the pooling square by only two states, R_1 and R_2. Similarly, Occasions is represented by O_1 and O_2 and Dimensions by D_1 and D_2. In the square variances are symbolized by the letter v and covariances by c. The subscripts of an element are determined by the concomitance or lack of it of the row and column symbols for that element. For example, in the first row and second column we write c_{ro} because this term stands for a covariance in which the same respondent has rated occupations* on the same occasion. The subscript d is omitted because the ratings are on two different dimensions. The term c without subscript signifies the covariance between different respondents rating different dimensions on different occasions. The symmetry of the square (or rather half-square as it is given in Table 15; the missing lower triangle is of course the mirror image of the upper triangle) is such that every covariance appears four times, but no distinction is to be drawn among these four appearances. In every case a particular covariance represents the same number, namely the average of all covariances which satisfy the subscripts of c. It is easy to see that, with three dimensions†, there are $3(3 - 1)/2 = 3$ covariances for each person on each occasion which satisfy the subscripts of c_{ro}. And so, taken over all ten respondents and both occasions, c_{ro} stands for a mean of $10 \times 2 \times 3 = 60$ covariances.

It is a simple matter to compute the value of each element of the pooling square from a consideration of the variance components which do and do not contribute to it. All elements involve component j for Occupations. In addition c_{ro}, for example, involves the interaction components jr, jo and jro, so that we write

$$c_{ro} = j + jr + jo + jro$$

The constitution of each element of the pooling square is indicated by plus signs in Table 16.

It can be seen that v_{rod} is simply the sum of all variance components. In the case of a design in which all four factors are random the value of v_{rod} is necessarily unity (when all the columns of the matrix of ratings have been standardized), and the covariance elements of the pooling square represent means of product-moment correlations among appropriate columns of the data matrix. Having assumed that Dimensions is a fixed effect we find that $v_{rod} = 1 \cdot 04$ and we divide this into each covariance to obtain a correlation coefficient r (Table 17). These correlations may

---

* No subscript for Occupations is employed because Occupations is universally present in every element of the pooling square.

† It will be noted that Value to Society is omitted from the calculation of reliability.

TABLE 16

Elements of the pooling square in terms of variance components.

Variance component

Element	j	jr	jo	jd	jro	jrd	jod	$jrod$
c	+							
c_r	+	+						
c_o	+		+					
c_d	+			+				
c_{ro}	+	+	+		+			
c_{rd}	+	+		+		+		
c_{od}	+		+	+			+	
v_{rod}	+	+	+	+	+	+	+	+

TABLE 17

Elements of the pooling square and corresponding correlation coefficients.

Coefficient	Element	Correlation
c	0·7032	0·6733
c_r	0·8135	0·7789
c_o	0·7040	0·6741
c_d	0·7554	0·7233
c_{ro}	0·8288	0·7936
c_{rd}	0·9440	0·9039
c_{od}	0·7588	0·7266
v_{rod}	1·0444	1·0000

be employed as estimates of reliability. For example, $r_{rd} = 0·90$ is the reliability with which a respondent will repeat his ratings of occupations on a given dimension. The reliability or extent of agreement between different respondents rating the same dimension on the same occasion is $r_{od} = 0·73$, which scarcely differs from the correlation between two different respondents rating the same dimension on two different occasions $r_d = 0·72$. The degree of correlation between a particular respondent's assessment of different dimensions is given by $r_{ro} = 0·79$ and $r_r = 0·78$. The correlation between different respondents' ratings on different dimensions is $r_o = 0·67$ and $r = 0·67$.

The negligible influence of Occasions enables us to simplify the findings of this section. Table 18 contains a reduced pooling square, lacking the factor of Occasions, with Dimensions and Respondents interchanged, and with r_{rd} in the diagonal. The other elements of the

TABLE 18

*Reduced pooling square with reliabilities rather than unities
in the diagonal.*

Dimensions		D_1		D_2			
Respondents	R_1	R_2	R_1	R_2			
	0·90	0·72	0·78	0·67	R_1	D_1	
		0·90	0·67	0·78	R_2		
			0·90	0·72	R_1	D_2	
				0·90	R_2		

square are r_d, r_r and r. In interpreting these coefficients it must be borne
in mind that they estimate the reliability of a single set of ratings by a
single rater. The reliability of the mean of several sets of ratings is of
course higher than the reliability of the individual sets which have been
averaged.

Each of the seven estimated correlations in Table 17 may be compared with the corresponding estimate derived from the completely random model (which is a mean of product-moment correlations among the
appropriate columns of the standardized data matrix). Discrepancies
between corresponding estimates derived from the two models vary
within the limits $-0·015$ and $+0·010$, that is, they are negligible.

The coefficients in Table 18 may be used to determine the 'true'
correlation between different dimensions, that is to find the extent to
which the three dimensions splay out from one another, on average. The
coefficient $r_r = 0·78$ indicates the mean correlation between ratings of
different dimensions by the same person, but we would expect this to
contain a halo effect. The coefficient $r = 0·67$ represents the mean correlation between different dimensions rated by different persons, and
the difference between the two, $0·11$, is an indication of the extent to
which halo effects occur (Chi, 1937). Since r_{rd} is the reliability with
which an individual respondent rates occupations on a particular dimension we may use it to correct r for attenuation due to unreliability. Then
$r/r_{rd} = 0·74$ represents an estimate of the average 'true' or 'objective'
correlation between different dimensions of occupational status, an
e stimate which discounts both halo effects and effects of unreliability.

Appendix:

A further pilot study

The data which have been analysed in the second part of this paper were
derived from relatives and acquaintances of the authors who were socially fairly
heterogeneous. To try the procedure under different, and in some ways, more
testing, conditions another pilot study, also of ten persons, was carried out on
a sample drawn randomly from the electoral register for a working-class area of

Oxford. The sample was constrained to contain equal numbers of men and women. Eighteen people had to be approached before ten respondents were obtained. The administration of the task was undertaken by Miss Anne Sharp.

Apart from the nature of the sample, the only difference between the two tasks was the omission from the second of 'Prestige in the Community' (P) and its replacement by 'the Interest of the Work' (W). The dimensions were always administered in the order S, W, I and V, and the interval between the first and second occasions was again about one week.

Table 19 shows the analysis of variance of the three dimensions S, W and I, and is comparable with the analysis of S, P and I shown in Table 6. The two outstanding changes are first, an increase of about 20 per cent in error (from 8 per cent to 27 per cent) and second, a decrease of 28 per cent in the common-general term (from 67 per cent to 39 per cent). Apart from these two changes the only differences worthy of mention are that the Occupations × Respondents term is rather larger and the Occupations × Respondents × Occasions term is not as close to zero as it was in the original analysis. These two differences suggest that there is more personal-general variance but that it is not as stable as in the former analysis (the coefficient of stability is 0·83, as against 0·88 formerly). The stability of the sample's common-general ratings is again 1·00.

However, the most important feature of the second pilot study is the relatively large second-order interaction for the new dimension, W, analysed in isolation from its companions. In the comparable analyses of the previous study S, P and I had error (second-order interaction) variances of 8—12 per cent and V had an error variance of 22 per cent. In the new study the error variances of the individual dimensions are (S) 21 per cent, (W) 49 per cent, (I) 26 per cent and (V) 44 per cent. While all errors have increased, in consequence of the nature of the sample, the substitution of W for P has introduced a dimension whose error is of the same order of magnitude as the error of V. The analysis of S, W and I is less valid than the analysis of S, P and I because the former is heterogeneous with respect to error while the latter is homogeneous. We may surmise that people find it hard to grade 'the Interest of the Work' because they are at two removes from the characteristic they are being asked to consider. In the first place they are only imperfectly aware of the nature of the tasks undertaken in a particular job, and in the second place they find the estimation of the subjective interest of those tasks difficult. Indeed, they may not concede that there can be an agreed assessment *in abstracto* of the subjective and interactive relations between a man's character and the tasks he is called upon to perform in fulfilling his occupational roles.

There is no reason to suppose that P would not have behaved like S and I if it had been included in place of W. The main contrast, therefore, between our first, highly selected, respondents and a random sample of a working-class area is an increase of the error variance of the non-normative dimensions from about 10 per cent to about 25 per cent. An increase was to be expected and the existence of about 25 per cent error in the grading of an occupation by a single respondent is not discouraging, since it implies that a very high degree of reliability may be obtained by averaging over only a small number, say ten or fifteen, of respondents.

Besides giving us a more realistic estimate of error the second pilot study has warned us to pick our dimensions with an eye to the uniformity of their error components. This admonition emerged from the data only after they had been subjected to lengthy and detailed analysis. We feel that this point illustrates the value of our rather unusual proceeding in which we have, as it were, carried out the analysis in advance of collecting the data. It is our contention that piloting

TABLE 19

Analysis of gradings of occupations by ten respondents (randomly sampled from a working-class area) on three dimensions: Standard of Living (S), the Interest of the Work (W), and Power and Influence over other people (I). cf. Table 6 for an identical analysis of gradings on S, P and I by ten selected respondents.

Source	d.f.	Sum of squares	Mean square	Variance component
Occupations	39	1019·1755	26·1327	0·4124
Occupations × Respondents	351	507·1394	1·4448	0·1757
Occupations × Occasions	39	13·1106	0·3362	−0·0018
Occupations × Dimensions	78	121·6800	1·5600	0·0580
Occupations × Respondents × Occasions	351	137·1089	0·3906	0·0359
Occupations × Respondents × Dimensions	702	326·1421	0·4646	0·0909
Occupations × Occasions × Dimensions	78	17·0990	0·2192	−0·0064
Error	702	198·5446	0·2828	0·2828
Sum	2340	2340·0001	—	1·0475

the analysis is at least as important as piloting the data-collection procedures, and that both must be carried out if the suitability of the one to the other is to be adequately assessed.

References

BARBER, B. (1957). *Social stratification*. Harcourt, Brace & Co., New York.

BURT, C. (1955). Test reliability estimated by analysis of variance. *Brit. J. Statist. Psychol.*, **8**, 103–18.

CHI, P.L. (1937). Statistical analysis of personality rating. *J. exp. Educ.*, **5**, 229–45.

DAVIS, K. (1945). Some principles of stratification. *Amer. Sociol. Rev.*, **10**, 242–9.

DUNCAN, O.D. (1961). A socioeconomic index for all occupations. In A.J. Reiss, *Occupations and social status*. Free Press of Glencoe. New York.

DUNCAN, O.D. and ARTIS, J.W. (1951). *Social stratification in a Pennsylvania rural community*. Pennsylvania State College: Agricultural Experiment Station Bulletin 543.

FISHER, R.A. (1958). *Statistical methods for research workers* (13th edn). Oliver and Boyd, Edinburgh.

GERSTL, J. and COHEN, L.K. (1964). Dissensus, situs and egocentrism in occupational ranking. *Brit. J. Sociol.*, **15**, 254–61.

GOFFMAN, E. (1963). *Stigma*. Prentice Hall, Englewood Cliffs.

GOLDTHORPE, J.H., LOCKWOOD, D., BECHHOFER, F. and PLATT, J. (1969). *The affluent worker in the class structure*. Cambridge University Press.

GUSFIELD, J.R. and SCHWARTZ, M. (1963). The meaning of occupational prestige: reconsideration of the NORC scale. *Amer. Sociol. Rev.*, **28**, 265–71.

HALL, J. and JONES, D.C. (1950). The social grading of occupations, *Brit. J. Sociol.*, **1**, 31–55.

HODGE, R.W., TREIMAN, D.J. and ROSSI, P. (1966). A comparative study of occupational prestige. In *Class, Status and power* (2nd edn). (ed. R. Bendix and S.M. Lipset). Free Press of Glencoe, New York.

HOPE, K. (1964). The constancy of hostility. Paper delivered to the Edinburgh University Group for Defence Studies, conference on aggression.

HOPE, K. (1968). Handbook of multivariate methods programmed in Atlas Autocode, which forms the appendix to the hardbacked edition of *Methods of multivariate analysis*. University of London Press.

HOPE, K. (1969a). The study of hostility in the temperaments of spouses: definitions and methods. *Brit. J. Math. Statist. Psychol.*, **22**, 67–95.

HOPE, K. (1969b). The Complete Analysis of a data matrix. *Brit. J. Psychiat.*, **115**, 1069–79.

HOPE, K. (1970). The Complete Analysis of a data matrix: application and interpretation. *Brit. J. Psychiat.*, **116**, 657–66.

HOPE, K. and CAINE, T.M. (1968). The Hysteroid–Obsessoid Questionnaire: a new validation. *Brit. J. soc. clin. Psychol.*, **7**, 210–5.

INKELES, A. and ROSSI, P. (1956). National comparisons of occupational prestige. *Amer. J. Sociol.*, **61**, 329–39.

KENDALL, M.G. (1962). *Rank correlation methods* (3rd edn). Griffin, London.

LENSKI, G.E. (1954). Status crystallization: a non-vertical dimension of social status. *Amer. Sociol. Rev.*, **19**, 405–13.

MAHMOUD, A.F. (1955). Test reliability in terms of factor theory. *Brit. J. Statist. Psychol.*, **8**, 119–35.

MOSER, C.A. and HALL, J. (1954). The social grading of occupations. In *Social mobility in Britain* (ed. D.V. Glass). Routledge, London.

N.O.R.C. (1947). Jobs and occupations: a popular evaluation. *Opinion News*, 9th September. Reprinted in *Class, status and power* (1st edn). (ed. R. Bendix and S.M. Lipset). Free Press of Glencoe, New York.

OSSOWSKI, S. (1963). *Class structure in the social consciousness.* Routledge, London.

PILLINER, A.E.G. (1965). The application of analysis of variance in psychometric experimentation. Unpublished Ph.D. thesis, University of Edinburgh.

REISS, A.J. (1961). *Occupations and social status.* Free Press of Glencoe, New York.

SCHULTZ, E.F. (1955). Rules of thumb for determining expectations of mean squares in the analysis of variance. *Biometrics*, **11**, 123–35.

SHILS, E.A. (1968). Deference. In *Social stratification* (ed. J.A. Jackson). Cambridge University Press.

STANLEY, J.C. (1961). Analysis of unreplicated three-way classifications, with applications to rater bias and trait independence. *Psychometrika*, **26**, 205–20.

SVALASTOGA, K. (1959). *Prestige, class and mobility.* Gyldendal, Copenhagen.

TAFT, R. (1953). The social grading of occupations in Australia. *Brit. J. Sociol.*, **4**, 181–8.

TIRYAKIAN, E. (1958). The prestige evaluation of occupations in an underdeveloped country: the Phillipines. *Amer. J. Sociol.*, **63**, 390–9.

TURNER, R. (1958). Life situation and subculture. *Brit. J. Sociol.*, **9**, 299–320.

SOCIAL MOBILITY AND FERTILITY

by K. HOPE

Summary. In several recent studies the effects of mobility or status inconsistency on a dependent variable have been quantified by means of an additive model in which sets of constants have been fitted to two principles of classification. In examining a particular application of this model the following paper begins by suggesting the possibility that the underlying hypothesis may be more adequately represented by a symmetrical model which fits one and the same set of constants to both principles of classification.

The second purpose of the paper is to show that, *whether or not the symmetrical model is deemed to be the more appropriate*, the basic hypothesis can be adequately tested only by the formulation of likely alternatives and the employment of tests which are specific to those alternatives.

Thirdly, a consideration of two alternatives to the basic model, one of which is simply a linear transformation of the other, implicitly demonstrates that some of the problems (of 'multicollinearity' or 'identification') which are associated with quantitative studies of difference variables such as inconsistency or mobility are analogous to the pseudo-problems generated by the concept of rotation in factor analysis.

The generalization of the methods employed to more than two principles of classification, and to more than one dependent variable, is obvious.

This paper will appear in the *American Sociological Review*, 1971, vol. 77.

Preamble

In their outstanding work on *The American occupational structure* Professors Blau and Duncan devote a number of pages to a discussion of what they call 'the mobility hypothesis', particularly to the form* in which it was advanced by R.A.Fisher in *The genetical theory of natural selection*. Various formulations of the hypothesis are cited. It is claimed that the hypothesis is refuted if the data exemplify a particular pattern, which they term 'the additive hypothesis'. In this paper data which have previously been held to satisfy the additive hypothesis are re-examined to see whether in fact they satisfy that hypothesis, either in its original form or in a modified form.

The analysis is carried out entirely within the terms laid down by the preceding work and the form of the analysis is a repetition and extension of that work. These limitations have been observed quite deliberately in order to ensure that the two sides of the argument come adequately to grips with one another.

It should, however, be said here that the Blau and Duncan argument might perhaps be side-stepped altogether by a refusal to acknowledge that the truth of the additivity hypothesis disposes of the social mobility hypothesis, in another sense of the term. It might be said that, given that fertility decreases with increasing social class among the non-mobile, the truth of the additivity hypothesis implies that those who rise out of a particular class are less fertile and those who fall out of the same class are more fertile. Sociologists might feel that the establishment of a simple additive law would have a miraculous quality which would cry out for intensive investigation of the mechanisms which bring it about. Indeed, the fact that the additive hypothesis is even approximately true leads one to wonder how it is that the values and life-styles of former and newly-encountered social aggregates lawfully modify conception-decisions, when movement between those aggregates appears so various in its abruptness, its finality, its extent, its salience and its temporal relations to the child-bearing period.

To investigate the social mobility hypothesis, as they have defined

---

* In considering their argument it is important to note that the mobility which Blau and Duncan subject to empirical test is mobility of the present generation. They make only passing reference to the Galton—Fisher hypothesis of the inheritance of (voluntary or involuntary) infertility, which is a mechanism whereby the mobility of an antecedent generation might affect the fertility of the following generation. This restriction is apparent in their argument that if differential fertility were completely explained by social mobility then there would be no differential fertility by class among persons who do not change their class.

it, Blau and Duncan carry out four analyses, three of which yield significant departures from additivity. They say 'we are not satisfied to
observe that significant deviations $\overline{Y}_{ij} - \hat{Y}_{ij}$ occur; it must be shown
that these deviations are in some systematic way related to the notion
of mobility' (p.377). In this paper the challenge is taken up in a twofold
sense. In the first place we begin by re-analysing data which do not, by
Blau and Duncan's criterion, show significant departures from additivity,
and we show that, by a more appropriate criterion such departures are in
fact present. And in the second place we show that the departures are
systematically related to the notion of mobility, indeed that they instantiate that form of the mobility hypothesis with which additivity is incompatible. The nub of the argument is that the criterion of departure from
additivity is blunt-edged: it lumps together likely and unlikely departures
in such a way that the former are swamped by the latter. The sociologist
and the non-sociologist (e.g. Fisher) alike, faced with a table which re-
lates mobility to fertility (such as Table 1 below) would begin by distinguishing the mobile from the non-mobile and the upwardly-mobile from
the downwardly-mobile. He would ask whether mobility as such is related
to fertility, whether direction of mobility affects fertility, and whether
fertility varies with extent of movement. To quote Westoff's discussion
(1956), 'In its most simple outline, there is a three-point continuum:
upward mobility, immobility or stability, and downward mobility. In addition to direction, there is the question of intensity or degree of movement'. These questions are posed below as explicit alternatives to the
additive hypothesis. They are not factitious consequences of a desperate
search for significance. On the contrary they arise naturally, and have
arisen, in advance of any empirical examination of the facts*.

* This preamble grew out of comments and criticisms on the following sections of the
paper which were made by Mrs. Jean Floud and Professor O.D. Duncan. As a reward for
my attack on his hypothesis Professor Duncan has, with his usual generosity, supplied
me with data on which further studies of fertility and mobility may be carried out. Although
we appear to disagree on several points he and I are in entire agreement on the need to
replicate findings such as those reported here. The additive hypothesis, in an approximate form, has already stood up to several replications and is to that extent on a surer
footing than the mobility effect which I claim to detect.

Introduction

Empirical studies of the relations between fertility and social mobility have led demographers to induce that 'the average fertility of those who move up or down the socio-economic scale appears to be intermediate between that of the class from which they came and that of the class into which they have moved' (Maxwell, 1953, 101n; see also chapter 11 of Blau and Duncan, 1967). Precision may be given to this observation by replacing the word 'intermediate' by the word 'halfway'. The first purpose of this paper is to design a model which adequately expresses the proposition that the fertility of socially mobile couples is halfway between the fertility of the class from which they remove and the fertility of the class into which they move. The second purpose of the paper is to suggest alternatives to the hypothesis whose empirical plausibility may be assessed as a means of testing the basic hypothesis, which we shall call the Halfway hypothesis.

In the following two sections we begin by considering a model which Professor O.D. Duncan employed to test for the existence of a mobility effect on fertility. This model is regarded as not entirely appropriate to the test of the Halfway hypothesis though it is closely related to the model which is found to be more appropriate, and the two do not differ significantly in their degree of fit to the data which are subjected to analysis.

Duncan refers to his model, which is called here model one, as an exemplification of the additivity hypothesis. The refined version which constitutes our second model exemplifies what we call the Halfway hypothesis. These names may cause some confusion because both models are in fact additive. Our purpose in presenting these two, slightly differing, models is to challenge theorists to define the hypothesized consequences of their theories so precisely that the empirical worker can decide a priori which model better represents a certain hypothesis.

The particular (additivity) model which is investigated below is of wider interest than our concentration on a single study of fertility might suggest, since it is relevant, for example, to any study whose aim is to decide whether a person with two discrepant sources of status stands halfway between persons who are crystallized at his higher level and other persons who are crystallized at his lower level (e.g. Hodge and Treiman, 1966). Generalization of the model to three or more stratification axes is a very simple matter.

The data

The relations between social mobility and fertility were investigated by Berent (1952) in a paper which Professor Duncan has described as 'the only worthwhile discussion of its subject' (Duncan, 1966). Berent's

TABLE 1

Mean number of live births per couple, by present social class and class of origin of husband

Present social class

		I	II	III	IV	All
	I	1·74	1·79	1·96	2·00	1·81
Social origin	II	2·05	2·14	2·51	2·97	2·38
of	III	1·87	2·01	2·67	3·69	2·81
husband	IV	2·40	3·20	3·22	3·68	3·44
	All	1·88	2·17	2·73	3·56	2·77

TABLE 2

Numbers of couples from which the means in Table 1 were derived.

Present social class

		I	II	III	IV	All
	I	65	43	23	11	142
Social origin	II	38	197	150	68	453
of	III	37	154	431	244	866
husband	IV	5	45	162	220	432
	All	145	439	766	543	1893

data were derived from a sample representing the population of England and Wales taken in 1949. He reported the mean fertilities* of 1893 married couples, classified by the occupational class of the husband's father and the occupational class of the husband himself (Tables 1 and 2). He also presented an analysis of variance of these data. Duncan repeated the analysis of variance (or 'multiple classification analysis', as it is sometimes known, perhaps in allusion to the title of Yates's original (1934) paper on analyses of variance with unequal numbers in the cells) and he reports the constants of the model which is implicit in Berent's analysis. On the basis of this analysis Duncan concludes that there is no need to postulate an effect of social mobility on fertility. He finds that the fertility of a couple may be regarded as a combination of the fertility of their class of origin (class of husband's father) and the fertility of their destination class (husband's own class). There is no significant deviation of the observed mean fertilities from those estimated on the basis of this hypothesis. Duncan's analysis is employed in the following section to give a lead into the test of the Half-way hypothesis.

* number of live births to couples married for more than twenty years, neither member having been previously married.

The first model

In his analysis Duncan assumes that a class can have two fertilities, one when it is an origin class and the other when it is a destination class. His model, which is the first to be considered here may be written;

$$\hat{Y}_{ij} = \mu + a_i + b_j$$

where $\hat{Y}_{ij}$ is the estimated mean fertility of couples in origin class i and destination class j, $\mu = 2 \cdot 77$ represents the general mean, a_i represents the fertility of the ith class of origin, and b_j represents the fertility of the jth destination class. Table 3 shows that the sum of squares of the deviations from the model, that is the sum of squares of $(\overline{Y}_{ij} - \hat{Y}_{ij})$ where $\overline{Y}_{ij}$ represents an observed cell mean in Table 1, is $66 \cdot 72$.*

TABLE 3

Test of the first model of the effect of class on fertility. The fitted constants are the a_i and b_j of the model $\hat{Y}_{ij} = \mu + a_i + b_j$

Source	d.f.	SS	MS
Fitted constants	6	729·60	121·60
Residual	9	66·72	7·41
Within cells	1877	9311·50	4·96
Total	1892	10 107·82	

This model has been employed in a very similar analysis of comparable American data in chapter 11 of Blau and Duncan's (1967) *The American occupational structure*. There it is argued that 'it is plausible to assume that there are separate effects for the two statuses because differential fertility is observed when couples are classified either by husband's first job or by current occupation' (page 374). The argument from differential fertility for both origin and destination implies that both should be taken into account in arriving at an estimate of the effect of class on the fertility of a married couple. It does not, however, imply that, because origin and destination each has its effect, the magnitude of a class effect should differ according to whether it is an origin or a destination class. A supplementary proposition is required to justify the postulation of two separate effects for one and the same class. One such supplement might run as follows: class i considered as an origin will differ from class i considered as a destination because the former antedates the latter by a period of time which may be quite lengthy.

* It should be noted that Berent gives the Between cells sum of squares as 762·8 whereas Table 3 shows that it should be 729·60 + 66·72 = 796·32. Berent's error may imply a corresponding overestimation of the Within cells sum of squares (if that was obtained by subtraction) but an error of this magnitude in the Within term is negligible. Alternatively there may be a slight error in the data as reported.

The second model

It might, however, be thought that the class effects will be roughly constant over time, and a second model, incorporating this assumption, may be constructed:

$$\hat{Y}_{ij} = \mu + c_i + c_j$$

This fits a constant effect for a class whether that class is an origin or a destination class. Naturally, the explained sum of squares for the second model is less than that for the first, but there is a compensating increase in the residual degrees of freedom. In the first model eight constants are fitted, six of them being independent. In the second model four constants are fitted, three of them being independent.

We may assess the importance of the difference between the two models by testing the discrepancy between the residuals, which yields a sum of squares of $89 \cdot 68 - 66 \cdot 72 = 22 \cdot 96$ with 3 degrees of freedom. This is not significant, but it is sufficiently large to make us hesitant about accepting the hypothesis of no difference. The marginal constants for the two models are given in Table 4. It should be observed that the second model is a subset of the first in that the sum of squares explicable by the two models acting together is identical with the sum of squares attributable to the first model alone.

TABLE 4

Constants of two models: first model $\hat{Y}_{ij} = \mu + a_i + b_j$
second model $\hat{Y}_{ij} = \mu + c_i + c_j$

		First model		Second model
		a	b	c
	I	$-0\cdot58$	$-0\cdot60$	$-0\cdot59$
Class	II	$-0\cdot20$	$-0\cdot50$	$-0\cdot35$
	III	$-0\cdot01$	$-0\cdot07$	$-0\cdot03$
	IV	$0\cdot42$	$0\cdot66$	$0\cdot55$

$$\mu = 2 \cdot 77$$

On the whole the second model seems to be a better interpretation of the proposition that the fertility of a couple is an additive combination or averaging of the fertility of their class of origin and that of their class of destination. This may be inferred from a comparison of the estimates of fertility which emerge from the two models. The second model, the one which ascribes a single effect to each class, yields a symmetric matrix of estimates, that is, it implies that the fertility of couples moving up from i to j is the same as the fertility of couples moving down from j to i. The first model, the one which assigns two constants to each class, does not lead to symmetric estimates. The proposition in its verbal form seems to imply symmetry in any model which purports to embody it.

Furthermore, the second model, unlike the first, yields an estimate of fertility for couples moving from i to j which is the unweighted mean of the estimate for couples remaining in i and the estimate for couples remaining in j. For example, the estimated value for stationary* couples in class one is 1·598, that for stationary couples in class two is 2·076, and the estimate for those who move, in either direction, between these two classes, is 1·837.

The effect of mobility on fertility

If we accept that model 2 is an adequate formulation of the Halfway hypothesis, it remains for us to test the fit of the hypothesis to the data. In fitting a three-dimensional model to fifteen-dimensional[†] data we are left with a large number of respects in which deviations from the model might occur. It is desirable, therefore, to examine the hypothesis to see whether any deductions may be drawn from it which may be tested in some specified subset of the residual twelve dimensions. The subset which we shall choose is one which has the property of isolating possible effects of mobility on fertility, after allowing for the class effects incorporated in the model. (The word 'effect' in the term 'mobility effect on fertility' is used here in its technical sense. The finding of a mobility effect would not imply that mobility is the *cause* of differences in fertility.)

A single dimension along which deviations from the model might occur is that contrasting the mean of all stationary couples with the mean of all mobile couples. Let us, therefore, fit a constant m which has a positive value for the diagonal cells of Table 1 and a negative value for the remaining cells. Adding this constant to the equation for the second model augments the explained sum of squares by only 2·84, which is certainly not significant. A similar constant added to the equation of the first model augments the sum of squares by 1·67.**

Two further contrasts may be drawn, one between the upwardly mobile and the rest, and the other between the downwardly mobile and the rest. Since comparison among the three means (those of the upwardly

---

* that is, stationary so far as the data allows us to determine. A couple may have moved in and out of a class several times between the two points in time for which their class is recorded. And it must be remembered that the status of a couple is defined entirely by reference to the husband's origins and occupation, omitting any reference to the wife.

† The sixteen means in the body of Table 1 may be regarded as points generating a space of fifteen dimensions.

** The absence of a contrast between the mobile and the non-mobile does not necessarily instantiate the Halfway hypothesis because the mean of the mobile is based on more downward than upward movers.

mobile, the downwardly mobile and the immobile) can be made in a space of only two dimensions it is convenient to combine these last two contrasts into a single contrast between the upwardly mobile and the downwardly mobile, with the deviation of the non-mobile from the mean of the mobile taken care of by the constant m. Let us write d for the constant which expresses the effect of direction of movement. d has a positive value for the downwardly mobile and a negative value for the upwardly mobile. Clearly, it stands for a classical sociological effect. Hawthorn and Busfield (1968, p. 193) report Berent's analysis in support of the conclusion that fertility is negatively associated with upward mobility and positively associated with downward mobility. But Hawthorn (1970 p. 109) later accepted Duncan's interpretation of Berent's data in which no mobility effect, equivalent to our constant d, is postulated.

We have now constructed a simple alternative to the second model by adding two constants to the original set. The alternative takes the forms:

for the upwardly mobile $(i > j)$ $\quad \hat{Y}_{ij} = \mu + c_i + c_j - m - d$

for the non-mobile $\qquad\qquad\quad \hat{Y}_{ii} = \mu + 2c_i + m$

for the downwardly mobile $(i < j)$ $\quad \hat{Y}_{ij} = \mu + c_i + c_j - m + d$

The sum of squares accounted for by the alternative model is 736·26, which exceeds the sum of squares attributable to the second model by 29·62. Tested against the Within mean square* of 4·96 this yields a variance ratio of $F_{2,1877} = 2·99$ which lies almost exactly at the 5 per cent point. If we test d against all the remaining effects (including m) we obtain a sum of squares of $736·26 - 709·48 = 26·78$ which, with one degree of freedom, is significant at the 2½ per cent level. Clearly, the sum of squares remaining to m is of no account.

The introductory discussion of the two models, although it tended to suggest that the second is a better embodiment of the Halfway hypothesis, did suggest a rationale for the first, namely that the fertility effect of a class may vary over time and so should be estimated separately for the class considered as an origin and for the class considered as a destination.[†] We may, therefore, ask whether the mobility effect which has been demonstrated when the hypothesis is schematized in the second model is abolished if we reincorporate into the analysis the

---

* It is convenient to employ a constant error term in all tests of significance, and the Within mean square is a good enough approximation when the value of R^2 (the ratio of the Between cells to the Total sum of squares in Table 3) is as low as 0·08. If the reader prefers an error term which errs on the conservative side he may substitute the Total mean square, which is 5·34. It is not possible to take account of the effect of the sampling design on variances.

† Other mechanisms which would imply the first model may easily be imagined. These take the form of supposing that a class is more salient to conception in one of its manifestations than it is in the other, for example as origin rather than destination, as higher rather than lower, or as some combination of the terms of these two dichotomies.

effects which are taken into account by the first model. Let us, therefore, construct an alternative to the first model. Employing the letters m and d as before we write:

for the upwardly mobile $(i > j)$ $\hat{Y}_{ij} = \mu + a_i + b_j - m - d$

for the non-mobile $\hat{Y}_{ij} = \mu + a_i + b_j + m$

for the downwardly mobile $(i < j)$ $\hat{Y}_{ij} = \mu + a_i + b_j - m + d$

The sum of squares for the first model is 729·60 (Table 3). When m is added this becomes 731·28. The sum of squares for the alternative, including both m and d, is 753·89. Once again, there is significant evidence of a difference between the fertility of the upwardly mobile and that of the downwardly mobile ($F_{1,1877} = 4·56; p < 0·05$).

Whichever model we take as representative of the effects of class on fertility we arrive at the conclusion that there is a mobility effect over and above the class effect. The mobility effect takes the form of higher fertility for the downwardly mobile and lower fertility for the upwardly mobile, with the non-mobile scarcely deviating from the weighted mean of the two. In the alternative to the second model the extent of this mobility effect on fertility is $\pm d = \pm 0·1665$ of a child, a discrepancy of one third of a child, on average, between the upwardly mobile and the downwardly mobile. The remaining values of the constants in the alternative to the second model are shown in Table 5. In the alternative to

TABLE 5

Values of the constants in the model which is an alternative to the second model.

μ	2·77
c_1	−0·59
c_2	−0·35
c_3	−0·03
c_4	0·54
m	−0·03
d	0·17

the first model $\pm d = \pm 0·0512$ of a child, a discrepancy of one tenth of a child between the upwardly and the downwardly mobile. It appears, therefore, that the first model comes closer to accounting for the mobility effect than does the second, but neither succeeds completely.

We have now disproved the Halfway hypothesis by showing that, whichever model we choose to represent it, a mobility effect which is inconsistent with the hypothesis can be detected. It should be made clear, however, that what we have proved is the existence of a mobility effect as a deviation from the Halfway hypothesis. In order to establish the existence of a mobility effect *simpliciter* we fit the model:

for the upwardly mobile $(i > j)$ $\hat{Y}_{ij} = \mu - m - d$

for the non-mobile $\hat{Y}_{ij} = \mu + m$

for the downwardly mobile $(i < j)$ $\hat{Y}_{ij} = \mu - m + d$

and we find that

$$m = -0 \cdot 0293$$
$$d = 0 \cdot 2194$$

and the explained sum of squares is 49·78 with two degrees of freedom, which establishes the existence of a mobility effect and shows that the original interpretation of the data is justified.

The Halfway hypothesis and the mobility effect hypothesis differ in the extent of their falsifiability, the former being disproved by a wider array of circumstances than the latter. If we reduce the precision of the Halfway hypothesis by reverting to some such proposition as that the fertility of mobile couples tends to lie somewhere between the fertility of their class of origin and the fertility of their destination class, then, it might be argued, the undoubted explanatory power of the hypothesis may be salvaged. The difficulty with this formulation is that the explanatory power of the hypothesis can be assessed only if it is expressed in a precise form, and it is not clear on what basis a model of this formulation (which is much vaguer than Duncan's hypothesis) could be constructed. A better statement of our conclusion is that the Halfway hypothesis comes close to being true but its applicability is modified by the existence of a mobility effect.

The third model

In the preceding sections we have referred to the constants a, b and c as 'class effects'. This is not a felicitous term. Consider a_1 and a_4 in Table 4. The former is directly derived from the fertility of couples who have stayed in class one or moved downward from class one into other classes. The latter is directly derived from the fertility of couples who have stayed in class four or risen from it into other classes. No upwardly mobile couples contribute to a_1, and no downwardly mobile couples contribute to a_4. Similar observations may be made on the b coefficients. It is only because Tables 1 and 2 are roughly symmetrical that each a_i is roughly similar to the comparable b_i and c_i is close to both.

So far we have treated Table 1 as a row × column analysis of variance table. Let us now rid ourselves of this paradigm, turn the table through 45°, and treat the diagonal as the axis of major interest, that is the set of four cells containing the non-mobile couples. If we are to find class effects in the table these ought surely to be estimated by

these cells. We must, of course, assume either that there is little movement out of the classes and back into them again, or that the effects of
such movements are balanced out.

The mental activity of turning our attention from the rows and
columns to the principal diagonal of the fertility table may be paralleled
by a similar change in our model, a change which factor analysts would
call a rotation to a new set of axes. It has been observed that the four
constants of the second model lie in a three-dimensional space, one of
them being redundant. We shall, therefore, in the course of performing
the rotation, reduce the number of constants from four to three. The
transformation matrix for carrying out the proposed rotation is neatly
furnished by the set of orthogonal polynomials for a set of four points:

	linear	quadratic	cubic
c_1	-3	1	-1
c_2	-1	-1	3
c_3	1	-1	-3
c_4	3	1	1

As an example of the employment of this matrix let us look at the
equation for estimating the contents of cell two/three in the second
model. This may be written,

$$\hat{Y}_{23} = \mu + 0c_1 + 1c_2 + 1c_3 + 0c_4$$

Multiplying the coefficients in this equation by each of the columns of
the transformation matrix in turn yields the equation,

$$\hat{Y}_{23} = \mu + 0 \text{ linear} - 2 \text{ quadratic} + 0 \text{ cubic}$$

It happens that all the coefficients of the new model are even numbers
and so the model may be more succinctly expressed by halving each
coefficient.

It is of interest to write out the equations for the diagonal cells
explicitly (the terms 'linear', 'quadratic' and 'cubic' are replaced by
x_1, x_2, and x_3 respectively):

$$\hat{Y}_{11} = \mu - 3x_1 + x_2 - x_3$$
$$\hat{Y}_{22} = \mu - x_1 - x_2 + 3x_3$$
$$\hat{Y}_{33} = \mu + x_1 - x_2 - 3x_3$$
$$\hat{Y}_{44} = \mu + 3x_1 + x_2 + x_3$$

The equation of the estimate $\hat{Y}_{ij}$ for any off-diagonal cell, $i \neq j$, is the
mean of the equations for the appropriate diagonal cells $\hat{Y}_{ii}$ and $\hat{Y}_{jj}$.

*It must be made quite clear that this, third, model is merely the
second model in a new guise. The degree and nature of the fit to the
data are the same and so are the estimates which the model yields.*

The differences between the estimated and the observed values for the diagonal cells have a sum of squares of 11·06, which is not significant. The estimates derived from the model may, therefore, be taken as estimates of class effects on fertility.

Apart from its conceptual simplicity, and the reduction in the number of constants, an advantage of this model is that it points to ways of achieving further simplification. The sum of squares attributable to the linear component is 671·75. When the quadratic element is added this rises to 704·40. The addition of the cubic element adds only a further 2·24 and this element may be ignored.

The main advantage of introducing this model which is no more than an algebraic variant of its predecessor is that it comminutes our natural set towards a two-dimensional table, which leads us to treat it as a row by column table in the analysis of variance. Changing the standpoint from which we view the table is of psychological, though not logical, assistance in that it suggests an alternative model which differs from the alternative to model two. Although it is perhaps placing too much weight on a single table of means to subject it to another set of tests it is nevertheless instructive to spell out the new alternative hypothesis and show how it may be tested.

Our former alternative hypothesis considered only two compendious contrasts, the one between mobile and non-mobile, and the other between upwardly mobile and downwardly mobile. The new alternative hypothesis takes into account extent, as well as existence and direction, of mobility. Having established the principal diagonal of Table 1 as the axis of primary sociological interest and as the base axis for generating the constants of the Halfway hypothesis, we now take the dimension at right-angles to that diagonal as specifying the first dimension of deviation from the hypothesis to be explored. By assigning to the cells the weights shown in Table 6 we, in effect, impose an axis

TABLE 6

Constants defining a possible linear effect of direction and extent of mobility on fertility.

		Present social class			
		I	II	III	IV
	I	0	1	2	3
Social origin of husband	II	−1	0	1	2
	III	−2	−1	0	1
	IV	−3	−2	−1	0

along which the cells are distributed according to the direction *and* *extent* of movement of their members. Non-movers are at the point of balance, those who move one class down are one step to the right of

the non-movers, those who move one class up are one step to the left of
the non-movers, and so on as far as the most mobile couples who move
three class steps in one direction or the other. This axis is a linear
polynomial which distinguishes number of classes moved but does not
distinguish between, say, those who move from class one to class two
and those who move from two to three or three to four. Subsequent axes
defined by higher-order polynomials also have these two properties.
The second, quadratic, polynomial is given in Table 7. The reader may

TABLE 7
*Constants defining a possible quadratic effect of direction and extent
of mobility on fertility*

		Present social class			
		I	II	III	IV
Social origin of husband	I	-4	-3	0	5
	II	-3	-4	-3	0
	III	0	-3	-4	-3
	IV	5	0	-3	-4

readily construct the remaining tables by consulting a table of orthogonal polynomials such as that in the *Biometrika tables for statisticians.**

Taking first the linear deviations represented by Table 6 we find
that these contribute a sum of squares of 13·85 over and above that
accounted for by the linear and quadratic elements of the third model
(we have already decided that the cubic term of the model may safely
be ignored because its sum of squares is only 2·24). The linear component of the alternative model has 1 degree of freedom and is, therefore, not significant. The quadratic component contributed by the constants in Table 7 adds only a negligible 1·57 to the explained sum of
squares. This is not surprising, since the main contrast provided by
the term is between the immobile or the one-step movers on the one
hand, and the long distance movers on the other. We have already seen
that the fertility of the mobile does not differ appreciably from that of
the non-mobile.

The third, cubic, component, whose constants appear in Table 8,
is significant, contributing a sum of squares of 23·23 over and above
the combined effects of the earlier terms in the analysis. The regression
coefficient for this term is positive. An examination of Table 8 shows

* In practice it is convenient to generate orthogonal polynomials by a computing routine.
It should be observed that the second set of polynomials is orthogonal to the first. Since
the first set has three members and the second set has six members the space spanned
by the axes of the alternative model has nine dimensions. In the analysis no two polynomials remain quite orthogonal when fitted because the number of couples differs from
cell to cell in no systematic manner, nevertheless the analysis remains nine-dimensional.
The degree of overlap between the two sets of polynomials may be gauged from the fact
that the sum of squares for the first set is 706·64, that for the second set is 72·54, and
the sum of squares jointly explained by the two sets is 755·57.

TABLE 8

Constants defining a possible cubic effect of direction and extent of mobility on fertility

		Present Social Class			
		I	II	III	IV
Social origin of husband	I	0	1	1	−1
	II	−1	0	1	1
	III	−1	−1	0	1
	VI	1	−1	−1	0

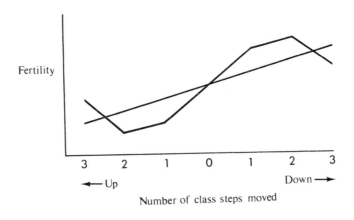

Number of class steps moved

FIG. 1.

what this means: the model ascribes high fertility to five out of the six sets of downwardly mobile couples and it ascribes low fertility to five out of the six sets of upwardly mobile couples. The two exceptions are the two smallest cells in the table, containing sixteen couples in all (Table 2). This, cubic, term is identical with the *d* term of the altern-ative to the second model, apart from the weights assigned to the two extreme cells. The two analyses have, therefore, arrived at practically identical conclusions. If the linear term of the second alternative model had proved to be significant this would have indicated that degree, as well as direction, of social movement is related to fertility.

A further three orthogonal polynomials may be fitted but, taken together, these add no more than 10·54 to the explained sum of squares, from which we may infer that none of them considered individually can attain significance.

It may be desirable to indicate in more detail the nature of the con-clusion we have demonstrated from our exploration of an alternative to the third model. We have established the significance of only one term, namely the cubic, but the first linear term, although not significant, is not negligible. In any statement of conclusions it is unwise to ignore lower-order terms with moderately high sums of squares because the sequential nature of the testing implies that each higher-order term is to be considered as a deviation from, or modification of, the earlier terms. The conclusions of the analysis may, therefore, be represented as in Figure 1, which incorporates a straight line with a small positive slope to indicate the existence of a possible linear component on which the downwardly mobile have a higher projection than the upwardly mobile (the regression coefficient of the linear component is positive). The cubic component represents a degree of wobble about this line, but the overall effect is again to contrast the two directions of mobility.

The two forms of alternative hypothesis

We have examined two possible alternatives to the basic model (model 2 or its equivalent model 3)*: one in terms of effects *m* and *d*, and the other in terms of polynomials. An examination of the constants of the two alternatives has led us to suppose that there is considerable overlap between them, and this is borne out by the calculation of the additional sums of squares which they explain, acting jointly and severally. The addition to the basic model of the linear and cubic

---

* It should be noted that the polynomial deviations for model 3 could equally well have been tested as deviations from model 2 since (so long as we retain all three polynomials which specify model 3) the two models are completely equivalent, yielding the same prediction for each cell of the data and hence explaining the same proportion of the over-all sum of squares. Many of the difficulties which research workers find themselves in when handling difference concepts such as mobility or inconsistency would dissolve if they would learn to ask not 'are these two sets of equations identical?' but 'are the *spaces* mapped by these two sets of equations identical?'

components of the alternative adds 38·25 to the explained sum of squares. The addition of m and d adds 29·26. The addition of all four terms adds 43·55, which is little more than the contribution of the polynomials acting alone.

Summary of the analyses

Our analysis of the third model and its alternative has reiterated the conclusions which we reached in explaining the second model and its somewhat cruder alternative. Both analyses result in the rejection of the Halfway hypothesis and in the acceptance of an alternative which involves an effect of direction of social mobility on fertility, the downwardly mobile being more fertile than the upwardly mobile, with the non-movers in the middle.

The third analysis has added a couple of refinements to the conclusion of the second. The first refinement consists in the observation that the class effects specified by the Halfway hypothesis may be represented in only two dimensions, although four classes have been defined. The two dimensions are a linear ranking of the classes in their expected order and a quadratic element which may reflect no more than the particular choice of cut-off points between neighbouring classes.

The second refinement is the suggestion that the d effect of the second alternative has a flick in its two tails, namely the deviation of the extremely mobile from the pattern of those who move in the same direction but to a less extreme degree. These tails are based on very few couples and their anomalous values are best ignored. Indeed, the anomaly is in fact confined to only one of the tails, namely that consisting of the highly downwardly mobile. If this effect were to recur in an analysis of further fertility tables we should probably want to examine individual cases before offering an explanation.

As an indication of the nature of the effects which have been demonstrated Table 9 contains the deviations of the estimated from the observed values when the estimates are derived from the Halfway hypothesis (ignoring the cubic term in the specification of the hypothesis)

TABLE 9
Observed minus estimated mean fertilities of couples, where the estimates are derived from the Halfway hypothesis.

		Present social class			
		I	II	III	IV
	I	0·08	− 0·05	− 0·24	− 0·76
Social origin	II	0·21	0·13	0·13	0·04
of	III	− 0·33	− 0·37	− 0·07	0·39
husband	IV	− 0·36	0·27	− 0·08	− 0·17

TABLE 10

*Observed minus estimated mean fertilities of couples, where the
estimates are derived from an alternative to the Halfway hypothesis.*

		Present social class			
		I	II	III	IV
	I	0·06	−0·25	−0·33	−0·09
Social origin of husband	II	0·40	0·13	−0·06	−0·03
	III	−0·26	−0·17	−0·06	0·21
	IV	−1·02	0·35	0·13	−0·16

and Table 10 contains similar values for the alternative hypothesis
which incorporates the linear and quadratic elements of the Halfway
hypothesis plus the linear and cubic elements of the deviations. It will
be observed that, when the values in Table 9 are subtracted from those
in Table 1, the result is a symmetrical table of estimates such that the
fertility of couples moving from i to j is the same as the fertility of
couples moving from j to i.

The residual sum of squares for the Halfway hypothesis, so specified, is 91·92 with 13 degrees of freedom. That for the alternative
(including the linear as well as the cubic component) is 53·51 with 11
degrees of freedom. If this reduction seems unimportant it should be
borne in mind that the mean deviation of the downwardly mobile from
the Halfway hypothesis is 0·1897, and that of the upwardly mobile is
0·1431, giving a difference between the two of 0·3314 or one third of a
child. (This difference is almost but not quite identical with twice the
value of d in the alternative to the second model.) In quantitative
terms this means that the 539 downwardly mobile couples have 102
children more than the Halfway hypothesis implies, and the 441 upwardly mobile couples have 63 children less than the hypothesis implies, a difference of 165 in a sample of approximately 5250 children.

Appendix:

A note on criticisms and queries

A number of enquiries and criticisms have been made concerning the
methods and conclusions of this paper and some of these are of sufficiently
general import to merit brief discussion. I shall deal with the criticisms first
and then explain the technical procedures which have aroused interest.

One criticism which has been levelled against the paper is that the Halfway hypothesis, as schematized in model two, is too rigid and has less
sociological justification than model one. My reply is that this may be true,
but the proposition as commonly stated (a) does not specifically allow that a
class may have more than one effect, and (b) appears to say that the fertility
of those moving from class i to class j is literally halfway between the fertility

of those in i and the fertility of those in j. To the best of my knowledge this paper is the first to point out that two models are possible and, in consequence, it is the first to recognise the need for, and provide, possible sociological justifications of the *first* model. Sociologists are now free to name their preferred model in the light of the preceding explorations of the properties of the two schematizations. Both models must be supplemented by a mobility effect.

A second criticism has been that examination of the residuals of either model (for example the deviations from model two reported in Table 9) does not reveal uniformly positive values for the downwardly mobile and negative values for the upwardly mobile. This is obviously true: it is unlikely that eye-assessment of residuals would suggest the existence of the d effect. It is not clear, however, what we are supposed to infer from the criticism. Do we throw overboard the concept of the variance of a mean when some means have the temerity to pass over to the wrong side of the magic number zero? This cannot be taken seriously, particularly when the deviations in question are based on fairly small numbers. Alternatively, the criticism might imply that a more complex effect than a simple contrast between the upward and downward movers is at work; but it was at finding just such an effect that the second (polynomial) alternative model was aimed, without any real success. It should be evident that any relatively small effect is going to be consistent with the presence of deviations with 'wrong' signs.

A third criticism is that some of the deviations of the observed cell means from the means given by the (basic plus) alternative models are quite large and some are greater than the deviations of the same means from the means given by the basic model (model one or model two). My reply is that the requirement that the fit should improve in any and every cell is unreasonable and its non-fulfilment is not sufficient to invalidate a model. The greatest deviations (whether enlarged or reduced by the addition of the alternative model) occur in the cells with the smallest numbers of couples, and therefore have the largest standard errors and contribute only moderately to the residual sum of squares.

Following upon this criticism is the suggestion that one should examine individual cells to see if any sense can be made of the deviations from a proposed model. While not entirely rejecting this recommendation I would point out that, if results of any generalizability are to be achieved, it is desirable to start by postulating effects which (a) have a basis in sociological theory and (b) span as many of the data as possible, so that their fit is to the generality of the available evidence rather than to certain aspects only. (Of course, the possibility of satisfying (b) may be circumscribed by a degree of specificity in the theory mentioned in (a).)

Some queries have arisen over the nature of the polynomials employed as an alternative to models two and three. The computing procedure for applying values such as those in Tables 6, 7 and 8 is described below. Here it is sufficient to point out that a variable such as fertility may be linearly related to class (if we are looking at the basic model) or to extent of mobility (if we are looking at the alternative model) but higher-order polynomials are required to supplement the linear polynomial because our categorization of class or extent of mobility has not produced equal-interval groupings. Linearity is always relative to some scale.

An objection has been raised to the fitting of the d effect in the first alternative model. Why, it has been said, should we not split it into two separate effects: (d_1) the difference between the downwardly mobile and the non-mobile, and (d_2) the difference between the upwardly mobile and the non-mobile? It will, of course, be observed that only two degrees of freedom are available for tests of differences among the three mobility categories. This means that the sum of squares explained by m and d will be the same as the sum of squares explained by m, d_1 and d_2. (The latter analysis is necessarily singular but singularity is a feature of several of the models in this paper and is easily handled by the methods described below.) The objection overlooks the fact that the sum of squares attributable to m has been shown to be very small indeed. From this we infer that the non-mobile lie at the weighted mean of the downwardly mobile and the upwardly mobile, and so all the remaining sum of squares (whether computed as the sum of squares due to d or the sum of squares due to d_1 and d_2) must be due to the fact that the downward movers lie on one side of the mean and the upward movers on the other. With allowances for the moderate excess of downward over upward movers we may say that downward and upward movement have equal and opposite effects on fertility.

Lastly, it has been asked how in fact it is possible to ensure that the constant for row i of a square table of means is the same as the constant for column i, and it is also asked how the singularity of several of the analyses is handled. To help us appreciate the answers to these questions let us first look at the computing procedure which was employed in the repetition of Professor Duncan's analysis.

The following design matrix is constructed for the table,

cell i,j	n_{ij}	a_1	a_2	a_3	a_4	b_1	b_2	b_3	b_4
1,1	65	1	0	0	0	1	0	0	0
1,2	43	1	0	0	0	0	1	0	0
1,3	23	1	0	0	0	0	0	1	0
1,4	11	1	0	0	0	0	0	0	1
2,1	38	0	1	0	0	1	0	0	0
2,2	197	0	1	0	0	0	1	0	0
2,3	150	0	1	0	0	0	0	1	0
2,4	68	0	1	0	0	0	0	0	1
3,1	37	0	0	1	0	1	0	0	0
3,2	154	0	0	1	0	0	1	0	0
3,3	431	0	0	1	0	0	0	1	0
3,4	244	0	0	1	0	0	0	0	1
4,1	5	0	0	0	1	1	0	0	0
4,2	45	0	0	0	1	0	1	0	0
4,3	162	0	0	0	1	0	0	1	0
4,4	220	0	0	0	1	0	0	0	1

n_{ij} is the number of couples in the cell in row i and column j (Table 2). An 8×8 sums of squares and sums of products matrix $\mathbf{W}$ is computed from the eight columns of the design matrix, employing the n_{ij} as weights. This matrix is singular in that its last two latent roots are necessarily zero. Let us write λ_i for the ith latent root of $\mathbf{W}$. Then we may write the well-known equality,

$$\mathbf{W} = \Sigma \lambda_i \mathbf{w}_i \mathbf{w}_i'$$

where the $\mathbf{w}_i$ are column latent vectors with unit sums of squares and the $\mathbf{w}_i \mathbf{w}_i'$ are matrix products known as unit hierarchies. It is perhaps not so well known that

$$\mathbf{W}^k = \Sigma \lambda_i^k \mathbf{w}_i \mathbf{w}_i'$$

where k is any power, and in particular that*

$$W^{-1} = \Sigma \lambda_i^{-1} w_i w_i'$$

We use this last equation to construct a pseudo-inverse for W by calculating its latent roots λ_i and their associated latent vectors w_i and, omitting both zero roots, computing,

$$W_*^{-1} = \Sigma \lambda_i^{-1} w_i w_i'$$

where i runs from 1 to 6.

We now calculate the vector p each of whose eight elements is a sum of products for a variable of the design matrix and the observed cell mean fertilities weighted by the n_{ij}.

Then the calculation,

$$W_*^{-1} p$$

gives us the constants of model one which Professor Duncan obtained by the conventional method.

The computing procedure described avoids all problems of multicollinearity and singularity and has a number of incidental advantages. The writer has adopted some variant of it in all his computer programs which call for a regression analysis (programmers are, however, warned that design matrices frequently throw up sums of squares and sums of products matrices with unhappy properties and tests must be made and compensating procedures introduced).

Now, in order to obtain a single set of constants c_i for the two principles of classification we simply average or sum corresponding a_i and b_i in the above table. The first quarter of the new design matrix then has the following appearance,

cell i,j	n_{ij}	c_1	c_2	c_3	c_4
1,1	65	2	0	0	0
1,2	43	1	1	0	0
1,3	23	1	0	1	0
1,4	11	1	0	0	1

The sums of squares and sums of products matrix for this design matrix has one zero root. The generalization to several principles of classification is obvious.

Finally, we may look at the design matrix for model three and its alternative (some of the polynomials for the alternative being given in Tables 6–8),

cell i,j	n_{ij}	x_1	x_2	x_3	linear	quadratic	cubic	quartic	quintic	sextic
1,1	65	-3	1	-1	0	-4	0	6	0	-20
1,2	43	-2	0	1	1	-3	-1	1	5	15
1,3	23	-1	0	-2	2	0	-1	-7	-4	-6
1,4	11	0	1	0	3	5	1	3	1	1
2,1	38	-2	0	1	-1	-3	1	1	-5	15
2,2	197	-1	-1	3	0	-4	0	6	0	-20
2,3	150	0	-1	0	1	-3	-1	1	5	15
2,4	68	1	0	2	2	0	-1	-7	-4	-6
3,1	37	-1	0	-2	-2	0	1	-7	4	-6
3,2	154	0	-1	0	-1	-3	1	1	-5	15
3,3	431	1	-1	-3	0	-4	0	6	0	-20
3,4	244	2	0	-1	1	-3	-1	1	5	15
4,1	5	0	1	0	-3	5	-1	3	-1	1
4,2	45	1	0	2	-2	0	1	-7	4	-6
4,3	162	2	0	-1	-1	-3	1	1	-5	15
4,4	220	3	1	1	0	-4	0	6	0	-20

It should be evident that, when the n_{ij} are employed as weights, the co-variances of the above columns will not be zero in general, and it may therefore be asked why we speak of 'orthogonal' polynomials. The answer is quite simply that the columns may be (and, in the case of the columns x_1 to x_3, explicitly were) produced by applying a matrix of orthogonal polynomials to a given design matrix. The uneasiness which may be felt about the non-orthogonality of the columns has its roots in the fear that something may be lost by failure to employ uncorrelated axes. This fear is, however, groundless because (a) k correlated axes may, and frequently do, lie in k dimensions; in other words correlation is not a sufficient condition of singularity, and indeed the presence of substantial correlation is consistent with non-singularity, and (b) the manner of arriving at the columns, by orthogonal transformation with a complete set of polynomials, ensures that the space of the original design matrix is preserved in its entirety.

References

BERENT, J. (1952). Fertility and social mobility. *Population Studies.* 5, 244–60.

BLAU, P.M. and DUNCAN, O.D. (1967). *The American occupational structure.* Wiley, New York.

DUNCAN, O.D. (1966). Methodological issues in the analysis of social mobility. In *Social structure and mobility in economic development* (ed. N.J. Smelser and M.S. Lipset). Aldine, Chicago.

HAWTHORN, G. (1970). *The sociology of fertility.* Collier-Macmillan, London.

HAWTHORN, G. and BUSFIELD, J. (1968). A sociological approach to British fertility. In *Penguin social sciences survey 1968* (ed. J. Gould). Penguin, London.

HODGE, R.W. and TREIMAN, D.J. (1966). Occupational mobility and attitudes towards negroes. *Amer. Sociol. Rev.,* 31, 93–102

MAXWELL, J. (1953). *Social implications of the 1947 Scottish mental survey.* University of London Press.

PEARSON, E.S. and HARTLEY, H.O. (1958). *Biometrika tables for statisticians,* vol. I. Cambridge University Press.

WESTOFF, C.F. (1956). The changing focus of differential fertility research: the social mobility hypothesis. In *Population theory and policy* (ed. J.J. Spengler and O.D. Duncan). Free Press of Glencoe, New York

YATES, F. (1934). The analysis of multiple classifications with unequal numbers in the different classes. *J. Amer. Statist. Assoc.,* 29, 51–66.

---

* a simple arithmetic example of these equations is given on page 193 of the hardback edition of Hope, K. (1968). *Methods of multivariate analysis.* University of London Press.

MARRIAGE MARKETS IN THE STRATIFICATION SYSTEM

by K. HOPE

Summary. Any bivariate distribution, expressed in the form of a contingency table, may be analysed into a number of additive component tables, to which the author has given the title 'contingency hierarchies'. A set of such hierarchies is here interpreted as a number of systems of marital conjunction. A related type of analysis shows that the pattern of constraints on choice of marriage partner closely parallels the pattern of constraints on intergenerational mobility. In both processes there is relatively high constraint at the top of British society, and a lower degree of constraint over most of the rest of the scale.

Analysis of an American table showing the relations between occupation of husband's father and occupation of wife's father reveals no tendency towards high constraint at any level of society, with the exception of farming. The contrast between Britain and the United States in terms of marriage is parallel to the contrast in terms of intergenerational social mobility which is reported in another paper in this volume.

Introduction

Oldman and Illsley (1966) report a table showing the relations between busband's social class and wife's occupational group. The population which they studied consisted of the 11,225 married couples in Aberdeen having their first child in the years 1951–1961. They use this table to show that variations in inter-marriage between groups can be employed as a method of ranking male occupations. The purpose of the new analysis of their table which is presented here is to tease out of the data patterns of inter-marriage which are additional to the general status-ordering which was the main interest of Oldman and Illsley.

Table 1 contains the data presented by Oldman and Illsley with the exception of 304 couples for whom one or other item of information was

TABLE 1

10921 primiparous married couples classified by wife's own occupation before marriage and husband's occupation at time of child's birth

		Husband's social class (R.G. 1950)					
		I	II	IIINm	IIIM	IV	V
	1 Professional & technical	281	301	142	188	17	3
	2 Clerical	177	449	738	1465	162	111
Wife's	3 Distributive	35	144	382	1156	220	181
occupational	4 Skilled manual	28	97	258	1288	301	364
group	5 Semi-skilled manual	3	31	132	810	241	275
	6 Unskilled manual	0	1	29	195	70	99
	7 Fish workers	0	4	22	242	115	164

unknown. It is reanalysed by the techniques described in the paper 'Quantifying constraints on social mobility'.* The latent hierarchies which are abstracted from the table may be thought of as marriage markets, or systems of marital exchange between status groups. The

---

* The reader is referred to the paper cited (page 121 below) for technical details. Although the techniques developed in 'Quantifying constraints on social mobility' are presupposed by the present paper readers who are more interested in the applications than the methods may wish to assure themselves that the methods are useful before tackling the complexities of the more technical paper. It is partly for this reason that the paper on marriage markets precedes the paper on quantification of constraints in this volume.

closest analogy is with labour markets, and the important aspect of the analogue is that an individual worker may, if he so wishes, or chance or social factors so determine, operate in more than one labour market while remaining within a single economy. We may, for example, distinguish a national labour market, a local labour market, and the labour market which operates through kin and friends. In deciding which market a man is operating in when he takes a particular job we might ask him how he came to hear of the job. The assumption of this approach is that we have some idea of what markets exist and the empirical problem is to quantify the importance or assess the salience of each. An alternative approach, which might be very difficult to adopt in practice, would be to confine our empirical work to the recording of job changes, and to induce from the aggregate of these movements the patterns of interchange which betray the existence of distinguishable markets forming whirlpools and eddies in the economic stream. It is the analogue of the latter of these two approaches which is adopted here in the isolation and examination of systems of marital conjunction.

Marriage markets

The data were subjected to canonical variate analysis and to explanatory variate analysis. The results of the two analyses were so similar as to be practically indistinguishable. We confine our report to the canonical analysis, which is summarized in the table in the appendix. The first three canonical correlations are 0·53, 0·24 and 0·05. All three are highly significant in terms of the usual chi square test, the fourth is not significant ($\chi^2_4 = 4\cdot07$)*. We therefore ignore the last two of the five possible canonical dimensions listed in the Appendix.

The results of the analysis may be presented in the form of three *contingency hierarchies*. In 1941 Maung, applying a technique based on work by Hirschfeld (1935) and Fisher (1940), showed how the observed value in an individual cell of a contingency table may be construed as the sum of a number of additive components derived from a canonical analysis. I have coined the term 'contingency hierarchy' to denote the table of such components which is uniquely associated with a particular canonical dimension.

The original contingency table (in the present analysis Table 1) is first split into two additive components. The first is the table of expected frequencies (Table 2) which are calculated by the usual chi square formula, familiar to sociologists because it has been used to define a situation of perfect mobility in an intergenerational mobility

---

* The test is of doubtful validity when the data are in the form of two discontinuous distributions, but the gap between the chi square for the third canonical correlation $\chi^2_6 = 31\cdot28$) and that for the fourth is considerable.

TABLE 2
Frequencies expected in Table 1 if the two classifications were independent

		Husband's social class (R.G. 1950)					
		I	II	IIINm	IIIM	IV	V
Wife's occupational group	1 Professional & technical	45	88	145	456	96	102
	2 Clerical	149	292	484	1518	320	340
	3 Distributive	102	199	330	1036	218	232
	4 Skilled manual	112	220	364	1143	241	256
	5 Semi-skilled manual	72	140	233	730	154	164
	6 Unskilled manual	19	37	61	193	41	43
	7 Fish workers	26	51	85	268	56	60

TABLE 3
Deviations from expectation. Each element is the difference between an observed number of couples in Table 1 and the corresponding expected number in Table 2.

		Husband's social class (R.G. 1950)					
		I	II	IIINm	IIIM	IV	V
Wife's occupational group	1 Professional & technical	236	213	−3	−268	−79	−99
	2 Clerical	28	157	254	−53	−158	−229
	3 Distributive	−67	−55	52	120	2	−51
	4 Skilled manual	−84	−123	−106	145	60	108
	5 Semi-skilled manual	−69	−109	−101	80	87	111
	6 Unskilled manual	−19	−36	−32	2	29	56
	7 Fish workers	−26	−47	−63	−26	59	104

table. The expected frequencies are, of course, not whole numbers but they are rounded into integer form in Table 2. The second component (Table 3) is simply the difference between the observed table and the table of expected frequencies, and is known as a table of deviations from expectation. The table of deviations may in turn be split into five additive tables known as contingency hierarchies, each hierarchy being uniquely associated with one of the five canonical roots and dimensions of the observed table. Tables 4–6 contain the contingency hierarchies associated with the three significant canonical roots. No element of the fourth and fifth hierarchies exceeds ±17.

The additive relations among contingency hierarchies simplify their

TABLE 4

First contingency hierarchy. Canonical correlation 0·53, χ^2_{10} = 3585

		Husband's social class (R.G. 1950)					
		I	II	IIINm	IIIM	IV	V
	1 Professional & technical	192	216	86	−210	−118	−167
	2 Clerical	125	141	56	−137	−77	−108
Wife's occupational group	3 Distributive	−37	−41	−16	40	22	32
	4 Skilled manual	−104	−117	−47	114	64	90
	5 Semi-skilled manual	−95	−107	−42	104	58	82
	6 Unskilled manual	−32	−36	−14	35	19	28
	7 Fish workers	−50	−56	−22	54	30	43

TABLE 5

Second contingency hierarchy. Canonical correlation 0·24, χ^2_8 = 658.
*Elements in brackets are largely, and elements in dotted brackets are
partly, correcting overcompensations introduced by the first contingency
hierarchy.*

		Husband's social class (R.G. 1950)					
		I	II	IIINm	IIIM	IV	V
	1 Professional & technical	42	0	(−85)	−67	(38)	(72)
	2 Clerical	(−87)	−0	173	(138)	−77	−147
Wife's occupational group	3 Distributive	−38	−0	75	60	(−34)	(−64)
	4 Skilled manual	(15)	0	−31	−25	14	26
	5 Semi-skilled manual	(24)	0	−48	(−39)	22	41
	6 Unskilled manual	(13)	0	−26	(−21)	12	22
	7 Fish workers	(29)	0	−57	(−46)	26	49

interpretation, but even so the message of a particular hierarchy must
be interpreted in the light of the information conveyed by its companions. The first hierarchy may be thought of as an emprically-derived
model which gives as good a fit as possible* to the original contingency
table (or, rather, to the deviations from expectation). Table 4, therefore,
contains a simplified outline of the main pattern of the deviations, with
excrescences removed and cavities filled in.

* The burden of the paper on the quantification of constraints on mobility is that
canonical dimensions do not, in general, optimize the fit of the model to the data. But
in the present analysis the explanatory variates, which do have a maximizing property,
are practically identical with the canonical variates. In every case the correlation
between a canonical variate and the corresponding explanatory variate exceeds 0·983.

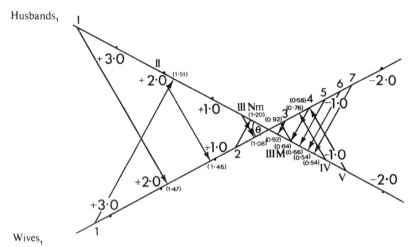

FIG.1. First canonical projection. The numbers in parentheses are
standard deviations, see the explanation in the text.

The information retained by the first canonical dimension may be
presented in quite a different form by means of a diagram which I propose to call a *canonical projection* (Figure 1). This is simply an application of the ordinary bivariate regression diagram to the case of a
canonical dimension. The two axes of figure 1 are the pair of canonical
variates defined by the six-element (husbands') vector and the seven-
element (wives') vector which also generate the first contingency hierarchy. The ordering of the classes and groups indicates that this dimension, which has been derived by analysis of frequencies of marital
conjunction, is also related to the general status hierarchy of society.

The arrows in the diagram indicate the mean projections of groups
or classes on to the axis of the opposite sex. For example, class II
men, who stand at a distance of 2·02 from the origin on their own axis
lie, on average, $2·02\theta = 1·07$* from the origin on the female axis, where
$\theta = 0·5291$ is the cosine of the angle between the two axes, and is the
value of the canonical correlation (the analysis has the property of
finding the two axes for which this angle is a minimum, i.e. the correlation is a maximum). If we accept these axes as status variates we can
learn from them that, to pursue the same example, the average wife of a
class II man has an occupational status slightly higher than the mean
of group 2, and so on, for each class and group.

Each axis had been standardized in such a way that the variance
(Within group mean square) of members of a group projected on to it
from the opposite axis is, on average, unity. The relative standard
deviation of each projected group is given in brackets beside the point

---

* This value is given in row II, column 1 of the table in the appendix, which contains
the position of the arrow heads on all possible canonical variates.

Husbands₂

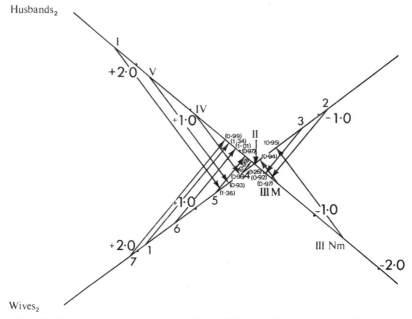

Wives₂

FIG. 2. Second canonical projection. The numbers in parentheses are standard deviations, see the explanation in the text.

of its arrow. The ratio of the Between groups (or Between classes) sum of squares to the Within groups (or Within classes) sum of squares is 0·39 (see the table in the Appendix).

The constraints to which the analysis is subjected by the model are indicated by the fact that all the arrows leading from the husbands' to the wives' axis are parallel to one another, as are the arrows going in the other direction. The parallelism corresponds to the smooth regularity of the contingency hierarchy in which every row is proportional to every other row and every column is proportional to every other column.

The unequivocal message of the first canonical dimension (a message which, at least in general outline, is equally well conveyed by an examination of the original contingency table or by Oldman and Illsley's Figure 1) is that the overall marriage market is one in which marital conjunction of the sexes is a function of their respective statuses to very much the same degree as a child's height is a function of his father's, or as one sib's IQ is a function of anothers.*

If we dichotomize the two arrays of the first contingency hierarchy

---

* If arbitrary, equally-spaced, weights are attached to the rows and the columns of the contingency table the product-moment correlation between the two arrays is 0·4652. This may be compared with the value of the first canonical correlation (0·5291) which is maximized by the weights assigned to the rows and columns by the canonical analysis.

between groups 2 and 3 and between classes IIINm and IIIM we get a clear picture of two marriage markets, one middle-class and the other working-class. Within a market the probability of marriage is always greater than the random probability, and between markets it is always less than the random probability. This is, of course, an oversimplified picture to the extent that the first canonical dimension is not a perfect fit to the data, but the pattern of the unanalyzed deviations (Table 3) largely confirms it. The modifications introduced by consideration of less general marriage markets are discussed below.

The fact that the second canonical correlation (0·24) is significant indicates that a second pair of axes, orthogonal to the first pair, must be examined. Figure 2 contains the second canonical projection, for which the ratio of Between to Within sums of squares is 0·06. The two figures may be considered in conjunction by imagining the sheet of paper bearing the second passing at right-angles through the sheet bearing the first, with the two origins coincident. Figure 3 shows the position of the arrow points from the husbands in the space of the orthogonal axes Wives$_1$ and Wives$_2$, and Figure 4 shows the reciprocal projection of the groups of wives into the husbands' class space (all figures are drawn to the same scale).

The figures reveal a neat curvilinear relationship which is reciprocal between the sexes. In this respect the analysis is very similar to the comparable analysis of the well-known intergenerational social mobility table reported by Glass and his co-workers (Glass, 1954). The first two canonical roots and their related vectors are remarkably similar in the two analyses (cf. page 156 below).

The second contingency hierarchy (Table 5) serves to explain the nature of the deviations from linearity. These are of two sorts. On the one hand some elements of the first hierarchy have partially explained the corresponding elements of the deviations from expectation. On the other hand some of the elements of the first hierarchy have carried the value predicted by the model further away from the true deviation. As an example of partial explanation: the number of marriages of group one females to class I males exceeds expectation by 236 (Tables 3). The first contingency hierarchy accounts for 192 of this deviation, leaving 44 marriages to be accounted for by subsequent hierarchies. The ratio of the observed to the expected number in this cell, $281/45 = 6·3$, has been explained to the extent of 1·0 (by the expectation itself) + $192/45 = 4·3$ (by the first contingency hierarchy). The remaining $6·3 - (1·0 + 4·3) = 1·0$ has yet to be accounted for. An example of a cell in which the first contingency hierarchy has worsened the fit between model and observation is the number of marriages between group one women and class III Non-manual men. An example of a cell where the correction introduced by the first hierarchy overshoots the

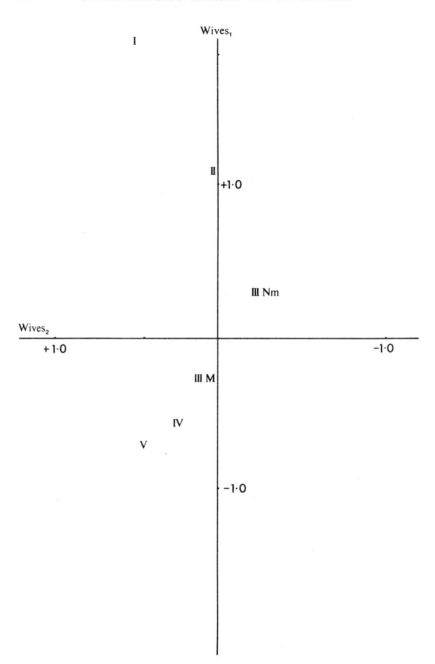

FIG. 3. Projections of social classes of husbands into the space of
the first two canonical variates of the wives.

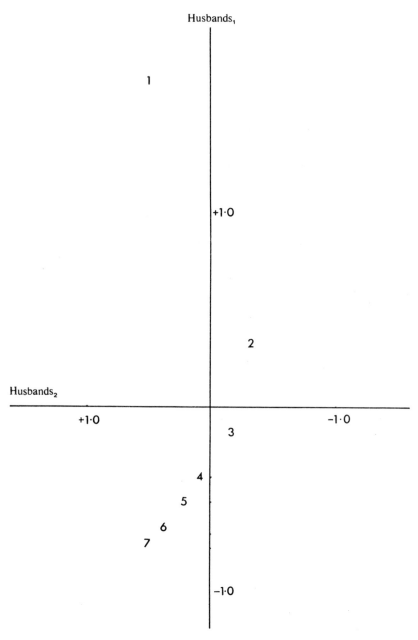

FIG. 4. Projections of occupational groups of wives into the space
of the first two canonical variates of the husbands

mark is cell 7, I.

Thus the second hierarchy has two tasks: it must further improve the fit between model and observation where improvement has already been introduced by the first hierarchy, and it must compensate for the increased deviations and over-corrections of the first hierarchy.

The first thing to be noted about the second hierarchy is that at the top of the social scale there is more endogamy than the simple linear ordering of the first status dimension implies. Group one females have a strong tendency to marry class I males (the second contingency hierarchy accounts for practically all the deviation from expectation in this cell which the first left unaccounted for). They do so at the expense of skilled manual workers.

The second point to be made is that there is a block of six positive elements in the bottom right-hand corner of the hierarchy. Interpreted as proportions of the corresponding expectancies these elements increase in importance as they descend from wives' group four to wives' group seven. They indicate the presence of another marriage market at the lower end of society, a market in which female manual workers meet and marry semi-skilled and unskilled men, rather than the clerks and tradesmen of class III.

The third system of exchange which is localized in the status hierarchy is that between female office and shop workers and male clerks, commercial travellers and shop workers (IIINm) and, to some extent, the craftsmen, drivers and soldiers of IIIM. From a functional point of view this market may be regarded as an equilibrating mechanism which helps to bring the positively skewed occupational distribution of the women into line with the negatively skewed class distribution of the men.

These three systems of exchange have been listed in descending order of their significance (ratio of number of marriages accounted for by the model to expected frequency of that type of marriage*) but in

---

* It may be shown (page 186 below) that the partitioning of the deviations from expectation is related to a comparable partitioning of the index of association (Glass, 1954). If we write o_{ij} for the observed frequency in cell i,j of a contingency table and e_{ij} for the corresponding expected frequency, then the index of association for that cell is the ratio o_{ij}/e_{ij}. The element of the kth contingency hierarchy for the cell is given by the product of e_{ij} and a term t_{ijk} where k runs from 1 up to the number of hierarchies h. If we write $t_{ijo} = 1$ for all i and j we can see that the product $e_{ij} \cdot t_{ijo}$ simply reproduces the expected frequencies. It has been shown that the elements of the contingency hierarchies sum to the observed deviations from expectation

$$e_{ij} \sum_{k=1}^{h} t_{ijk} = o_{ij} - e_{ij}$$

Taking the summation from zero instead of one is equivalent to adding the expected frequency and we obtain

$$e_{ij} \sum_{k=0}^{h} t_{ijk} = o_{ij}$$

If we divide both sides by e_{ij} we readily see that the terms t_{ijk} are simply partitions of the index of association, the zeroth partition being always unity. The values of t_{ijk} are the ratios of marriages accounted for to expected number of marriages which were employed above as indices of significance.

TABLE 6

Third contingency hierarchy. Canonical correlation $0 \cdot 05$, $\chi_6^2 = 31 \cdot 28$.
Elements in brackets are correcting over-compensations introduced by the first two contingency hierarchies.

		Husband's social class (R.G. 1950)					
		I	II	IIINm	IIIM	IV	V
	1 Professional & technical	2	−2	−5	(10)	−0	−4
Wife's occupational group	2 Clerical	(−9)	14	29	−58	1	(24)
	3 Distributive	5	−7	(−15)	31	−0	−12
	4 Skilled manual	7	−10	−22	43	−0	−17
	5 Semi-skilled manual	3	−4	−9	19	−0	(−8)
	6 Unskilled manual	−2	3	6	(−11)	0	5
	7 Fish workers	−5	8	(17)	−33	0	13

ascending order of their numerical importance (number of marriages accounted for).

The function of the third contingency hierarchy (Table 6) is, principally, to improve the fit of the model to certain cells of the table, of which the most important in numerical terms are the cells in the skilled manual column. These men tend to marry women in the distribution industry, or in skilled or semi-skilled work, rather than secretaries and receptionists (who gravitate towards white-collar class III men) or women in the fish industry.

It must be emphasized that the constraints introduced by this third instalment of the model are additional and supplementary to both the general status factor of the first dimension and the specific marriage markets of the second dimension. They are numerically so unimportant as to be detectable only in a very large sample. The ratio of Between to Within sums of squares on this third dimension is only $0 \cdot 003$.

Differential constraints on marital conjunction

In the paper on the quantification of constraints in social mobility tables to which reference has been made, a technique is introduced which is there called the method of 'percentage determinations'. The purpose of this technique is to obtain some rough-and-ready idea of the differential strength of constraints over the various levels of the stratification system. The method has been applied to Table 1 with results which are listed in Table 7. There is a strong resemblance between the 'percentage determinations' in Table 7 and the comparable percentages which emerge from an analysis of intergenerational social mobility tables for England and Scotland (page 136, below). A percentage for a

TABLE 7

Percentage accuracy with which membership or non-membership of a group or class may be ascribed to one spouse when the class or group membership of the other spouse is known.

	Group or class	Percentage predictability
	1	20·9
	2	5·9
	3	1·0
Women	4	2·8
	5	3·5
	6	1·6
	7	3·5
	I	14·2
	II	8·6
	IIINm	3·0
Men	IIIM	3·6
	IV	3·0
	V	6·5

particular category in Table 7 tells us the extent to which we can say whether or not a spouse belongs to that category if we are told which category the other spouse belongs to. The conferring or confirming of status by marriage resembles very closely the transmission of status to a son. There is the same high degree of constraint in the top category, with a somewhat lower degree in the second category, and very little constraint in the subsequent categories until we come to the bottom of the scale, where there is a slight upturn. The pattern for the men is less marked than that for the women in that the constraints on the marriages of class I men are less than the constraints on the marriages of group one women.*

Just as there is, at the top of society, an intensified degree of intergenerational transmission of opportunities for desirable occupations, so there is, at this level, an intensified degree of selection of socially and economically desirable spouses. We have, as yet, no means of relating the two.

Comparison with U.S. data

In the paper 'Quantifying constraints on social mobility' the constraints on intergenerational mobility at the upper end of British society are contrasted with the relative absence of such constraints in the

---

* No doubt many explanations of this difference might be offered. In choosing among them we should have to know how women enter the top occupational group, and how mode of entry is related to men's mode of entry into class I.

United States. The same contrast emerges from analysis of marriage tables. In Table J10.1 of *The American occupational structure* Blau and Duncan (1967) cross-tabulate husband's father's occupation and wife's father's occupation for a large national sample of married couples. The American and the British data differ in their categorization of occupation, in the principle by which wives are classified, and in the nature of the sample, the British sample being couples having their first child whereas the American is a sample of couples in which the wife is aged between 22 and 61 years. Nevertheless it is interesting to see the same comparative pattern emerging from analyses of marriage tables as from analysis of mobility tables. If we leave aside the farming category (for which the percentage predictability in both directions is 17 per cent) none of the American categories has a predictability greater than 4·18 per cent (and even this figure refers to farm labouring). The first canonical dimension is entirely dominated by farming parents and has a canonical correlation of 0·42. The second dimension, which contrasts the marriage markets for white-collar occupations (plus farming) and for blue-collar occupations (plus farm-labouring) has a canonical correlation of 0·26. This implies that, in the non-agricultural sectors of American society, one can, to the extent of 7 per cent of total variance, predict a man's occupational status from a knowledge of the status of a fairly remote affine: his child's father-in-law.

Appendix

Mean of each class or occupation group on each canonical variate, together with the canonical roots (μ), canonical correlations ($\mu^{\frac{1}{2}}$), and ratios of Between to Within sums of squares $[\phi = \mu/(1-\mu)]$. Each variate has been standardized by setting its Within mean square to unity.

		Canonical variate				
		1	2	3	4	5
	I	1·8649	0·5618	−0·0687	0·0118	0·0177
Husband's	II	1·0708	0·0006	0·0536	−0·0149	−0·0205
social	IIINm	0·2566	−0·3452	0·0689	0·0134	0·0099
class	IIIM	−0·1998	−0·0875	−0·0438	−0·0074	−0·0003
	IV	−0·5318	0·2328	0·0024	0·0474	−0·0093
	V	−0·7079	0·4165	0·0794	−0·0230	0·0059
	1	1·6913	0·4339	−0·0269	0·0042	0·0011
	2	0·3307	−0·2657	0·0469	−0·0071	−0·0024
Wife's	3	−0·1415	−0·1693	−0·0363	0·0269	0·0059
occupational	4	−0·3663	0·0631	−0·0461	−0·0287	0·0002
group	5	−0·5219	0·1548	−0·0317	0·0155	−0·0112
	6	−0·6608	0·3195	0·0729	−0·0038	0·0381
	7	−0·7452	0·5012	0·1512	0·0116	−0·0093
	μ	0·2799	0·0585	0·0029	0·0004	0·0001
	$\mu^{\frac{1}{2}}$	0·5291	0·2418	0·0535	0·0193	0·0091
	ϕ	0·3888	0·0621	0·0029	0·0004	0·0001

References

BLAU, P.M. and DUNCAN, O.D. (1967). *The American occupational structure*. Wiley, New York.

FISHER, R.A. (1940). The precision of discriminant functions. *Ann. Eugen.*, 10, 422–9.

GLASS D.V. (1954). *Social mobility in Britain*. Routledge and Kegan Paul, London.

HIRSCHFELD, H.O. (1935). A connection between correlation and contingency. *Proc. Camb. Phil. Soc.*, 31, 520–4.

MAUNG, K. (1941). Measurement of association in a contingency table with special reference to the pigmentation of hair and eye colours of Scottish school children. *Ann. Eugen.*, 11, 189–223.

OLDMAN, D. and ILLSLEY, R. (1966). Measuring the status of occupations. *Sociol. Rev.*, 14, 53–72.

QUANTIFYING CONSTRAINTS ON SOCIAL MOBILITY:
THE LATENT HIERARCHIES OF A CONTINGENCY TABLE

by K. HOPE

Summary. Methods associated with canonical analysis are developed and applied to intergenerational social mobility tables for England and Wales, Scotland, and the United States. The method of 'percentage determinations' is suggested as a means of showing the extent of mobility constraints at different rungs of the social or occupational ladder. The analysis of a contingency table into additive 'contingency hierarchies' is described, and it is shown that the well-known index of association may be subjected to a parallel analysis. Canonical methods form a link between the techniques employed in *Social mobility in Britain* and those employed in *The American occupational structure.*

However, canonical techniques are defective in ways which have not been previously realized because they maximize correlation without necessarily maximizing variance explained. A method called 'explanatory variate analysis' is derived which has the property of maximizing the variance explained by each dimension of regression in turn, and its relations to canonical analysis are described. Numerical taxonomy is applied to distance matrices in order to detect the class structure as this is manifested in terms of constraints on mobility. Tentative comparisons are made among the three intergenerational mobility tables analysed. The paper concludes with a discussion of ways of organizing mobility data for the most effective deployment of these techniques.

PART I.   THE METHOD OF PERCENTAGE DETERMINATIONS

Among the many attempts which have been made to quantify social or occupational mobilities we may distinguish those which are directional and those which are symmetric. Let us suppose that we are faced with a typical table of intergenerational mobility, which is a contingency table in which rows represent fathers' occupational categories and columns represent sons' occupational categories. Then the Markovian approach initiated by Prais (1955) and the regression approach of Blau and Duncan (1967) involve an assumption, or at least an attitude, of directionality, whereas the index of association (Glass, 1954; Rogoff, 1953) is essentially symmetrical. The directional approach looks to father's occupation for an explanation of son's occupation whereas the symmetric approach asks how far the two are associated.

The purpose of this paper is to develop a method of analysis which has some of the properties of both the symmetrical and the directional approaches. It might be called a bi-directional method. It might, indeed, be regarded as a generalization both of the index of association and of the regression methods employed by Blau and Duncan. Although it is complex in its calculations some of the conclusions which it reaches are very simply stated in terms of percentages. And the questions which these percentages answer are not subtle, operational, questions thrown up by the method of analysis, but straightforward questions of relative importance which might be posed by any sociologist or demographer.

In the following introductory paragraphs an attempt is made to introduce the multivariate procedures involved in the method by generalization from simple bivariate regression methods with which the sociologist might be supposed to be familiar. (The slightly more complicated procedures required for an actual analysis are not given explicitly but are described in geometrical terms.)

Statistical introduction

Many users of bivariate statistical methods will be familiar with the procedure for calculating the extent to which the sum of squares of one variable, y say, is accountable for by, or predictable from, another variable, say x. We first of all calculate the regression coefficient for predicting a person's position on y from a knowledge of his position on x,

$$b_{y.x} = \frac{\Sigma xy}{\Sigma x^2} \tag{i}$$

and then multiply it by the sum of products Σxy

$$\text{Sum of squares due to regression} = (\Sigma xy)b_{y.x} = \frac{(\Sigma xy)^2}{\Sigma x^2} \tag{ii}$$

That part of Σy^2 which cannot be explained by x, namely the deviation from regression, is then,

$$\Sigma y^2 - \frac{(\Sigma xy)^2}{\Sigma x^2} \tag{iii}$$

Now, to help us in generalizing the method to the case of many x variables and many y variables, let us write,

$$\Sigma x^2 = c_{xx}$$
$$\Sigma y^2 = c_{yy}$$
$$\Sigma xy = c_{xy} \text{ or } c_{xy}$$

These symbols may be written in the cells of a partitioned matrix as follows:

c_{xx}	c_{xy}
c_{yx}	c_{yy}

The regression coefficient may then be written

$$b_{y.x} = c_{xx}^{-1} c_{xy} \tag{ia}$$

and the sum of squares attributable to regression,

$$c_{yx} b_{y.x} = c_{yx} c_{xx}^{-1} c_{xy} \tag{iia}$$

and the deviation from regression,

$$c_{yy} - c_{yx} c_{xx}^{-1} c_{xy} \tag{iiia}$$

In each case the formula which is flagged by a number followed by an 'a' is identical with the formula flagged by the same number without an 'a'.

The generalization to the multivariate case is now quite straightforward. Our 2×2 partitioned matrix expands into a matrix with $p + q$ columns, where p is the number of x variables and q is the number of y variables. Each section of the matrix is itself a matrix, and so we represent the sections by capital letters,

$\mathbf{C}_{xx}$	$\mathbf{C}_{xy}$
$\mathbf{C}_{yx}$	$\mathbf{C}_{yy}$

To predict the y variables from the x variables we require a $p \times q$ matrix of regression coefficients

$$\mathbf{B}_{y.x} = \mathbf{C}_{xx}^{-1}\mathbf{C}_{xy} \qquad \text{(ib)}$$

The part of the sums of squares and sums of products matrix $\mathbf{C}_{yy}$ which can be accounted for by the x variables is,

$$\mathbf{C}_{yx}\mathbf{B}_{y.x} = \mathbf{C}_{yx}\mathbf{C}_{xx}^{-1}\mathbf{C}_{xy} \qquad \text{(iib)}$$

and the deviation from regression is

$$\mathbf{C}_{yy} - \mathbf{C}_{yx}\mathbf{C}_{xx}^{-1}\mathbf{C}_{xy} \qquad \text{(iiib)}$$

If we now take each y variable in turn, and employ it as the dependent variable in a multiple regression analysis where the x variables are the predictor variables, we obtain q squared multiple correlation coefficients, one for each y variable. These coefficients, sometimes called coefficients of determination, are commonly symbolized by R^2 where R is not a matrix but a simple scalar quantity. R^2 is the proportion of the variance or the sum of squares of the y variable which is explained by the set of x variables. The elements of the principal diagonal of $\mathbf{C}_{yy}$ represent sums of squares of y variables, and R^2 for the ith y variable is equal to the ratio of the ith diagonal element of $\mathbf{C}_{yx}\mathbf{C}_{xx}^{-1}\mathbf{C}_{xy}$ to the ith diagonal element of $\mathbf{C}_{yy}$.

If all the variables have been standardized before calculating the partitioned sums of squares and sums of products matrix then this matrix is in a fact a correlation matrix, and all the diagonal elements of $\mathbf{C}_{yy}$ are unity. Each diagonal element of $\mathbf{C}_{yx}\mathbf{C}_{xx}^{-1}\mathbf{C}_{xy}$ is then equal to R^2 for the corresponding y variable. This is a multivariate analogue of the familiar fact that, when both x and y have been standardized (i.e. $\Sigma x^2 = \Sigma y^2 = 1$), then

$$b_{y.x} = r_{xy}$$

$$\text{and} \qquad (\Sigma xy)\, b_{y.x} = r_{xy}^2$$

Application to a social mobility table

A table which has been extensively analysed in the literature is the intergenerational contingency table reported by Glass et al. (1954). This is reproduced here as Table 1. The total of the entries in the table is 3497.

In order to apply our generalized regression method to such a table we must imagine a data matrix made up of the scores of 3497 persons on fourteen variables, seven dummy variables for the fathers ($p = 7$) and seven dummy variables for the sons ($q = 7$). This matrix is reproduced in skeleton form in Table 2. Each person in the matrix has a positive score on one of the paternal variables and on one of the filial variables.

TABLE 1

Contingency table relating occupational category of father to occupational category of son (Glass, 1954).

		Son's occupational category						
		1	2	3	4	5	6	7
	1	50	19	26	8	18	6	2
Father's	2	16	40	34	18	31	8	3
occupational	3	12	35	65	66	123	23	21
category	4	11	20	58	110	223	64	32
	5	14	36	114	185	714	258	189
	6	0	6	19	40	179	143	71
	7	0	3	14	32	141	91	106

TABLE 2

Skeleton of a 3497 × 14 data matrix derived from Table 1.

	Paternal variables								Filial variables					
n_{ij}	f_1	f_2	f_3	f_4	f_5	f_6	f_7	s_1	s_2	s_3	s_4	s_5	s_6	s_7
50	1	0	0	0	0	0	0	1	0	0	0	0	0	0
19	1	0	0	0	0	0	0	0	1	0	0	0	0	0
26	1	0	0	0	0	0	0	0	0	1	0	0	0	0
8	1	0	0	0	0	0	0	0	0	0	1	0	0	0
18	1	0	0	0	0	0	0	0	0	0	0	1	0	0
6	1	0	0	0	0	0	0	0	0	0	0	0	1	0
2	1	0	0	0	0	0	0	0	0	0	0	0	0	1
16	0	1	0	0	0	0	0	1	0	0	0	0	0	0
40	0	1	0	0	0	0	0	0	1	0	0	0	0	0
34	0	1	0	0	0	0	0	0	0	1	0	0	0	0
.	.													
.	.													
.	.													
91	0	0	0	0	0	0	1	0	0	0	0	0	1	0
106	0	0	0	0	0	0	1	0	0	0	0	0	0	1

His remaining scores are all zero. In constructing the matrix we take each cell of the contingency table in turn. If a cell is in the *i*th row and *j*th column we assign a positive score to the *i*th paternal variable and the *j*th filial variable, we assign zero scores to the remaining twelve variables, and we reiterate this pattern of scores as many times as there are persons in the cell (n_{ij}).

Each dummy variable has the property of contrasting membership of a particular occupational category with membership of all other categories, and each set of dummies systematically runs through all possible contrasts. Thus the data matrix contains all the information which is given in the contingency table, though in a long-winded fashion. The one can be completely reconstituted from a knowledge of the other.

It should be evident that the technique of employing dummy variables* is not confined to the analysis of square contingency tables, or to contingency tables in which rows and columns both relate to the same variable. Nor does it make any assumptions about the ordering of the marginal categories. Like the ordinary chi square test, but unlike a rank correlation coefficient, the method gives unchanged results if two or more rows are interchanged, or if two or more columns are interchanged.

We now imagine† ourselves centring each dummy variable about its mean, that is expressing every score in Table 2 as a deviation from the column weighted mean, and we may also standardize each variable by dividing the deviation scores by their sum of squares. If we now calculate the sums of squares and sums of products matrix of the fourteen centred and standardized variables we obtain the partitioned correlation matrix whose sub-matrices are C_{xx}, C_{xy}, C_{yx}, and C_{yy}. This matrix has certain characteristic properties. The correlations within the sub-matrices C_{xx} and C_{yy} are necessarily negative, since membership of one category precludes membership of another.** The smaller the number of variables in a set the larger are the negative correlations between variables within the set. For example, in the 7×7 matrix C_{yy} of the present analysis the correlations vary between -0.0380, for categories one and two, and -0.3756, for categories five and six. Although it is not a necessary property of the matrix, in fact the diagonal elements of C_{yx} (Table 3, note that C_{yx} is identical with the transpose of C_{xy}) tend to be larger than the off-diagonal elements. It is shown below that these diagonal elements give us direct access to the quantification of occupational inheritance. The pattern of signs in C_{yx} is an unmistakable indication of the nature of interchange between categories. The near-symmetry of the matrix, which distinguishes it from matrices similarly derived from other societies, may be interpreted as an indication of a particular type of equilibrium in the system.

* Fisher (1958) presents an interesting example of an analysis of a special type of table containing serological data (cf. Bartlett, 1951, 1965a). It was after re-working Fisher's example by means of dummy variables that the application to generalized regression suggested itself to the author. He was helped in this re-working by useful discussions with Miss A-M. Skrimshire. In a third paper Bartlett (1965b) observes that 'because in this example we are in effect working with dummy or pseudo-variables for both sets of variables, we can hardly claim to have normal distributions for them. In spite of this, it is believed that they [the canonical roots] are broadly correct provided the tests of significance are not taken too precisely.'

† In practice it is not of course necessary to write out the matrix at all. There are much quicker routes to the partitioned sums of squares and sums of products matrix. The computing method evolved by Lancaster and described in volume 2 of *The advanced theory of statistics* (Kendall and Stuart, 1967) is a quick and easy way of arriving at the roots and vectors of the canonical analysis but it will do no more. The types of analysis developed in this paper call for a much more extensive body of computation of which canonical analysis is only one aspect.

** Though this constraint might, for some purposes, be relaxed in studies which are designed with this type of regression analysis in mind. We might, for example, have a category of foremen and supervisors, and a man might belong to that, as well as to a trade category.

TABLE 3

Correlations between filial and paternal variables (matrix $\mathbf{C}_{yx}$)

Paternal variables

		1	2	3	4	5	6	7
	1	0·4146	0·0967	0·0104	−0·0203	−0·1041	−0·0676	−0·0615
	2	0·0957	0·2248	0·0889	−0·0137	−0·0905	−0·0603	−0·0639
	3	0·0718	0·0958	0·1064	0·0251	−0·0563	−0·0702	−0·0702
Filial	4	−0·0401	−0·0071	0·0588	0·1001	−0·0226	−0·0505	−0·0507
variables	5	−0·1071	−0·0870	−0·0351	0·0185	−0·1139	−0·0141	−0·0318
	6	−0·0642	−0·0656	−0·0907	−0·0511	0·0030	0·1476	0·0616
	7	−0·0634	−0·0657	−0·0612	−0·0760	0·0105	0·0402	0·1650

It has been pointed out that the more variables there are in a set, the nearer to zero are the correlations among the variables. Conversely, if the number of variables falls to two, these two necessarily have a correlation of minus one. The reason for this is that the variables of a set are necessarily linearly dependent on one another. Although we have p, x-axes, each representing membership of a row-category, these p axes lie in a space of $p - 1$ dimensions. Similarly the q, y-axes lie in a space of $q - 1$ dimensions. Thus the matrices $\mathbf{C}_{xx}$ and $\mathbf{C}_{yy}$ are singular matrices.

Singularity is the limiting case of a condition which is often discussed in the sociological literature under the title 'multicollinearity'. Readers of this literature might be forgiven for supposing that multicollinearity is a defeat and singularity a disaster in any regression analysis. And it is certainly true that multicollinearity renders regression equations equivocal (Kendall, 1961) and so must be regarded as a danger signal by those who are accustomed to interpreting regression coefficients as guides to the relative importance of variables. However, in the paper on path analysis in this volume it is pointed out that regression equations have inherent defects for this purpose, whether or not collinearities are present. In the case of a singular matrix, it is possible to choose two or more sub-sets of predictor variables which serve to define one and the same dimension, even though the same variable may appear in two subsets with quite different regression weights. But this apparent discrepancy does not alter the relation between the defined dimension and all other dimensions or axes, including the variables employed in the regression equations. The stability of relationships becomes manifest if we concentrate on the cosines of the constant angles between the axes or dimensions, that is if we look at the correlations between dimensions, whether those dimensions are variables or linear combinations of variables such as emerge from regression or other weighting equations.

Both C_{xx} and C_{yy} are singular matrices. But this says no more than that each lies in one less dimension than it has rows and columns. Since it is not possible to invert a singular matrix we must proceed by reducing the dimensionality of our analysis until inversion becomes possible and then translate the analysis back into the terms of the original dummy variables. This somewhat technical procedure is not described in detail here. In the paper 'Path analysis: supplementary procedures' it is shown that an examination of the steps which are involved may help in deciding how far a particular regression equation may be taken as a guide to the relative importance of its constituent variables.

The rigidity of an occupational category

Having inverted C_{xx} we calculate $C_{yx}C_{xx}^{-1}C_{xy}$, which is that part of matrix C_{yy} which is accounted for by the set of x variables. Each diagonal element is the R^2 or coefficient of determination for the corresponding y variable. Since each y variable is uniquely associated with membership or non-membership of a particular occupational category we have, in effect, devised a simple, straightforward measure, expressed as a proportion or percentage, of the extent of rigidity or immobility associated with each occupational category. These *percentage determinations* are given in Table 4. It will scarcely be denied that the precise quantification of the relative concentration of constraints on intergenerational mobility at the top of the ladder* is an important social datum. The existence of this relative rigidity[†] can of course be detected in the original contingency table and in any number of indices or analyses which might be derived from it. The contention advanced here is that a percentage statement emanating from a multivariate regression analysis has a peculiar directness and comparative force which other measures lack.

Rigidity in the society

Having established a measure of rigidity for individual occupational categories we may wish to calculate an average for the society as a whole. A number of weighting systems might be devised for the derivation of such an average. We might, for example, weight a category by

* The reader is reminded that the analysis does not assign any ordering to the categories. It is on extraneous grounds that we call category one the top of a ladder. On the other hand an extension of the analysis to the calculation of distances between occupational categories shows that the seven categories of this study are indeed ordered in mobility terms exactly as they are in terms of 'prestige'. Although the two orderings are identical there is, in the mobility ordering, a startling gap between categories one and two such that, for both sons and fathers, the distance between categories one and two is about 65 per cent of the distance between categories one and seven. This is simply another reflection of the exceptional position of the first category in Table 4.

[†] The use of the terms 'constraint' or 'rigidity' to mean an observed pattern of relations, rather than a factor which brings about that pattern, should not puzzle sociologists, who are accustomed to refer to social movement as social 'mobility'.

TABLE 4

The extent of intergenerational constraints on mobility associated with each occupational category, together with a measure of their relative importance.

		Percentage of variance predictable from knowledge of father's occupation	Variance
	1	18·84	0·0286
	2	7·59	0·0434
Occupational	3	3·50	0·0855
category	4	1·81	0·1140
	5	2·81	0·2417
	6	4·00	0·1408
	7	4·20	0·1065

its income or status level in such a way as to give greater weight to the upper categories. However, for the more mundane purpose of arriving at an estimate of the social constraints faced by a man drawn at random from the population as a whole we need to weight the rigidity of a class or category by a factor related to the relative size of that class. Since our rigidity measures are percentages of variance explained, the obvious weight to apply to each value is the total variance of the variable which is being explained. The variables are dummy variables taking only two values. It is well known that the variance of a two-valued variable is pq, where p is the proportion of persons having one value and q is the proportion having the other value (the use of the letters p and q here has no relation to their use earlier in the paper). The closer these proportions come to 0·5 the greater the variance of the variable. Conversely, a category which has proportionately few members will be associated with a variable which has a small variance. Because category 1 is the smallest of the seven categories its degree of rigidity has the smallest weight in the calculation of overall or average rigidity (Table 4). Taking the sum of products of the two columns of Table 4, and dividing by the sum of the variances, gives us a figure of 4·03% as the extent of constraints on mobility, or intergenerational predictability of occupational category, in England and Wales.

It will be appreciated that figures such as this depend on the particular classification which is employed and that they do not take into account what is known of the ordering of occupations in the social scale. They should not be taken very seriously and should never be employed out of their context, which is essentially the quantification of movement for individual collectivities.

Occupational transmission

It was stated above that the diagonal elements of the matrix $\mathbf{C}_{yx}$ enable us to quantify extent of occupational inheritance. The typical diagonal element is a product-moment correlation between two corresponding binary variables, f_i and s_i. It is well known that such a correlation is equivalent to the phi coefficient, or fourfold point correlation coefficient (Yule, 1912). The square of phi is sometimes known as the mean-square contingency (Pearson, 1904), and displays the identity

$$\phi^2 = \frac{\chi^2}{n}$$

where χ^2 is calculated from the 2×2 table for the two point variables from which phi is calculated, and $n = 3497$ is the total number of persons. Since n is constant for all values of phi we have a strict proportionality between the mean-square contingency and chi squared.

If phi is positive, in the sense that a score of 1 on f_i tends to be associated with a score of 1 on s_i, then the range of phi is limited in so far as the ratio p/q is different for the two variables, where p is the proportion of persons scoring 1 and $q = 1 - p$. Although this limitation applies to all the elements of the partitioned correlation matrix, in so far as the proportion of the population in a category differs from category to category, it is not an important consideration in the interpretation of the diagonal elements of $\mathbf{C}_{yx}$ because the variance of each paternal variable is very similar to the variance of the corresponding filial variable (Table 6). From this it follows that the square of a diagonal element of $\mathbf{C}_{yx}$ is not only an indication of the extent to which a particular filial variable can in practice be predicted from knowledge of the corresponding paternal variable, but it is also an indication of the strength of the intrinsic relation between father's membership of a particular class and son's membership of the same class.

The estimates of occupational inheritance derived from diagonal elements of Table 3 are reported in Table 5. The term 'inheritance' must be taken as short-hand for 'being in the same occupational category as father', rather than 'inheriting father's job' or 'following father's trade'. The extent of occupational inheritance of a category (Table 5) is a constituent of the total predictable variance of the variable associated with that category (Table 4). This follows from the fact that f_i is always one of the seven variables which are employed in the prediction of s_i. Only if none of the other six paternal variables was contributing to the prediction* would occupational inheritance account for the whole

* i.e. contributing a specific element, over and above the element which it shares with f_i. The set of six variables from which f_i has been omitted predicts S_i to exactly the same extent as the full set of seven variables because every paternal variable lies entirely in the space of its six companions. This says no more than that in an exclusive and exhaustive seven-fold classification, the statement that a person is not in any of six classes is logically equivalent to the statement that he is in the seventh.

TABLE 5

Degree of occupational 'inheritance' associated with each occupational category, together with the weighted average (weights given in the 'variance' column of Table 4)

Occupational category	Percentage of variance attributable to occupational inheritance
1	17·19
2	5·05
3	1·13
4	1·00
5	1·30
6	2·18
7	2·72
Overall	2·41

of the predictable variance. Thus the difference, say, between the 19 per cent predictability of the top category and the 17 per cent inheritance of that category is a measure of the extent to which variables f_2 to f_7 contribute after allowing for the influence of f_1.

A comparison between the extent of inheritance of a category (Table 5) and its overall predictability (Table 4) suggests that the more constraints there are on membership of a category the greater is the part which inheritance plays in those constraints. Categories three and five display the least proportionate effect of inheritance. Calculation of inflow percentages shows that 10 per cent of class three persons had their origins in class two, and 8 per cent originated in class one, the corresponding figures for all sons being 4 per cent for both classes of origin. Membership of category five has no strong positive association with any other particular family background (Table 3) but it is negatively related to the two top categories. Only 1 per cent of category five sons come from a class one background, and 2 per cent from class two, compared with 4 per cent for all sons. We have here evidence which suggests the presence of certain pins in the social bagatelle (cf Farber, 1965) which divert the downwardly-mobile sons of the top two classes away from skilled manual or routine clerical work (category five) and into higher-grade supervisory and other non-manual employment (category three). The need for an early start to an apprenticeship is one obvious negative explanation. Education and apprenticeship were for long incompatible, and the top 8 per cent of boys would naturally receive the former in preference to the latter, thus acquiring formal or informal qualifications which would, in some cases, be disproportionate to their capacities. Another, closely related, explanation might lie in the exercise of 'influence' to assure a competence for sons who were thought to be incapable of 'making the grade'.*

It should be observed, however, that there is a sense in which the importance of predictable inter-category movement is underestimated relative to the importance of category inheritance. This incommensurability of the two quantities follows from the observation that the diagonal elements of $\mathbf{C}_{yx}$ are closer to their arithmetic maxima than are the off-diagonal elements. And this discrepancy, in turn, follows from the facts (a) that the proportion of the population in a category is not constant for all categories, and (b) that the proportion in category i is roughly equal for fathers and sons. If, in a square table with k columns, each row and column contains $1/k$ of the total number of entries in the table, then the variance of each dummy variable is $(k - 1)/k^2$, and the sum of the variances for either set of variables is $(k - 1)/k$. If every entry in the 'a' columns of Table 6 were $6/49 = 0.12$ then ϕ_{max} for every element of the partitioned correlation matrix would be unity.

It is important to realize that the limitation which these considerations place on the predictability of inter-category movement, as opposed to continuance of category membership, is not a limitation which is inherent in the methods employed, but is imposed by the information contained in the original contingency table. All the available information is used, but more might have been made available.

It is possible to place too much emphasis on the limitations of phi as a measure of intrinsic relation. The two categories most divergent in size are paternal category five ($n = 1510$) and filial category one ($n = 103$). The maximum possible positive correlation between the corresponding dummy variables f_5 and s_1 is

$$\phi_{max} = 0.20$$

But this low value accurately reflects the fact that if all 103 class one sons had class five fathers there would still be $1510 - 103 = 1407$ sons of class five fathers outside class one.

The finding that inheritance accounts for most of the constraints on mobility is analogous to Goodman's (1965, 1969) finding of quasi-independence (quasi-perfect mobility) when the diagonal elements of a reduced (3×3) version of Table 1 are blocked out. In a recent paper Duncan (1968, p. 697) has pointed out that 'son's status may depend upon that of the father to a degree, even if the son ends up in a different classification' and, alluding to the work of Goodman (1965) and White (1963), he says 'I seriously doubt the generality of results that appear to imply the contrary'.

Our concept of 'constraints on mobility' takes account of both terms of Duncan's distinction. The preceding discussion has indicated the

* These explanations are developed more fully in part IV of this paper as alternatives to the frequently-proposed explanation of a willingness to sacrifice income for status.

difficulties involved in reaching a satisfactory numerical statement of the relative importance of inheritance and predictable inter-category movement. The problem posed by unequal category membership can, in principle, be largely overcome by re-classification of occupations. Against this it must be pointed out that, if the rows and columns of the mobility table represent collectivities then re-grouping would serve only to obscure the realistic limits to the maximum possible degree of association between particular paternal and particular filial categories.

The problem which faces us may be clarified by deploying the model which has been developed in the introduction to this volume. In a study of two societies (or of a single society at two points in time) we may find (a) that they are similar in the pattern of relations among a set of stratification axes, (b) that each stratification space* has a distribution of clusters representing social collectivities, (c) that the two distributions are similar, and (d) that similar proportions of the two populations fall into analogous collectivities. If all four conditions hold no problem of re-grouping arises. If condition (d) alone does not hold we shall probably carry out our comparative analysis after an initial standardization (perhaps standardizing each table in terms of the other). If condition (b) alone holds we may carry out the two separate analyses and make verbal comparisons between their conclusions. If, for at least one of the societies, none of the conditions, or (a) alone, holds, that is, if we are faced with a multidimensional continuum in which no collectivities can be discerned, then we are reduced to the necessity of defining some axis of interest (which may differ between the two societies but which will, in all probability, be defined so as to maximize inequalities) and arbitrarily grouping the projections of individuals along it. (Clearly, if mobility is to be the object of analysis, the grouping of individuals and the ordering of groups should not be arrived at by analysis of mobility data.) One method of grouping would be to define categories with fairly equal membership. Another would be to chop the inequality axis, if it could be regarded as an interval scale, into equal lengths.

Retrodiction

So far we have talked entirely in terms of the predictability of son's occupational category from a knowledge of his father's category. But the method of percentage determinations is symmetrical or bi-directional. We may equally calculate that part of the paternal matrix C_{xx} which is accounted for by the filial variables, namely, $C_{xy}C_{yy}^{-1}C_{yx}$.

It must at once be admitted that the two calculations are not on an entirely equal footing, in so far as sampling is sampling of sons, and father's chances of appearing in the sample vary according to his

---

* The choice between the 'economic' and the 'subcultural' spaces defined in the introduction, and the choice of axes, depend on the interest of the analyst.

number of sons. This asymmetry is inherent in intergenerational tables. It was pointed out by one of the original authors of these data (Mukherjee, 1954) and has been discussed in detail by Duncan (1966). It will not be discussed further here.

Table 6 contains a summary report of the predictive and the retro-dictive analyses. Column 'c'—the extent of occupational inheritance—is the same for both fathers and sons because the elements are simply the squares (multiplied by one hundred) of the diagonal elements of $C_{y x}$. The means at the feet of the two 'c' columns are different because the columns of weights 'a' are slightly different. It is evident that this par-ticular table is to a high degree arithmetically, as well as formally, sym-metric.

Although it has been pointed out that little importance can be attached to the figure of 4 per cent which represents overall predict-ability, it is instructive to note that, in both analyses, as much as 40 per cent of this figure is attributable to constraints on mobility other than direct inheritance.

Comparisons between societies

Tables 7 and 8 contain summary reports of analyses of Scottish and American data. The three intergenerational studies summarized in Tables 6, 7 and 8 are, respectively, (a) the study of England and Wales by Glass and his co-workers (Glass, 1954, table of percentages on page 183 converted back to frequencies) (b) the Scottish Mental Survey (Maxwell, 1969, Table 18*), and (c) the study of occupational changes in a generation carried out by the United States Bureau of the Census for Blau and Duncan (1967, Table J2.1 on page 496 with the 'no answer' row and column omitted). All three studies were carried out with a high level of technical competence but they differ somewhat in the definition of the population sampled, the questions asked, response rate, and the classification of occupations. The English study was a pioneer which has been much analyzed and serves as a bench-mark for new methods of analysis. The data consist of occupational category of father's last main job and occupational category of son's job in 1949, both reported by the son. The American data consist of occupational category of father when son was sixteen years old and occupational category of son in 1962, both reported by the son. The frequencies reported in Table 8 are in-flations of the sample numbers to represent the U.S. male population in thousands. The Scottish data, collected for a much smaller sample, represent a remarkable and meticulous follow-up of a sample of eleven-year-old boys drawn in 1947. Each boy's father's occupation was

* I am indebted to Mr. Maxwell and to the Committee of the 1947 Scottish mental survey for allowing me to see the manuscript of this report before publication.

TABLE 6

Percentage determination analysis of both fathers and sons (English data, $\Sigma n = 3497$)

Occupational category	Fathers					Sons				
	n	a	b	c	d	n	a	b	c	d
1 Professional and high administrative	129	0·04	20	17	2	103	0·03	19	17	2
2 Managerial and executive	150	0·04	8	5	3	159	0·04	8	5	3
3 Inspectoral, supervisory and other non-manual, higher grade	345	0·09	3	1	2	330	0·09	4	1	2
4 Inspectoral, supervisory and other non-manual, lower grade	518	0·13	2	1	1	459	0·11	2	1	1
5 Skilled manual, and routine grades of non-manual	1510	0·25	3	1	2	1429	0·24	3	1	2
6 Semi-skilled manual	458	0·11	3	2	1	593	0·14	4	2	2
7 Unskilled manual	387	0·10	4	3	1	424	0·11	4	3	1
Weighted mean			4·05	2·51	1·55			4·03	2·41	1·62

Note: a variance of the dummy variable associated with the occupational category

b percentage of a predictable from the other array (percentage determination)

c percentage of a attributable to occupational inheritance

d $b - c$, percentage of a which involves predictable inter-category movements (discrepancies are due to rounding)

TABLE 7
Percentage determination analysis of Scottish data ($\Sigma n = 513$)

Occupational category	Fathers					Sons				
	n	a	b	c	d	n	a	b	c	d
1 Professionals and large employers	16	0·03	17	16	0	65	0·11	23	16	7
2 Small employers and self-employed	24	0·04	7	3	4	11	0·02	4	3	1
3 Non-professional salaried employees	27	0·05	5	2	3	48	0·08	3	2	1
4 Non-manual wage earners	33	0·06	3	0	2	65	0·11	3	0	3
5 Skilled manual wage earners	207	0·24	9	5	4	132	0·19	7	5	2
6 Semi-skilled manual wage earners	86	0·14	7	1	5	118	0·18	5	1	3
7 Unskilled manual wage earners	73	0·12	6	4	2	44	0·08	9	4	5
8 Farmers	15	0·03	45	42	3	10	0·02	43	42	1
9 Agricultural workers (including crofters)	32	0·06	10	8	2	20	0·04	11	8	3
Weighted mean			8·98	4·81	4·17			8·92	5·56	3·36

See Table 6 for notes on column headings.

TABLE 8

Percentage determination analysis of U.S. data ($\Sigma n = 33972$; this is 2·17 times the actual sample size)

Occupational category	Fathers					Sons				
	n	a	b	c	d	n	a	b	c	d
1 Self-employed professionals	473	0·01	3	2	1	573	0·02	3	2	1
2 Salaried professionals	1160	0·03	2	2	1	3883	0·10	6	2	4
3 Managers	1314	0·04	2	1	2	2941	0·08	4	1	3
4 Salesmen, other	732	0·02	2	1	1	1197	0·03	2	1	1
5 Proprietors	2687	0·07	4	1	3	2576	0·07	1	1	0
6 Clerical	1151	0·03	1	0	1	2241	0·06	0	0	0
7 Salesmen, retail	633	0·02	1	0	1	562	0·02	0	0	0
8 Craftsmen, manufacturing	2113	0·06	1	1	1	2669	0·07	2	1	1
9 Craftsmen, other	2371	0·06	1	0	1	2577	0·07	1	0	0
10 Craftsmen, construction	1790	0·05	2	1	1	1809	0·05	1	1	0
11 Operatives, manufacturing	2805	0·08	2	1	1	3580	0·09	2	1	1
12 Operatives, other	2437	0·07	1	0	1	2751	0·07	1	0	1
13 Service	1626	0·05	1	0	0	1857	0·05	1	0	1
14 Laborers, manufacturing	648	0·02	1	0	1	764	0·02	1	0	1
15 Laborers, other	1562	0·04	1	0	1	1456	0·04	1	0	1
16 Farmers	9508	0·20	15	10	5	1997	0·06	10	10	0
17 Farm laborers	962	0·03	2	1	1	625	0·02	3	1	2
Weighted mean			4·71	2·83	1·88			2·56	1·30	1·26

See Table 6 for notes on column headings.

TABLE 9

Contribution of each occupational category to the weighted mean percentage rigidity of three societies. The column sums are the weighted means of the 'b' columns of Tables 6, 7 and 8.

England and Wales			Scotland			United States		
Occupational category	Fathers	Sons	Occupational category	Fathers	Sons	Occupational category	Fathers	Sons
1	0·93	0·73	1	0·65	3·11	1	0·05	0·05
2	0·42	0·43	2	0·39	0·09	2	0·09	0·64
3	0·38	0·39	3	0·32	0·32	3	0·10	0·32
4	0·29	0·27	4	0·20	0·39	4	0·05	0·07
5	0·96	0·89	5	2·88	1·70	5	0·36	0·11
6	0·52	0·74	6	1·19	0·98	6	0·05	0·03
7	0·55	0·59	7	0·93	0·85	7	0·01	0·01
			8	1·64	0·99	8	0·09	0·13
			9	0·78	0·49	9	0·07	0·05
						10	0·09	0·08
						11	0·16	0·19
						12	0·06	0·09
						13	0·04	0·05
						14	0·02	0·02
						15	0·07	0·06
						16	3·34	0·61
						17	0·06	0·05
Sum	4·05	4·03	Sum	8·98	8·92	Sum	4·71	2·56

ascertained at that date and his own occupation was ascertained in frequent follow-ups, ending in 1963. Thus the Scottish respondents differ
from the English and American in that they are homogeneous in age. The
age at which their own occupation was finally determined (27) is only
two years above the minimum age of the American respondents (25).

Looking first at the farming category it can be seen that there is
considerable rigidity here both in Scotland and in the United States.
Farming does not feature as a distinct category in the English data and
so nothing can be said about it. The percentage immobility for Scotland
is based on small numbers: eight out of fifteen fathers who are farmers,
factors, or grieves have sons who are similarly employed. Leaving aside
the difference in magnitude between the Scottish and American rigidities
we can detect the effect on immobility of rapid change in the economic
structure. Whereas more than a quarter of Americans have fathers who
are farmers, this is true of only 3 per cent of young Scotsmen. Because
the drift from the land has been so much smaller in Scotland than in the
United States occupational 'inheritance' accounts for most of the backward, as well as the forward, rigidity in Scotland, but for less of the
backward rigidity in the United States.

When an occupational category is decanting its sons they flow into
a number of other categories. The predictability of son's category is
therefore diffused while that of father's category is concentrated.
Exactly the opposite effect occurs with the top Scottish category. Of
the 16 fathers in this category 14 have sons in the same category, but
51 sons enter it from other categories. And so occupational 'inheritance'
explains almost all of the fathers' predictability but not so much of that
of the sons. The discrepancy between overall rigidity and occupational
inheritance occurs in the one case because sons of farmers move selectively into other jobs, and in the other case because top category sons
are drawn selectively from the remaining categories.

In computing the mean overall rigidity of a society the rigidity of
an individual category is weighted by the variance of the dummy variable for that category, or rather, by the proportion which that variance
bears to the sum of the variances for all the dummy variables. The additive weighted contributions to the overall rigidities are reported in
Table 9 for all three societies. It can be seen that, when farming is
deducted from the calculation of overall immobility the predictability of
the occupation of American fathers falls from 4·71 per cent to 1·37 per
cent, and that of American sons from 2·56 per cent to 1·95 per cent.

Leaving aside farming, the outstanding difference among the three
tables is the contrast between the two British studies on the one hand
and the American study on the other in the degree of rigidity associated with the top one or two categories. It is, of course, possible that
there is in American society an élite which displays a degree of rigidity

comparable to that of the British, but that this élite, or its source categories, has not been unequivocally identified in the American categorization.

It may be pointed out that the British studies employ a classification which approximates to a set of social collectivities, whereas the
American study categorizes men according to their economic function.
If, in fact, constraints on mobility are primarily related to prestige then
they may be obscured in so far as the functional census categories overlap in terms of prestige. Clearly, it would be most valuable to be able to
determine this question empirically by performing two analyses of a
single set of data, the first with men allotted to prestige strata, and the
second with the same men re-grouped according to function.* It may even
be found that the incidence of constraints is on different systems in
different societies. The outcome of the present analyses suggests that
the functional category of agricultural work should always be retained
in the search for constraints, even though the primary principle of grouping is prestige or status. It would, in fact, be an easy matter to sub-
divide functional categories into prestige[†] strata and to test the effects
of (a) functional categorization alone (b) prestige categorization alone,
and (c) the combination of the two. More complicated investigations
would involve the employment of different categorizations for fathers
and sons.

The evidence of the present analyses is that British society differs
from American in its relatively high degree of constraint in the top one
or two classes. Such rigidities as the United States possess tend to
be associated with farming. Differences in the populations sampled pre-
vent us drawing any conclusions from a comparison of the absolute
figures for Scotland and England.

In no case does the overall extent of rigidity exceed 9 per cent. It
is instructive to contrast this quantification with a more impressionistic reading of an earlier collection of evidence by Buckley (1958),
who states that 'the empirical data Barber gathers together in later
chapters show overwhelmingly that, even in modern democratic societies, the social positions of the majority of adults are at the same or

* Professor O.D. Duncan has kindly supplied the cross-tabulations of the same men
classified in terms of five-point intervals on his socio-economic scale (Duncan, 1961).
The analysis of the data in this form is very similar to the analysis reported in Table 8.
The two highest percentage predictabilities for the sons are 6.42 for interval 10—14 and
3.86 for interval 90+. For the fathers the two highest predictabilities are 10.67 and 2.69
for the intervals of 10—14 and 90+ respectively. Thus, for both generations, predictability
is highest for the socio-economic range which includes farmers (who have a position of
14 on the index), and the next highest predictability is for men of highest status. But ,
leaving aside farming, these percentage determinations are quite low and are close to
the comparable figures in Table 8. Thus two different classifications of the American
data have failed to reveal differential constraints of the sort found in two independent
British studies.

[†] For a discussion of the sociological concept of occupational prestige see the first
paper in this volume.

very similar levels in the hierarchy as those of their parents'. Sons' occupations may be highly predictable even though no son belongs to the same category as his father (a constraint on mobility is not the same thing as immobility), but intergenerational similarity of status implies at least a moderate degree of predictability.

Throughout the first part of this paper we have interpreted predictability as evidence of rigidity or constraint. These concepts should not be confused with immobility or transmission of similar status. It is conceivable that transmission of status might be highly determinate even though inheritance of status was rare. As an illustration: a society consisting of a small number of lineages may practice a form of exogamy with rules so restrictive that the lineal identification of a married woman is completely determined by the lineal origins of her parents. More fancifully, one can imagine a two-class society in which the children of upper-class people are always lower class, and the children of lower-class people are always upper class. Here class membership is completely constrained but there is no class-inheritance. The term *continuation constraints* might be used to stand for predictable occupational 'inheritance', and the term *departure constraints* might be used to refer to predictable movement between categories. The extent of departure constraints may be measured by the residual which is obtained when the percentage continuation constraint is subtracted from the percentage determination of a category. Although the effect of these relations is to assign as much of the predictable variance as possible to continuation constraint it is nevertheless the case that, in each of our three analyses, the overall extent of departure constraint is of the order of forty per cent.

It might be hypothesized that much of the departure constraint may be due to a certain kind of movement, for example movement from one particular class to another, or one-step upward movement from all classes except the top. Effects of this nature may be investigated by constructing models like those in the paper 'Social mobility and fertility'.

The main conclusion of the first part of this study is that, although Britain may, on average, possess marginally more intergenerational transmission of status than the United States (and this is by no means proved), when we look at the upper end of the social scale, which is qualitatively though not quantitatively important, British society appears to show markedly more constraints and greater rigidity than American.

The relation between father's occupational category and son's occupational category is stronger in the Scottish than in the English data, in part, we may surmise, because the Scottish sons, unlike the English, form a temporally-homogeneous cohort, in part because the Scottish data are more reliable, and in part because the lapse of time between the occupational assessments of the two generations is probably less in the Scottish than in the English survey. Nevertheless the distribution of constraints on mobility suggests that the forces at work in Scottish society are very similar to those in England, but significantly different from those in the United States.

PART II.   DIMENSIONS OF CANONICAL REGRESSION

Canonical hierarchy

The method of analysis which we have been examining may be described in geometrical terms as relating a space of $p - 1$ dimensions to another space of $q - 1$ dimensions and showing how far the two overlap. In this section we show how the space which is common to the paternal and the filial spaces may be explored in detail. In general this common space has either $p - 1$ or $q - 1$ dimensions, whichever is the smaller.

Students of factor analysis who are familiar with the concept of a 'unit hierarchy' (Burt, 1938) will be aware that, by means of a 'spectral analysis', a covariance or correlation matrix can be decomposed into a set of matrices which sum to the original matrix. Each matrix in the set is uniquely associated with an axis of the multidimensional space of the original matrix, and the axes form an orthogonal set. They will also be aware that, in general, the analysis of a covariance matrix is not identical with nor transformable into the analysis of the corresponding correlation matrix. In the method of generalized regression it is possible to carry out a similar type of spectral analysis which has the property of yielding the same set of axes whether we start from a correlation or a covariance matrix.

A unit hierarchy in factor analysis is so called because it is a matrix with a single non-zero latent root. In other words, the whole matrix can be generated from the square roots of its diagonal elements. In canonical regression too the unit hierarchies have this property, and it is possible to summarize each hierarchy, and hence the axis to which it corresponds, by reporting the square roots of its diagonal elements. Since every axis has a dual representation, one in the paternal space and the other in the filial space, two sets of axes must be reported.

The axes given in Table 10 (and in the analogous Tables 11 and 12) are those for the standardized variables. In other words, by squaring the ith element of a vector we obtain the proportion of the variance of the ith dummy variable which lies along the axis. The percentage of the variance of all (non-standardized) variables which each one-dimensional space accounts for is given below the vector describing the axis of

TABLE 10

Vectors representing axes of the canonical space of the English data. The dummy variable for an occupational category is weighted by its variance (Table 6) in calculating the overall percentage of variance associated with an axis.

		Fathers							Sons				
Dimensions	1	2	3	4	5	6	1	2	3	4	5	6
Occupational category 1	0·41	-0·15	0·04	0·00	0·00	-0·00	0·40	-0·15	0·05	0·00	0·00	0·00
2	0·24	0·09	-0·11	-0·02	-0·01	0·01	0·23	0·10	-0·11	-0·01	-0·01	0·01
3	0·11	0·13	-0·01	0·03	0·02	-0·02	0·16	0·09	-0·01	0·01	0·01	-0·02
4	0·01	0·10	0·08	-0·00	0·04	0·02	0·01	0·11	0·06	0·01	0·05	0·01
5	-0·15	0·00	0·05	-0·00	-0·06	-0·00	-0·13	0·04	0·08	-0·01	-0·06	0·00
6	-0·14	-0·09	-0·04	-0·07	0·03	-0·01	-0·14	-0·11	-0·05	-0·07	-0·02	-0·00
7	-0·14	-0·11	-0·07	0·07	0·02	0·01	-0·14	-0·11	-0·07	0·07	0·01	0·00
% variance	2·56	0·80	0·38	0·14	0·16	0·01	2·42	0·86	0·44	0·17	0·14	0·01

TABLE 11

Axes of the canonical space of the Scottish data (see legend of Table 10 for explanations and Table 7 for titles of occupational categories)

	Fathers								Sons							
Dimensions	1	2	3	4	5	6	7	8	1	2	3	4	5	6	7	8
1	−0·08	0·37	0·12	0·01	−0·08	−0·03	0·02	−0·00	−0·13	0·45	0·11	0·01	−0·04	−0·02	0·01	0·00
2	−0·05	0·20	0·02	−0·07	0·12	−0·05	−0·04	−0·00	−0·02	0·06	−0·02	−0·05	0·16	−0·05	0·01	0·00
3	−0·05	0·17	−0·07	−0·00	−0·02	0·10	−0·04	−0·00	−0·05	0·11	−0·07	0·04	0·03	−0·09	−0·03	−0·00
4	−0·06	0·10	−0·04	0·02	0·07	0·05	0·06	0·00	−0·05	−0·01	−0·15	0·03	0·01	0·05	−0·00	0·00
Occupational 5	−0·14	−0·12	−0·14	0·19	−0·02	−0·05	−0·01	−0·00	−0·12	−0·17	−0·04	0·15	−0·02	−0·07	−0·04	−0·00
category 6	−0·06	−0·18	0·15	−0·06	0·04	0·03	0·02	−0·00	0·00	−0·19	0·04	−0·02	−0·02	0·03	0·08	−0·00
7	−0·03	−0·17	0·13	−0·10	−0·06	−0·00	−0·02	0·00	−0·02	−0·17	0·22	−0·12	0·00	0·01	−0·04	0·00
8	0·66	0·04	0·06	0·06	0·01	0·01	−0·00	0·00	0·65	0·05	0·05	0·07	0·02	0·01	−0·00	0·00
9	0·18	0·02	−0·20	−0·16	−0·04	−0·02	0·02	−0·00	0·23	0·02	−0·16	−0·17	−0·06	−0·05	−0·00	−0·00
% variance	2·65	2·50	1·70	1·59	0·26	0·21	0·07	0·00	1·78	4·58	1·16	0·81	0·13	0·27	0·18	0·00

TABLE 12

Axes of the canonical space of the American data (see legend of Table 10 for explanations and Table 8 for titles of occupational categories. Only nine of the sixteen pairs of axes are reported. None of the omitted axes accounts for more than 0·014% of variance.)

	Fathers									Sons								
Dimensions	1	2	3	4	5	6	7	8	9	1	2	3	4	5	6	7	8	9
1	0·11	−0·08	−0·09	−0·07	0·00	−0·04	0·02	−0·01	0·00	0·11	−0·09	−0·06	−0·08	−0·01	−0·05	0·02	−0·02	−0·00
2	0·13	−0·03	−0·06	0·03	0·02	0·02	−0·01	0·01	−0·02	0·21	−0·04	−0·09	0·03	0·04	0·01	−0·02	0·00	−0·02
3	0·14	−0·05	−0·00	0·02	0·01	0·00	−0·02	0·01	0·01	0·17	−0·06	0·06	0·02	−0·03	0·01	−0·02	0·01	0·01
4	0·12	−0·06	0·02	−0·00	−0·02	0·02	0·01	0·01	0·04	0·12	−0·04	0·01	−0·01	−0·01	0·02	0·02	0·02	0·04
5	0·16	−0·08	0·09	−0·02	−0·05	−0·00	0·00	−0·01	−0·03	0·04	−0·05	0·09	−0·00	−0·03	−0·01	0·00	−0·02	−0·03
6	0·10	−0·01	−0·03	0·02	0·03	0·02	−0·00	−0·02	−0·00	0·04	0·04	0·01	0·00	0·03	0·01	0·01	0·02	−0·00
7	0·05	−0·01	0·03	0·01	−0·02	0·01	0·01	0·02	0·01	0·03	−0·01	0·02	−0·00	−0·03	0·01	0·01	−0·00	−0·00
8	0·06	0·07	−0·01	0·04	0·01	−0·04	−0·03	−0·00	0·00	−0·01	0·10	−0·01	0·03	0·00	−0·06	−0·03	−0·00	0·02
9	0·05	0·05	0·02	0·01	0·03	0·02	0·01	−0·04	0·02	−0·02	0·04	0·02	0·00	0·03	0·02	0·01	−0·04	0·02
10	0·01	0·06	0·07	−0·04	0·06	−0·05	−0·01	0·02	0·00	−0·05	0·02	0·06	−0·04	0·06	0·04	−0·01	0·02	−0·00
11	0·00	0·11	−0·03	0·02	−0·06	−0·04	0·00	−0·01	0·01	−0·08	0·08	−0·03	0·02	−0·06	−0·02	0·00	−0·00	−0·00
12	0·01	0·07	−0·01	−0·01	0·02	0·03	0·01	−0·04	−0·02	−0·07	0·04	−0·01	−0·00	0·02	0·04	0·01	−0·03	−0·01
13	0·02	0·06	0·01	−0·00	−0·00	0·01	0·03	0·03	−0·02	−0·04	0·06	−0·01	−0·01	−0·00	0·02	0·02	0·03	−0·02
14	−0·03	0·07	−0·03	0·01	−0·04	−0·00	0·01	0·01	−0·01	−0·05	0·05	−0·03	0·00	−0·04	−0·01	0·01	0·01	−0·01
15	−0·04	0·09	−0·01	−0·04	−0·00	0·03	0·02	0·02	0·01	−0·10	0·03	−0·01	−0·05	−0·00	0·02	0·00	0·02	0·01
16	−0·35	−0·16	−0·01	0·03	0·01	−0·01	0·01	0·00	0·00	−0·25	−0·19	−0·01	0·05	0·01	−0·02	0·02	0·01	0·00
17	−0·10	0·02	−0·01	−0·06	−0·03	0·04	−0·06	0·00	0·00	−0·13	−0·05	−0·02	−0·04	−0·02	0·03	−0·06	−0·00	0·00
% variance	3·26	0·95	0·14	0·08	0·09	0·07	0·03	0·03	0·02	1·43	0·52	0·22	0·07	0·10	0·08	0·03	0·04	0·02

Occupational category

that space. Because the axes represent orthogonal dimensions of the canonical space the percentages add up (separately for fathers and sons) to the overall percentages of predictable variance reported in Table 6.

It is proposed that, by analogy with the unit hierarchy of factor analysis, the vectors of Table 10 should be called *bases of canonical hierarchies*. Canonical hierarchies, unlike unit hierarchies, have a double constitutive role, in that they combine additively to reproduce both the original partitioned correlation matrix **C** and also the elements of the two sub-matrices $\mathbf{C}_{xx}$ and $\mathbf{C}_{yy}$ which are attributable to regression. If we symbolize the ith paternal column of Table 10 by $\mathbf{x}_i$, and the jth filial column by $\mathbf{y}_j$ we may construct an individual canonical hierarchy from the matrix products $\mathbf{x}_i \mathbf{x}_i'$, $\mathbf{y}_i \mathbf{y}_i'$ and $\mathbf{x}_i \mathbf{y}_i'$. The diagonal sub matrices of the original partitioned matrix are given by

$$\mathbf{C}_{xx} = \sum_{i=1}^{v} \frac{1}{R_i^2} \mathbf{x}_i \mathbf{x}_i'$$

$$\mathbf{C}_{yy} = \sum_{i=1}^{v} \frac{1}{R_i^2} \mathbf{y}_i \mathbf{y}_i'$$

where $\sum_{i=1}^{v}$ stands for summation of the following matrix products over all v canonical dimensions and R_i^2 is the ith canonical root. The off-diagonal sub-matrix of the partitioned matrix is given by

$$\mathbf{C}_{yy} = \sum_{i=1}^{v} \frac{1}{R_i} \mathbf{x}_i \mathbf{y}_i'$$

The canonical hierarchies also combine to reproduce the variance attributable to regression as follows:

$$\mathbf{C}_{xy} \mathbf{C}_{yy}^{-1} \mathbf{C}_{yx} = \sum_{i=1}^{v} \mathbf{x}_i \mathbf{x}_i'$$

$$\mathbf{C}_{yx} \mathbf{C}_{xx}^{-1} \mathbf{C}_{xy} = \sum_{i=1}^{v} \mathbf{y}_i \mathbf{y}_i'$$

If we write all v vectors $\mathbf{x}_i$ as columns of a matrix $\mathbf{X}$, and all v vectors $\mathbf{y}_i$ as columns of $\mathbf{Y}$, we may write

$$\mathbf{C}_{xy} \mathbf{C}_{yy}^{-1} \mathbf{C}_{yx} = \mathbf{X} \mathbf{X}'$$

$$\mathbf{C}_{yx} \mathbf{C}_{xx}^{-1} \mathbf{C}_{xy} = \mathbf{Y} \mathbf{Y}'$$

Canonical regression and analysis by canonical correlations

Readers who are familiar with methods of analysis by canonical correlations (Hotelling, 1936) will no doubt have observed that the partitioned matrix from which this analysis started is also the usual starting-point of a canonical variate analysis, and they may wonder why the technique of canonical regression has been deployed in place of a straightforward canonical analysis.

The answer to this question is of importance for all regression analyses, whether they are concerned with continuous or dummy variables. It will be readily granted that analysis by canonical correlation has created many headaches for those research workers who have ventured to use it because of the difficulty of interpreting canonical roots and vectors. It is the writer's contention that a canonical variate analysis should always be supplemented by a canonical regression analysis. Indeed, he suspects that experience will show that the latter is usually more informative than the former, although the two are clearly intimately related. Canonical variate analysis should be looked upon as one facet of a larger body of analysis. It is dangerous to use it in isolation.

It may be asked why, in the past, attention has been one-sidedly concentrated on a partial aspect of a complex field. The answer would seem to be that users of multivariate methods have been misled by a paralogism which has its origin in factor analysis. The latent roots and vectors of an ordinary principal component analysis are doubly-orthogonal in a way that canonical roots and vectors are not. In consequence the former fulfil a double function: they assign both direction and importance to the underlying dimensions. Because a canonical root can be represented as a latent root of a certain matrix, and because it is the square of a correlation coefficient, which is a straightforward generalization of the ordinary multiple correlation coefficient R, it is assumed that, like a latent root or a squared multiple correlation coefficient, it tells us the importance of the dimension with which it is associated. This is not in fact so. Similarly, a canonical vector, unlike a latent vector, does not tell us (except in very special circumstances) the relative importance of variables in the dimension to which it is related. The method of canonical regression has been developed as a means of answering questions concerning relative importance. Although the method, as it is set out here, applies to data in the form of a contingency table, it applies equally well to the more usual analysis of continuous variables.

It may be objected that a correlation coefficient, whether canonical or not, is essentially a guide to importance. By squaring it we obtain the proportion of the variance of either variable which is accounted for by the other variable. In an ordinary multiple regression analysis R^2 is the proportion of the variance of the dependent variable y accounted for by the independent variables x_1, x_2, etc. A simple way of meeting this objection is to point out that in a canonical analysis the two sets of variables may have the same statistical status, and thus the relationship between them may, as in this example, be symmetric. Suppose now that one of the sets, y say, has only one member. Then R^2 for the regression of y on the x variables is the one and only canonical root. Can we therefore turn the interpretation round and claim that R^2 gives us the proportion of the variance of the x variables which is predictable from y? Clearly we cannot. The variance of which a proportion is explained by a canonical dimension is variance along a single dimension in a multidimensional space. The R^2 of a multiple regression analysis tells us the proportion of the y variance accounted for only because the projection of the canonical dimension into the y space is necessarily identical with the one and only dimension of that space, namely the y variable itself.

It should then be evident that there is no necessary relation between the size of a canonical correlation and its importance. A linear combination of one set of variables may yield a highly accurate prediction of position on a similar dimension of the other set, but the two closely-related dimensions may possess any degree of importance in their respective spaces. Nor is it the case that there is any necessary association between degree of importance in one space and degree of importance in the other.

In principal component analysis one and the same vector, namely a latent vector, serves as a guide both to the relative importance of variables in determining a component (an underlying dimension forming one of an orthogonal set of axes) and to the relative importance of a component in the constitution of a variable (see, for example, chapter 4 of Hope, 1968). Each of these functions has its analogue in canonical analysis but the canonical vector, although it has some relevance to the former, has no part to play in the latter.

Since we have been at pains to show the relations between canonical regression and canonical variate analysis it is perhaps necessary to point out the difference between the interpretation of canonical regression which is appropriate to our analyses and the interpretation of canonical regression which is appropriate to a bivariate normal surface. The coefficient of contingency and its relation to a correlation computed for a bivariate normal surface were first described by Pearson (1904)* The observation that Pearson's 'mean square contingency' χ^2/n is equal to the sum of squares of the canonical correlations led to the conclusion that 'in a contingency table with very narrow groups derived from a normal frequency surface, the canonical correlation obtained by using scores appropriate to the scale of the two variates is the same as the correlation coefficient for the two sets of variates' (Maung, 1941). The analysis of the Scottish table (see below) shows that the first canonical

---

* It is of some sociological interest that Pearson applied his new technique to data on the relation between occupations of fathers and occupations of sons, the sons being culled from the Dictionary of National Biography. He computed a correlation (contingency coefficient) of 0.63.

dimension of a social mobility table may bear little relation to any general dimension of correlation. And the canonical regression analyses of all three tables reveal striking departures from the typical pattern of a table derived from a bivariate normal surface where, with an equal-interval categorization, the contribution of a category to overall predictability (Table 9) is highest for the middle categories and falls off towards the outermost categories. The assumption of an underlying bivariate normality would obscure the sociologically important fact that correlation and predictability are localized at certain points of the occupational spectrum.

It has been pointed out that each axis in Table 10 is the base of a canonical hierarchy, that is that the matrix product of each column vector and its transpose is a one-dimensional matrix. And the sum of the hierarchies is the dispersion matrix attributable to regression,

$$\mathbf{X}\mathbf{X}' = \mathbf{C}_{xy}\mathbf{C}_{yy}^{-1}\mathbf{C}_{yx}$$
$$\mathbf{Y}\mathbf{Y}' = \mathbf{C}_{yx}\mathbf{C}_{xx}^{-1}\mathbf{C}_{xy}$$

Substituting from (ii) and its analogue for the reverse analysis we may write,

$$\mathbf{X}\mathbf{X}' = \mathbf{C}_{xy}\mathbf{B}_{x.y}$$
$$\mathbf{Y}\mathbf{Y}' = \mathbf{C}_{yx}\mathbf{B}_{y.x}$$

where the $\mathbf{B}$ matrices are matrices of regression coefficients.

The last two equations serve to bring out an analogy with ordinary multiple regression analysis. The matrices $\mathbf{X}$ and $\mathbf{Y}$ have the property that each of their elements is a correlation between a canonical variate and the dummy variable for an occupational category. A set of canonical variates is by definition an orthogonal set. Each row of, say $\mathbf{Y}$ may therefore be regarded as giving both the correlation coefficients and the partial regression coefficients for the regression of a filial variable on an orthogonal set of paternal canonical variates. Hence the square of an element of $\mathbf{Y}$ is a coefficient of separate determination for the regression of a dummy variable on a paternal variate. The sum of squares for an occupational category is the proportion of the variance of that category which is predictable from knowledge of father's occupation, and these proportions are reported as percentages in the 'b' columns of Table 6. In calculating the percentage of variance accounted for by each canonical dimension the dummy variables are weighted by their standard deviations. The percentages of variance add up to the weighted means for the 'b' columns in Table 6.

Because $\mathbf{X}$ and $\mathbf{Y}$ are correlation matrices, i.e. covariance matrices for the standardized dummy variables and the standardized canonical variates, we may regard a comparison between them as showing the extent of intergenerational symmetry after removing the effects of differences between the occupational structures of fathers and sons. The two matrices in Table 10 are in fact remarkably similar, which suggests that, after allowing for differences in the occupational structure, there is a very high degree of stability in the quantity and pattern of intergenerational transmission of status.

In Table 6 the overall predictability of father's occupation is given as 4·05 per cent and that of son's occupation as 4·03 per cent. We may recalculate these two percentages on the assumption of an identical occupational structure, which may be arrived at by simply summing the marginal distributions of fathers and sons in the original contingency table (given in Table 6). The resulting common set of variances may be applied to the 'b' columns of Table 6 or, equivalently, to each of the columns of Table 10. The overall predictability figures are then 4·00 per cent for fathers and 4·07 per cent for sons. The analogous figures for Scotland are 8·93 per cent and 8·73 per cent (cf. Table 7).

The assumption of a common occupational structure makes only a small difference to the percentage predictabilities in both England and Wales and Scotland. In the United States, on the other hand, it reduces the predictability of father's occupation from 4·71 per cent to 3·77 per cent and increases the predictability of son's occupation from 2·56 per cent to 3·19 per cent. The intergenerational decline in the farming category, and in its predictability, are more than sufficient to account for the change. The contributions of farming to the two paternal percentages are 3·34 per cent and 2·24 per cent respectively, and its contributions to the two filial percentages are 0·61 per cent and 1·56 per cent respectively.

The axes of the American data (Table 12) display less symmetry than those of the English data (Table 10), indicating that the United States is further from occupational equilibrium than England and Wales.* Combining these pointers with the findings of Tables 8 and 9, we may infer that, although the relatively closed category of farming is in steep decline in the United States, certain growth categories are subject to moderate degrees of mobility constraint, and this factor counteracts the effects of the decline in farming. The two most important categories which combine growth and relative predictability are salaried professional and technical workers and salaried managers and officials. These are groups in which appointment is most dependent on paper qualifications which testify to prolonged exposure to education. We may surmise that differential educational opportunity plays a part in raising the intergenerational predictability of membership of these categories.

---

* It must be remembered that the two enquiries are separated by an interval of thirteen years, and that the American mobility table is organized in terms of economic function to a greater degree than the English. The inference from symmetry to equilibrium is not explicitly defended here.

The analysis shows that, when allowance is made for differences in the marginal distributions, the English system, unlike the American, is virtually reversible between the generations, and this implies that it is in equilibrium. Further evidence of equilibrium may be adduced from a comparison of the five cohorts of respondents reported by Glass and Hall (1954, pp. 186–7). The intergenerational contingency tables for these birth cohorts sum to a collapsed 5×5 version of Table 1. When a test is made of the hypothesis that all five cohorts are realizations of the same Markov transition process we obtain $\chi^2_{80} = 90\cdot09$, which implies that there is no significant evidence of change over the fifty years spanned by the cohorts.

The axes of canonical hierarchies reported in Tables 10–12 are informative both because their elements are correlations between dummy variables and canonical dimensions and also because they have the algebraic properties which have been set out in this part of the paper. But future experience with the method of canonical regression may suggest that a table of axes should be supplemented, or even replaced, by a derivative table of percentages of variance accounted for. Table 13 is derived from Table 10 by expressing the elements of the 'a' columns of Table 6 as percentages of their column totals, and multiplying the square of each element of a row of Table 10 by the corresponding percentage. This calculation is performed separately for the paternal and the filial variables.* The resulting table has the useful properties: (a) that the row sums represent the contribution of each category to overall predictability, weighted by the numerical importance of that category (Table 9), (b) that the column sums represent the relative importance of the canonical dimensions (Table 10), and (c) that the elements of the table as a whole add up to the overall percentage constraint on mobility (Table 6). In view of the potential usefulness of this type of table it seems desirable to give it a name and, because its elements are related to a species of coefficient of separate determination, it is proposed that is should be called a table of *percentage determinations in canonical hierarchies.*

PART III. ANALYSIS OF THE CONTINGENCY TABLE

We have shown how the variance and covariance attributable to regression may be broken down into a set of additive unit hierarchies, each hierarchy being associated with one of an orthogonal set of canoncal dimensions. R.A. Fisher (1940) pointed out that every canonical

* The percentage weights may of course be derived from some other source. In particular as has already been indicated, it is possible to apply a common set of weights to both the paternal and the filial variables, thus eliminating the effects of differences in the occupational distributions.

TABLE 13

Percentage determinations for the English data, i.e. additive contributions of elements of the axes of canonical regression (Table 10) to the overall weighted percentage of variance accounted for by regression.

Occupational category	Dimensions								Dimensions						
	1	2	3	4	5	6	Sum		1	2	3	4	5	6	Sum
1	0·81	0·11	0·01	0·00	0·00	0·00	0·93		0·61	0·09	0·01	0·00	0·00	0·00	0·71
2	0·30	0·05	0·07	0·00	0·00	0·00	0·42		0·30	0·06	0·07	0·00	0·00	0·00	0·43
3	0·16	0·20	0·00	0·01	0·00	0·01	0·38		0·28	0·10	0·00	0·00	0·00	0·01	0·39
4	0·00	0·16	0·10	0·00	0·02	0·01	0·29		0·00	0·18	0·05	0·00	0·03	0·00	0·27
5	0·75	0·00	0·10	0·00	0·12	0·00	0·96		0·56	0·04	0·19	0·00	0·10	0·00	0·89
6	0·28	0·12	0·03	0·08	0·01	0·00	0·52		0·38	0·22	0·04	0·09	0·01	0·00	0·74
7	0·26	0·17	0·07	0·06	0·00	0·00	0·55		0·27	0·17	0·07	0·07	0·00	0·00	0·59
Sum	2·56	0·80	0·38	0·14	0·16	0·01	4·05		2·42	0·86	0·44	0·17	0·14	0·01	4·03

dimension is associated with one of an additive set of contingency
tables. Although this observation was made thirty years ago it has been
put to little use by research workers. The overall variance attributable
to regression has its analogue in the table which contains the deviation
of each observed cell frequency from its expected value, the latter being calculated in the usual way on the assumption of independence of
fathers' and sons' occupational categories. Just as the former may be
broken down into a set of variance-covariance matrices which have been
called 'canonical hierarchies', so the latter may be broken down into a
set of contingency tables which might, by extension, be called *contingency hierarchies*. Each dimension of canonical regression forms a
canonical hierarchy and is uniquely associated with a contingency hierarchy. The contingency hierarchies sum to the deviations of the observed from the expected cell frequencies. Thus the observed contingency
table is a simple sum of the table of expected frequencies plus the contingency hierarchies.

In laying a set of contingency hierarchies before the research worker
we are offering him an easily understood set of building blocks. Examination of them will save him from being too influenced by canonical correlation coefficients. The Scottish data contain a good illustration of
this point. The first canonical correlation is 0·6976 and the second is
0·5211. But the second dimension explains 4·58 per cent of the son's
variance whereas the first explains only 1·78 per cent (Table 11). There
is here a clear inversion between strength of relationship and quantitative
importance. The reason is obvious: the first canonical dimension, for
both fathers and sons, contrasts those who work on a farm with those
who do not work on a farm, and it shows that there is a strong tendency
for fathers in farming occupations (categories 8 and 9) to have sons in
farming occupations. Virtually all the explicable variance of category 8
and about half of the explicable variance of category 9 is explained by
the first dimension. The second dimension, although it does not reveal
so strong a degree of correlation, is more important because it spans all
of the seven remaining categories of society and is virtually a simple
ranking in terms of social class (Table 11, cf. Table 16). The contingency hierarchies associated with the first two dimensions (Table 14)
serve both to reveal the pattern of group interchange for the dimensions
and to illustrate their relative importance.

An example of analysis of a contingency table into its contingency
hierarchies is given in the paper 'Marriage markets in the stratification
system'.

It is again useful to indicate how the methods described in the
present paper apply to a bivariate normal distribution. If a contingency
table represents a grid laid over a bivariate normal surface the second
and subsequent canonical correlations are powers of the first (Kendall

TABLE 14

Contingency hierarchies for the first two canonical dimensions of the Scottish data.

First dimension

				Occupational category of sons					
	1	2	3	4	5	6	7	8	9
1	0·42	0·04	0·16	0·17	0·52	-0·00	0·05	-0·91	-0·44
2	0·34	0·03	0·13	0·14	0·42	-0·00	0·04	-0·73	-0·36
3	0·35	0·03	0·13	0·14	0·43	-0·00	0·04	-0·75	-0·37
4 (Occupational)	0·45	0·04	0·17	0·18	0·55	-0·01	0·05	-0·96	-0·47
5 (category)	2·12	0·18	0·80	0·85	2·60	-0·02	0·24	-4·54	-2·23
6 (of fathers)	0·74	0·06	0·28	0·30	0·90	-0·01	0·08	-1·58	-0·78
7	0·33	0·03	0·12	0·13	0·41	-0·00	0·04	-0·71	-0·35
8	-3·42	-0·29	-1·28	-1·37	-4·18	0·04	-0·39	7·31	3·59
9	-1·34	-0·11	-0·50	-0·54	-1·63	0·02	-0·15	2·86	1·40

Second dimension

				Occupational category of sons					
	1	2	3	4	5	6	7	8	9
1	9·56	0·56	2·12	-0·13	-4·80	-5·11	-2·94	0·47	0·27
2	6·32	0·37	1·40	-0·08	-3·17	-3·38	-1·95	0·31	0·18
3	5·75	0·34	1·27	-0·08	-2·88	-3·08	-1·77	0·28	0·16
4 (Occupational)	3·61	0·21	0·80	-0·05	-1·81	-1·93	-1·11	0·18	0·10
5 (category)	-8·51	-0·50	-1·88	0·11	4·27	4·55	2·62	-0·42	-0·24
6 (of fathers)	-9·87	-0·58	-2·18	0·13	4·95	5·28	3·04	-0·49	-0·28
7	-8·54	-0·50	-1·89	0·11	4·29	4·57	2·63	-0·42	-0·24
8	0·99	0·06	0·22	-0·01	-0·50	-0·53	-0·31	0·05	0·03
9	0·69	0·04	0·15	-0·01	-0·34	-0·37	-0·21	0·03	0·02

and Stuart, 1967, vol. 2, sec. 33.47). Under these circumstances the process of successive approximation which is illustrated by the contingency hierarchies in the paper cited is a process of fitting a surface by two sets of marginal polynomials.

PART IV.   QUANTIFYING PATTERNS OF CONSTRAINT

Importance versus correlation

Each contingency hierarchy corresponds to a pair of canonical hierarchies, and also to a pair of canonical variates. The pairs of canonical variates associated with the first two canonical correlations are shown for each of the three societies in Tables 15–17.* At first glance it might

TABLE 15

Means of the occupational categories on the first two canonical variates. English data.

		Fathers		Sons	
		1	2	1	2
	1	2·48	−0·80	2·72	−0·90
	2	1·30	0·45	1·23	0·47
Occupational	3	0·41	0·41	0·58	0·30
category	4	0·04	0·24	0·02	0·29
	5	−0·20	0·00	−0·19	0·05
	6	−0·41	−0·24	−0·37	−0·25
	7	−0·47	−0·33	−0·44	−0·31
Canonical correlation		0·53	0·27	0·53	0·27

seem that in Scotland, as well as in England and in the United States, the first canonical dimension is straightforwardly associated with a ranking of the occupational categories more or less in their expected order in terms of their socio-economic status. It has however already been demonstrated, by reference to the canonical hierarchies of Table 11, that, in the Scottish analysis, it is the *second* dimension which represents the usual social ordering, and that, in terms of predictability of son's occupation, the first dimension is a hybrid related in part to the social ladder and in part to the distinction between agricultural and

* Each variate is standardized in such a way that the weighted average of the *Within-category* mean squares is unity. It may be noted that, in reporting canonical variates in Table 2 of the following paper, Paul Duncan-Jones sets the *Total* mean squares of his variates to unity. A variate standardized by one method is proportional to the same variate standardized by the other.

TABLE 16

Means of the occupational categories on the first two canonical variates. Scottish data.

		Fathers		Sons	
		1	2	1	2
	1	−0·61	2·41	−0·46	1·38
	2	−0·33	1·06	−0·23	0·48
	3	−0·30	0·86	−0·23	0·41
Occupational category	4	−0·31	0·44	−0·18	−0·02
	5	−0·24	−0·17	−0·27	−0·34
	6	−0·20	−0·46	0·00	−0·41
	7	−0·11	−0·47	−0·08	−0·63
	8	5·28	0·27	6·33	0·44
	9	0·97	0·09	1·55	0·13
Canonical correlation		0·70	0·52	0·70	0·52

TABLE 17

Means of the occupational categories on the first two canonical variates. United States data.

		Fathers		Sons	
		1	2	1	2
	1	1·08	−0·72	1·00	−0·71
	2	0·77	−0·19	0·67	−0·12
	3	0·79	−0·25	0·60	−0·22
	4	0·87	−0·41	0·72	−0·22
	5	0·62	−0·28	0·17	−0·17
	6	0·60	−0·07	0·17	0·14
	7	0·44	−0·10	0·29	−0·07
Occupational category	8	0·25	0·26	−0·03	0·35
	9	0·20	0·18	−0·08	0·15
	10	0·03	0·24	−0·25	0·08
	11	0·01	0·38	−0·25	0·26
	12	0·03	0·25	−0·28	0·15
	13	0·08	0·29	−0·19	0·25
	14	−0·24	0·49	−0·40	0·32
	15	−0·20	0·42	−0·51	0·13
	16	−0·62	−0·27	−1·14	−0·77
	17	−0·66	0·12	−1·07	−0·42
Canonical correlation		0·45	0·28	0·45	0·28

other occupations. In fact farming alone accounts for 1·61 per cent of the 2·65 per cent paternal variance predictable by the first dimension, and for 0·96 per cent of the 1·78 per cent predictable filial variance. A single very small category, containing fifteen fathers and ten sons, dominates the first dimension because it happens to be highly predictable, and canonical analysis selects the 'most predictable criterion' no matter how much information is ignored in the process. Only after the Scottish analysis has accounted for this small, relatively closed, system does it take cognizance of the whole range of society.

A comparison of Table 15 with Table 10 shows that no such complications arise in the English analysis, where the first canonical ordering is straightforwardly related to the status of categories. The American analysis lies somewhere between the two. The predictability of farming is higher than that of other American occupations though not nearly so high as the Scottish value (cf. Tables 7 and 8). In the case of fathers continuation constraints (occupational 'inheritance') account for only part of the predictability of farming. The category is sending its sons selectively into other occupations and so it is possible to predict a farming father from the filial variables. Thus farming is in interchange with the rest of the occupational structure and the first canonical dimension, though it gives considerable weight to farming (the correlation in Table 12 is –0·35 and farming contributes 2·72 per cent of the 3·26 per cent of paternal variance predictable by the first dimension) yet assigns it to a position which is not too remote from its social degree (Table 17, cf. Table VII–4 in Duncan 1961 which shows that non-farm laborers rank below the farming categories). The second dimension also bears some relation to the expected occupational prestige ranking but here again (cf. Table 12) farming accounts for 0·59 per cent of the total of 0·95 per cent of the paternal variance predicted by the dimension.

Farming does not dominate the first filial dimension to the same extent (it accounts for 0·38 per cent out of a predicted variance of 1·43 per cent) because both its overall predictability and its size are lower among the sons than among the fathers. Indeed the category of salaried professionals has greater weight than farming in the second dimension: 0·50 per cent as agains 0·38 per cent out of 1·43 per cent.

It can be seen that, if a small category, such as farming in Scotland, dominates a canonical dimension, it will display an extreme mean on the associated variate (Table 16). If however a large category is dominant it may not stand out from the rest on the variate (e.g. farming in the first paternal variate of Table 17) but reveal its predictability only in the axis of a canonical hierarchy (Table 12) and its importance only when its degree of predictability is weighted by its size (i.e. by the variance of its associated dummy variable).

Explanatory variate analysis

It is evident that, while canonical regression is appropriate to the quantification of constraints on mobility, the ordinary canonical correlation methods associated with it have only a loose and contingent relation to questions of the relative importance of patterns or dimensions of such constraints. In this section of the paper, therefore, we introduce a new technique whose purpose is to detect the most explanatory dimensions of constraint, in the sense of those dimensions which account for as much variance as possible.* *Although the technique is applied here to the particular case of analysis of contingency tables it is, like canonical analysis, applicable to multivariate situations in general.*

Let us write M_{cy} for the matrix of scores of the sons on the original filial dummy variables (the last seven columns of Table 2) after it has been centred (and, if necessary, standardized) in such a way that $M_{yc}M_{cy} = nC_{yy}$ where n is the number of father-son pairs. (Note that we adopt a convention of indicating transposition either by reversing subscripts or by the more usual method of a superscript dash.) We write, similarly, M_{rx} for the centred scores of fathers on the paternal dummy variables (the first seven columns of Table 2), giving

$$M_{xr}\,M_{rx} = nC_{xx}$$

Note that both M_{cy} and M_{rx} have as many rows as there are father-son pairs in the original contingency table ($n = 3497$ for the English data), and so we may write,

$$M_{xr}\,M_{cy} = nC_{xy}$$

The regression coefficients for the prediction of the paternal (x) from the filial (y) variables are the elements of

$$C_{yy}^{-1}\,C_{yx}$$

and the regressed scores of the sons are

$$M_{cy}\,C_{yy}^{-1}\,C_{yx}$$

* An *a priori* or theoretical dimension may be explanatory in a different sense, while accounting for a relatively small proportion of variance. There should be no confusion, and certainly no quarrel, between the two types of explanation (see, for example, chapter 8 of Hope, 1968).

When faced with the problem of maximizing predicted variance the writer explored a number of possible techniques and found difficulty in choosing among them. The nature of the problem was put to Dr. D.N. Lawley who, with his customary helpfulness, and without knowledge of the writer's attempted solutions, indicated one of the approaches already considered as the one which he would recommend for further investigation. Further explorations of this approach seemed, to the writer at least, to confirm Dr. Lawley's intuition.

Although he might have saved himself a lot of trouble by consulting expert opinion at an earlier stage of the search the writer feels that his hit-and-miss search for a solution was not entirely in vain, since the bye-work suggested solutions to the interesting problems of (a) computing canonical correlations for a square table subject to the constraint that the weight of the ith row in a canonical vector is identical with the weight of the ith column, and (b) computing a kind of generalized canonical analysis of a three- or higher-order contingency table.

Since every son in a particular column (c) of the contingency table has the same regressed scores we may collapse the n rows of the matrix into the number of columns of the contingency table. We shall represent this collapse by underlining the subscript c.

The sums of squares and sums of products matrix of the regressed scores is

$$(\mathbf{M}_{cy}\mathbf{C}_{yy}^{-1}\mathbf{C}_{yx})'\ (\mathbf{M}_{cy}\mathbf{C}_{yy}^{-1}\mathbf{C}_{yx})\ =\ n\mathbf{C}_{xy}\mathbf{C}_{yy}^{-1}\mathbf{C}_{yx}$$

Omitting the scalar n we now calculate the latent vectors of this sums of squares and sums of products matrix and write them as columns of the matrix $\mathbf{V}_{xe}$. The sum of squares of each column may be taken to be unity. We write the latent roots corresponding to the columns of $\mathbf{V}_{xe}$ as diagonal elements of the diagonal matrix $\mathbf{L}_{ee}$.

The orthogonal variates

$$\mathbf{Z}_{\underline{c}e}\ =\ \mathbf{M}_{\underline{c}y}\mathbf{C}_{yy}^{-1}\mathbf{C}_{yx}\mathbf{V}_{xe}$$

have the property of successively explaining as much as possible of the predictable paternal variance. We propose to call them *explanatory variates.* In an exactly analogous way we may obtain the other set of explanatory variates

$$\mathbf{Z}_{\underline{r}f}\ =\ \mathbf{M}_{\underline{r}x}\mathbf{C}_{xx}^{-1}\mathbf{C}_{xy}\mathbf{V}_{yf}$$

where $\mathbf{V}_{yf}$ contains the latent vectors of

$$(\mathbf{M}_{rx}\mathbf{C}_{xx}^{-1}\mathbf{C}_{xy})'\ (\mathbf{M}_{rx}\mathbf{C}_{xx}^{-1}\mathbf{C}_{xy})\ =\ n\mathbf{C}_{yx}\mathbf{C}_{xx}^{-1}\mathbf{C}_{xy}$$

The corresponding latent roots are written as the diagonal elements of $\mathbf{L}_{ff}$.

The two sets of explanatory variates resemble canonical variates in that they are uncorrelated within sets, but they differ from canonical variates in that the correlation matrix between the two sets is not necessarily a diagonal matrix. In other words there will, in general, be a non-zero correlation between explanatory variate e_i and explanatory variate f_j whether or not $i=j$.

The sums of squares of the first set of explanatory variates may be written (using the subscript-inversion convention for transposition),

$$\mathbf{Z}_{ec}\mathbf{Z}_{ce}\ =\ n\mathbf{V}_{ex}\mathbf{C}_{xy}\mathbf{C}_{yy}^{-1}\mathbf{M}_{yc}\mathbf{M}_{cy}\mathbf{C}_{yy}^{-1}\mathbf{C}_{yx}\mathbf{V}_{xe}$$
$$=\ n\mathbf{V}_{ex}(\mathbf{C}_{xy}\mathbf{C}_{yy}^{-1}\mathbf{C}_{yx})\mathbf{V}_{xe}$$

Since the term in brackets is pre- and postmultiplied by its own normalized latent vectors we have

$$\mathbf{Z}_{ec}\mathbf{Z}_{ce}\ =\ n\mathbf{L}_{ee}$$

a diagonal matrix of sums of squares. Similarly we have

$$\mathbf{Z}_{fr}\mathbf{Z}_{rf}\ =\ n\mathbf{L}_{ff}$$

The cross-products matrix is

$$\mathbf{Z}_{ec}\mathbf{Z}_{rf} = n\mathbf{V}_{ex}\,\mathbf{C}_{xy}\,\mathbf{C}_{yy}^{-1}\mathbf{C}_{yx}\,\mathbf{C}_{xx}^{-1}\mathbf{C}_{xy}\,\mathbf{V}_{yf}$$

and the correlations between the two sets of explanatory variates are

$$\tfrac{1}{n}\,\mathbf{L}_{ee}^{-\frac{1}{2}}\mathbf{Z}_{ec}\mathbf{Z}_{rf}\,\mathbf{L}_{ff}^{-\frac{1}{2}}$$

The sum of squares of these correlations is equal to the sum of squares of the canonical correlations, that is to the sum of the canonical roots.

The matrices $\mathbf{Z}_{ce}$ and $\mathbf{Z}_{rf}$ represent the projections of either set of categories into the space of the other set. They are akin to the means of groups on canonical variates in a canonical analysis of discriminance (Hope, 1968). But the explanatory case differs from the canonical case in that, although the columns of means which comprise $\mathbf{Z}_{ce}$ and $\mathbf{Z}_{rf}$ are orthogonal, the columns of $\mathbf{S}_{re} = \mathbf{M}_{rx}\mathbf{V}_{xe}$ and $\mathbf{S}_{cf} = \mathbf{M}_{cy}\mathbf{V}_{yf}$, which are akin to the projections of categories into the space of their own canonical variates, are not, in general, orthogonal. Indeed the sums of squares and sums of products of the former matrix are

$$\mathbf{S}_{er}\mathbf{S}_{re} = (\mathbf{M}_{rx}\mathbf{V}_{xe})'\,(\mathbf{M}_{rx}\mathbf{V}_{xe})$$
$$= \mathbf{V}_{ex}\mathbf{C}_{xx}\mathbf{V}_{xe}$$

and those of the latter matrix are

$$\mathbf{S}_{fc}\mathbf{S}_{cf} = (\mathbf{M}_{cy}\mathbf{V}_{yf})'\,(\mathbf{M}_{cy}\mathbf{V}_{yf})$$
$$= \mathbf{V}_{fy}\,\mathbf{C}_{yy}\mathbf{V}_{yf}$$

$\mathbf{Z}_{ce}$ and $\mathbf{Z}_{rf}$ may be calculated from $\mathbf{S}_{re}$ and $\mathbf{S}_{cf}$ respectively. The mean of a column i on variate e_j, that is the element z_{ij} of $\mathbf{Z}_{ce}$, may be calculated from $\mathbf{S}_{re}$ by weighting each element of a column of $\mathbf{S}_{re}$ by the appropriate element of the original contingency table and dividing the weighted sum by the sum of the weights. The variance of the father-son pairs about this mean may then be computed, and $\mathbf{Z}_{ce}$ may be standardized by setting these deviation variances to a common value such as unity. In this way we obtain an orthogonal set of explanatory variates, each of which has unit error variance. The analogous standardized version of $\mathbf{Z}_{rf}$ may be calculated.

Tables 18–20 show the first two columns (four in the case of Scotland) of $\mathbf{Z}_{rf}$ and $\mathbf{Z}_{ce}$ for the three societies we have been studying. The tables may be compared with tables 15–17 which report the corresponding means on the first two canonical variates. The weighted average within-category mean square of each explanatory variate is unity. Table 21 contains the variance of each category on each of the explanatory variates reported in Table 18 and on each of the canonical variates reported in Table 15, that is, for the English data. It is of interest to see that the within-category dispersions about the category

TABLE 18

Means of the occupational categories on the first two explanatory variates. English data.

		Fathers		Sons	
		1	2	1	2
	1	1·49	0·48	1·60	0·65
	2	1·16	0·12	1·02	0·03
Occupational category	3	0·52	−0·17	0·53	−0·15
	4	0·13	−0·23	0·17	−0·27
	5	−0·19	−0·09	−0·17	−0·12
	6	−0·39	0·23	−0·32	0·24
	7	−0·40	0·31	−0·37	0·31
Between/Total sums of squares		0·18	0·04	0·17	0·05

TABLE 19

Means of the occupational categories on the first four explanatory variates. Scottish data.

		Fathers				Sons			
		1	2	3	4	1	2	3	4
	1	2·37	0·21	−0·58	0·35	−0·35	0·42	0·81	−0·23
	2	1·05	0·01	−0·09	−0·03	−0·31	0·21	0·50	0·15
	3	0·87	0·04	0·32	−0·33	−0·17	0·22	0·30	0·18
Occupational category	4	0·39	0·02	0·11	−0·23	0·22	0·30	−0·16	0·15
	5	−0·21	0·33	0·21	0·13	0·46	0·07	−0·27	−0·13
	6	−0·37	−0·11	−0·41	−0·10	0·06	−0·27	−0·09	0·02
	7	−0·35	−0·14	−0·41	−0·04	−0·30	−1·00	0·37	−0·01
	8	0·03	−2·03	0·29	0·66	−1·87	0·23	−1·92	−1·05
	9	0·05	−0·72	0·52	−0·40	−0·80	0·23	−0·66	1·06
Between/Total sums of squares		0·25	0·17	0·10	0·04	0·16	0·13	0·18	0·08

means are sensibly more homogeneous in the case of explanatory variates than in the case of the canonical variates. This is even more true of the Scottish data. In the United States analysis, however, the canonical variates display pretty uniform dispersions and the dispersions of the explanatory variates are not noticeably more homogeneous. Homogeneity of dispersions is, of course, desirable if a variate is to be employed as a yardstick of distance between categories in terms of outflow or recruitment.

TABLE 20

*Means of the occupational categories on the first two explanatory
variates. United States data.*

		Fathers		Sons	
		1	2	1	2
	1	0·89	−0·37	0·44	−0·60
	2	0·82	−0·14	0·43	−0·17
	3	0·78	−0·22	0·38	−0·39
	4	0·74	−0·34	0·45	−0·27
	5	0·52	−0·27	0·08	−0·30
	6	0·61	−0·06	0·20	0·07
	7	0·37	−0·11	0·23	−0·19
Occupational	8	0·22	0·27	0·14	0·33
category	9	0·14	0·15	0·02	0·14
	10	−0·03	0·19	−0·14	0·08
	11	−0·08	0·41	−0·06	0·30
	12	0·01	0·23	−0·13	0·19
	13	0·01	0·25	−0·00	0·23
	14	−0·26	0·44	−0·16	0·37
	15	−0·25	0·37	−0·30	0·22
	16	−0·50	−0·28	−1·38	−0·41
	17	−0·51	0·16	−0·95	−0·13
Between/Total sums of squares		0·16	0·07	0·16	0·07

It will be noted that the ratio of Between category sum of squares
to Total sum of squares is given for each explanatory variate.
In the case of an explanatory variate the ratio must be computed separately for each individual variate. Table 19 shows that the variates,
ordered in terms of their explanatory power, are not necessarily ordered
in terms of their discriminating power.

The correlations between row and column explanatory variates are
given in Tables 22–24. If these tables contained correlations between
canonical variates all off-diagonal elements would be zero, and the diagonal elements would be the canonical correlations in descending
order of size.

The means of the categories on the first two explanatory variates
are plotted in Figures 1–6. The plots for the United States data may
be compared with two graphs presented by Blau and Duncan (1967,
Figures 2.1 and 2.2) as analyses of the same contingency table. Blau
and Duncan proceeded by percentaging the table by rows (for the analysis of fathers' occupations) and by columns (for the analysis of sons'
occupations). A distance between two occupations was computed by

TABLE 21

Variance (mean square) of each category on the first two canonical variates and on the first two explanatory variates. English data. The weighted average of each column of mean squares is unity.

| | Canonical variates | | | | Explanatory variates | | | |
| | Fathers | | Sons | | Fathers | | Sons | |
Occupational category	1	2	1	2	1	2	1	2
1	5·39	4·68	4·50	4·33	1·33	0·66	1·18	1·23
2	2·99	2·36	2·91	2·25	1·51	0·60	1·47	0·82
3	1·68	1·16	2·30	1·62	1·57	0·70	1·57	0·84
4	1·08	0·90	0·89	0·89	1·27	0·82	1·24	0·81
5	0·67	0·75	0·66	0·75	0·94	1·06	0·99	0·94
6	0·27	0·63	0·53	0·67	0·59	1·25	0·66	1·20
7	0·23	0·64	0·35	0·66	0·51	1·24	0·57	1·25

TABLE 22

Correlations between the projections of father–son pairs on the row explanatory variates and the column explanatory variates $(\frac{1}{n}\mathbf{L}_{ee}^{-\frac{1}{2}}$ $\mathbf{Z}_{ec}\,\mathbf{Z}_{rf}\,\mathbf{L}_{ff}^{-\frac{1}{2}})$. *English data. The canonical correlations are given for comparison.*

		Explanatory variates for columns (f)					
		1	2	3	4	5	6
	1	0·51	0·05	0·06	-0·00	-0·02	-0·01
	2	0·03	0·25	0·08	0·02	-0·01	-0·00
Explanatory variates	3	0·04	0·03	0·19	0·02	0·04	0·00
for rows (e)	4	-0·01	-0·01	0·01	-0·09	0·02	-0·00
	5	-0·03	-0·01	0·02	0·03	0·08	0·00
	6	-0·00	-0·00	0·01	0·00	0·01	0·03
Canonical correlation		0·53	0·27	0·17	0·09	0·07	0·03

TABLE 23

Correlations between the projections of father-son pairs on the row explanatory variates and the column explanatory variates. Scottish data. The canonical correlations are given for comparison.

		Explanatory variates for columns (f)							
		1	2	3	4	5	6	7	8
	1	-0·22	0·50	-0·04	-0·13	-0·01	0·02	-0·00	0·00
	2	0·33	0·05	0·25	0·03	-0·03	0·01	-0·02	-0·00
Explanatory	3	0·32	0·38	-0·23	-0·17	0·02	0·00	-0·03	-0·00
variates	4	-0·06	0·06	0·08	-0·25	0·08	0·12	-0·01	-0·00
for rows (e)	5	0·06	0·01	-0·04	0·06	-0·00	0·11	0·11	0·00
	6	-0·02	0·00	0·03	-0·04	-0·09	-0·04	0·09	-0·00
	7	-0·01	-0·00	0·02	-0·01	0·07	-0·06	0·03	-0·00
	8	-0·00	0·00	0·00	-0·00	-0·00	-0·00	-0·00	0·01
Canonical correlation		0·70	0·52	0·33	0·26	0·18	0·14	0·09	0·00

summing the positive differences between corresponding percentages. Each triangular matrix of distances was then subjected to a Guttman–Lingoes 'smallest space analysis'. (See the paper 'MDSCAL and distances between socio-economic groups.') The purpose of this technique is identical with the purpose of the principal component analysis of explicable variances and covariances which is the heart of explanatory variate analysis, that is, it attempts to find the 'lines and planes of closest fit to systems of points' in space (Pearson, 1901).

TABLE 24

Correlations between the projections of father—son pairs on the row ex-
planatory variates and the column explanatory variates (first six vari-
ates only). United States data. The canonical correlations are given for
comparison.

		\multicolumn{6}{c}{Explanatory variates for columns (f)}					
		1	2	3	4	5	6
	1	0·31	0·16	0·03	–0·00	0·01	0·01
Explanatory	2	–0·11	0·23	–0·04	–0·00	–0·01	0·00
variates for	3	–0·04	0·00	0·13	–0·04	–0·01	0·02
rows (e)	4	–0·02	0·01	0·04	0·10	–0·00	0·01
	5	–0·01	0·00	0·01	–0·00	0·10	0·01
	6	0·00	0·00	–0·01	0·00	–0·02	0·09
Canonical correlation		0·45	0·28	0·17	0·13	0·12	0·11

The differences between the two approaches are threefold: (a) the
Guttman—Lingoes technique starts from a matrix of distances whereas
explanatory analysis starts with a system of projections of points on to
axes, (b) the Guttman—Lingoes technique considers only the rank order
of the distances, ignoring their relative size, whereas explanatory analysis treats the variates as interval scales, (c) Blau and Duncan's matrix
of distances is computed from percentaged inflows or outflows whereas
explanatory analysis arrives at its matrix of distances by the elaborate
techniques which culminate in the calculation of $\mathbf{Z}_{ce}$ and $\mathbf{Z}_{rf}$. A distance matrix may easily be computed from any subset of the columns of
these matrices by the usual method of calculating distances between
points referred to orthogonal axes.

In spite of these differences there is a similarity of general outline
between comparable plots derived from the two techniques, The explanatory method does, however, yield a clearer two-dimensional interpretation than the Guttman—Lingoes method. All four diagrams show the
occupational categories lying diagonally across the graph in rough order
of status, but the diagrams based on the explanatory technique separate
the two farm occupations from the rest. Looking at Figure 6 it is easy
to see that an orthogonal rotation through 45° would produce two dimensions, the one a status-ordering with white-collar categories at the top
and blue-collar categories at the bottom, and the other contrasting the
farm occupations with the rest. A similar rotation of Figure 5 would
yield similar rotated axes. Blau and Duncan were unable to offer a
satisfactory interpretation of the second dimension of their analysis.
The interpretation of our two figures is quite clear in both dimensions
after eye-rotation.

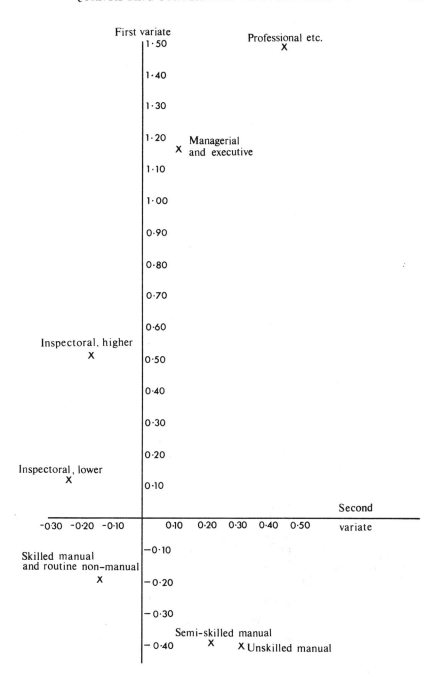

FIG. 1. Positions of occupational groups of fathers on the first two explanatory variates. English data.

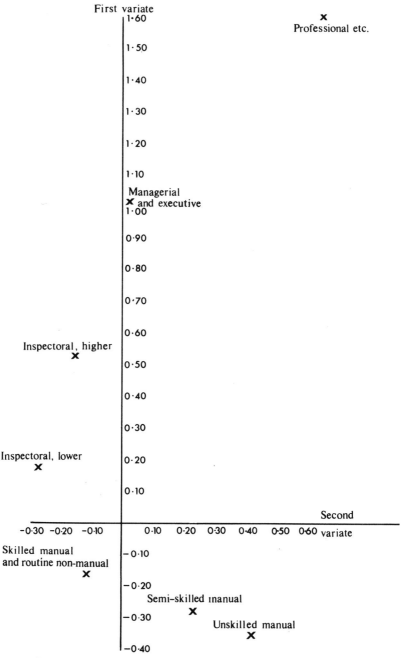

FIG. 2. Positions of occupational groups of sons on the first two
explanatory variates. English data.

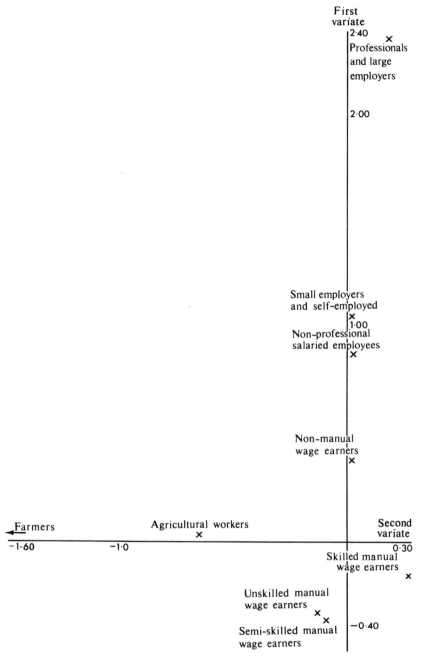

FIG. 3. Positions of occupational groups of fathers on the first two explanatory variates. Scottish data.

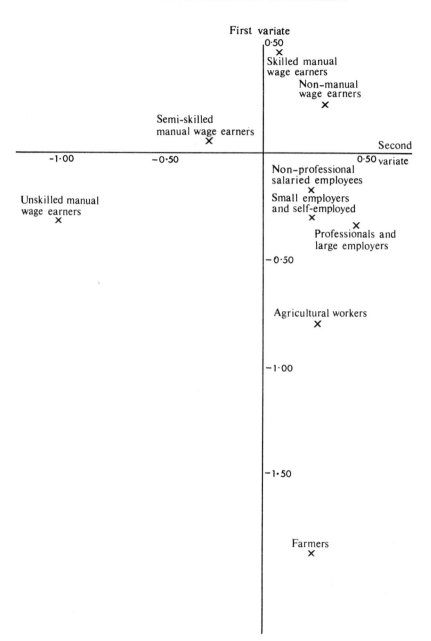

First variate
0·50
×
Skilled manual
wage earners
Non–manual
wage earners
×

Semi-skilled
manual wage earners
×

-1·00   −0·50   0·50 variate
Second

Non–professional
salaried employees
×
Unskilled manual   Small employers
wage earners   and self-employed
×   ×
                              ×
                          Professionals and
                          large employers
−0·50

Agricultural workers
×

−1·00

−1·50

Farmers
×

FIG.4. Positions of occupational groups of sons on the first two
explanatory variates. Scottish data.

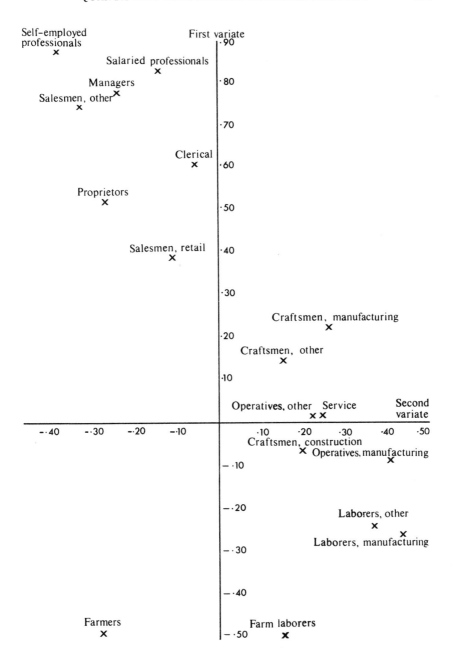

FIG. 5. Positions of occupational groups of fathers on the first two explanatory variates. United States data.

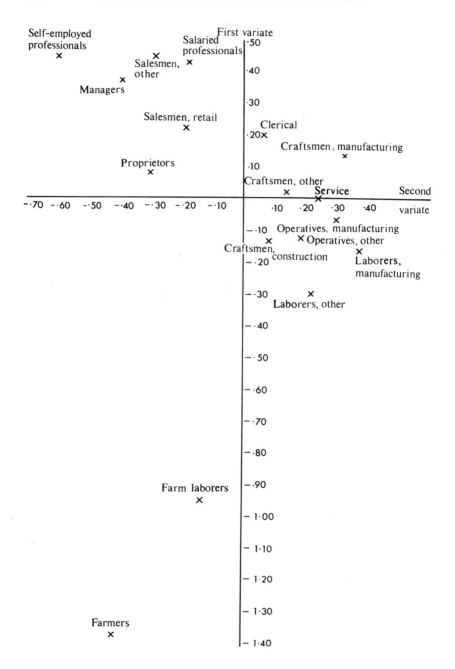

FIG. 6. Positions of occupational groups of sons on the first two
explanatory variates. United States data.

Class in the United States

In the second chapter of *The American occupational structure* Blau and Duncan suggest the existence of three classes whose occurrence is reflected in the flow of manpower between occupations. These are the conventional triad: middle class, working class and agricultural class. Blau and Duncan liken the two class boundaries to one-way screens which limit the extent of downward mobility while permitting upward mobility to occur to a degree which is, in some cases, in excess of the mobility expected on the assumption of complete independence of father's occupation and son's occupation.

If we group the seventeen categories of the U.S. intergenerational mobility table into Blau and Duncan's three classes we may compute the transition matrix (Table 25) for the hypothesized class system. Each

TABLE 25

Transition matrix for three classes. United States data. The percentage column contains row totals expressed as percentages of the grand total.

		Son's class				
		Middle	Working	Agricultural	Sum	Percentage
Father's class	Middle	0·71	0·28	0·01	1·00	24%
	Working	0·37	0·61	0·02	1·00	45%
	Agricultural	0·23	0·55	0·22	1·00	31%
	All	0·41	0·51	0·08	1·00	100%

element of this matrix represents the proportion of sons of a particular class of fathers who find themselves in one or other of the three classes. The percentage distribution of sons by father's class is shown in the last column. The last row shows the transition proportions for the average son, irrespective of his class of origin. The table succinctly summarizes Blau and Duncan's observations in that few sons move into farm work from the other classes, and the proportion of sons in class i who rise into class j is always greater than the proportion in j who fall* to i.

We propose now to attack the question of the American class system by a taxonomic approach which differs from that of Blau and Duncan in that it is based on explanatory variate analysis and is less subjective

---

* The order of the three classes is that employed by Blau and Duncan. It is obviously correct, even though one of the constituent groups of the working class (laborers except farm and mine) has a lower prestige than either of the two farm groups (Duncan 1961).

in application.* It is not claimed that this method is superior to that of Blau and Duncan, but it does serve as a partly independent check on their analysis and it sheds some additional light on their conclusion.

We wish to know whether there are discontinuities in the status ordering of the American occupational groups which would suggest the existence of stratification (a) by life-chances and (b) by social origins. These two types of discontinuity are, of course, conceptually quite distinct though, in a society which is in 'equal exchange' (i.e. in which movement from class i to class j is equal in amount to movement from j to i) they may be taxonomically identical. In the terms of the first paragraph of this paper, we are distinguishing two sorts of stratification by class, and the distinction is one of the direction in which we are looking: forwards or backwards. In this sense a single class system may embrace two quite distinct sets of classes.

The data matrices for our two analyses are the matrices $\mathbf{Z}_{\underline{c}e}$ and $\mathbf{Z}_{\underline{r}f}$ (all the explanatory variates are employed, not merely those reported in Table 20) and the taxonomic technique is a modified form of that described in Hope, 1969 and 1970. The latter is an approximately minimum-variance method employing a Euclidean metric. The modification consists in weighting the variate mean of an occupational category by its number of members whenever the joint mean of several categories is computed. Taxonomic analyses of all three societies are reported in Figures 7–12, but we shall here concentrate on the two American analyses. Figure 11 contains the classification of the categories of fathers in terms of the similarities of the life-chances of their sons. Once again, we are presented with the conventional three classes, but there is this interesting difference: the category of entrepreneurial professionals stands aside from the rest of the middle class.

Figure 11 must be interpreted in the light of the percentage constraints reported in the first 'c' column of Table 8 which show that the importance of class boundaries should not be over-emphasized. Furthermore, the reader must be warned that relatively small changes in the elements of a data matrix can produce large changes in a taxonomic analysis. But even with these caveats in mind one cannot but be struck by the sociological sense which the dendrogram makes.

An index of dispersion (Hope, 1969) may be computed for any

---

* The method employed by Blau and Duncan was to try out a number of partitions of the mobility table and to count up the number of ratios of observed to expected movements exceeding unity which occurred in the various sub-matrices of the partitioned table. The number of possible partitionings of a 17 × 17 table is, of course, enormous, and the success of the method depends (a) on having the categories in approximately the right order before one starts, and (b) on knowing what one is looking for. This comment is not intended to rule out the subjective approach, but only to suggest that it needs supplementing. As indicated in the text, the method of numerical taxonomy of explanatory variates has its own weakness, but this is to some extent independent of the weakness of the subjective approach, and so, if they give the same answer, the two methods reinforce one another.

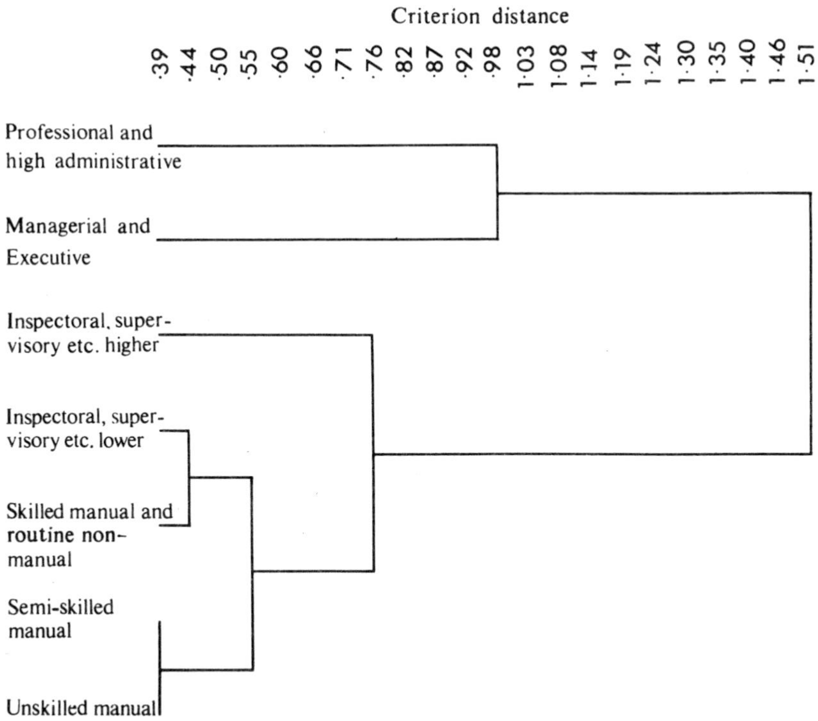

Criterion distance

FIG. 7. Similarities among categories of fathers in terms of the occupational destinations of their sons. English data.

aggregation of categories shown in the dendrogram. The index has the property that, when all the categories have, as they do at the end of the analysis, amalgamated to form a single aggregate, the dispersion of this all-embracing group is

$$\sum_{i=1}^{v} \frac{h_i^2}{1 - h_i^2}$$

where the h_i are the ratios of Between to Total sums of squares for the explanatory variates, and these are summed over the v variates. The overall dispersion of Figure 11 is 0·35.* The dispersion for the cluster of six white-collar groups (managers down to retail salesmen) is 0·14, that for the following eight blue-collar categories is 0·12, and that for the dyad of farming categories is 0·03. When the manual and farm classes

* The first two explanatory variates account for 66 per cent of this variance.

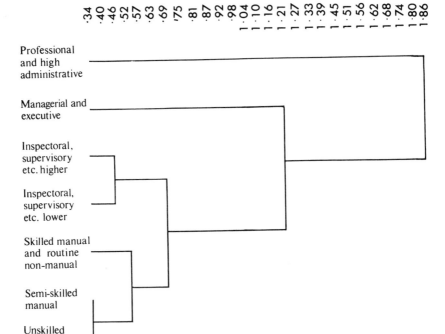

FIG. 8. Similarities among categories of sons in terms of their social
origins (occupation of father). English data.

amalgamate the joint dispersion rises to 0·21, and the further addition
of the white-collar cluster raises the figure to 0·33. The two sub-clusters
of the white-collar cluster have dispersions of (a) 0·06 for the managers,
salaried professional and clerical workers and (b) 0·05 for the salesmen
and proprietors. From the dendrogram it may be seen that the self-
employed professionals are at a distance of about 1·29 from the mean
of the remaining categories. In fact, they lie at a distance of 1·24 from
the mean of all groups including themselves. The next most extreme
group is the salaried professionals who lie at a distance of 0·95 from the
social centroid. The maximum distance between any two occupational
categories is 1·71, which separates self-employed professionals from
non-farm laborers. The group which is closest to the self-employed
professionals is the group of salaried professionals, and even they are
at a distance of 0·76. It may be seen that the self-employed professionals

Criterion distance

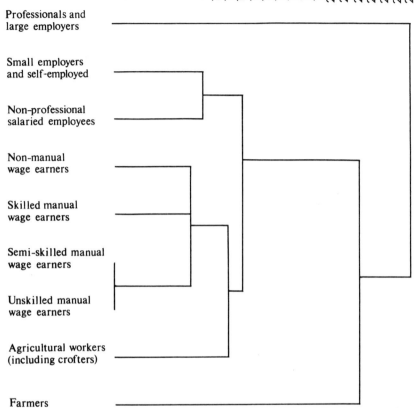

FIG. 9. Similarities among categories of father in terms of the occupational destinations of their sons. Scottish data.

TABLE 26

Transition matrix for the United States. The percentage column contains row totals expressed as percentages of the grand total.

		Son's class					
		Élite	Middle	Working	Agri-cultural	Sum	Percentage
	Élite	0·18	0·63	0·15	0·03	0·99	1%
Father's	Middle	0·03	0·67	0·28	0·01	0·99	23%
class	Working	0·02	0·35	0·61	0·02	1·00	45%
	Agri-cultural	0·01	0·23	0·55	0·22	1·01	31%
	All	0·02	0·39	0·51	0·08	1·00	100%

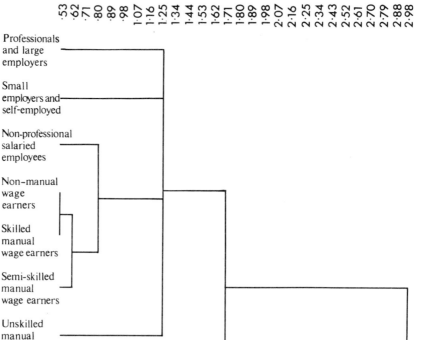

FIG. 10. Similarities among categories of sons in terms of their social origins (occupation of father). Scottish data.

are almost twice as far from the 'centre' of society, in terms of the life-chances of their sons, as their nearest neighbours. The cluster of managers, salaried professionals and clerical workers lies 0·79 from the centre and the cluster of salesmen and proprietors is only slightly nearer at 0·66. The cluster of manual occupations is 0·28 and the dyad of farming occupations is 0·56 from the centre.

The overall picture is one of a three-class society topped by an élite. This picture emerges from an analysis of distinctions between classes in terms of sons' occupational destinations. The percentage determinations in Table 8 have shown that there are no great differences between categories in degree of constraint, but the taxonomy has shown that patterns of dispersal of sons are distinct, and the distinctions show a class grouping. Table 26 contains the transition matrix for the

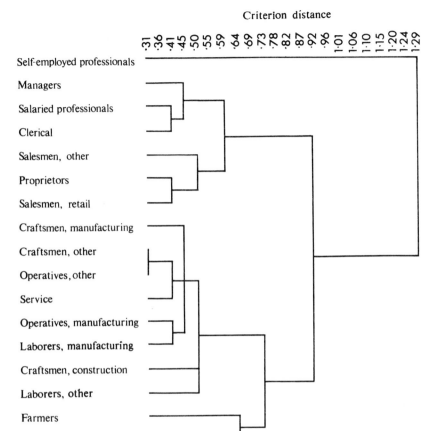

FIG. 11. Similarities among categories of fathers in terms of the occupational destinations of their sons. U.S. data.

four elements of American society.

The taxonomies for England and Scotland which correspond to the taxonomy of U.S. paternal categories are given in Figures 7 and 9. They are derived from fewer categories and are, therefore, more difficult to interpret. There does seem to be a broad similarity between the Scottish and the American analyses. English society, on the other hand, seems to be split into 'officers' versus the rest, the officers comprising the members of the two categories which display the highest percentage determinations (Table 6). The lack of comparability between the English and the Scottish occupational groupings prevents us drawing conclusions from the comparison of the two taxonomies.

Turning now to Figure 12, the clustering of American categories of sons in terms of similarities among their backgrounds, we obtain the same broad picture as we did for the clustering of fathers' occupations.

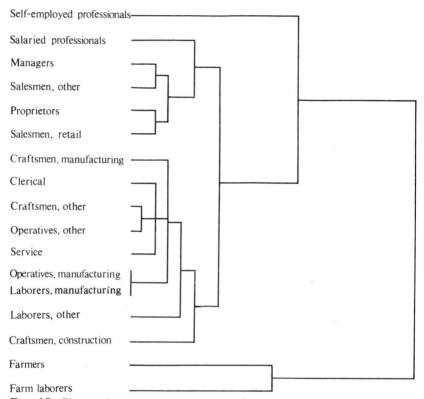

FIG. 12. Similarities among categories of sons in terms of their social
origins (occupation of father). U.S. data.

There are just two differences worthy of note. One is that the agricultural dyad has now become more isolated. This is, of course, simply a
consequence of the fact that many sons in all groups had fathers engaged in agriculture, but few sons now on the farm came from non-farm
backgrounds. The second difference is that clerical workers have been
demoted to the working class, in that they come from the same sorts of
background as blue-collar workers. This is of some interest since it
tends to run counter to an explanation put forward by Blau and Duncan.
In the discussion of their findings these authors ask why it is that the
downwardly mobile son of a white-collar worker chooses a low income
white-collar job in preference to a higher income blue-collar job. And
their answer is that he is trading income for status. The formulation of
the problem and its proposed solution may be attacked on two counts,
the first being that we do not know whether, in general, the downwardly

mobile man is presented with just this choice, and the second being that
we do not know whether, if he has it, he typically chooses as the formulation presupposes. The first line of attack depends on general considerations, the second gains some slight support from the observed clustering of clerical occupations with blue-collar occupations.

Does a downwardly-moving son of a white-collar worker typically
have the choice between lower income in a white-collar occupation and
higher income in a blue-collar occupation? Certainly in Britain he has
very often not had this choice. There is an obvious structural reason for
this in that, as a son of the middle class, he will very often have
acquired one or two years of additional education which have carried him
beyond the age at which he can be bound apprentice, and it is men who
have served their time who tend to have the higher, and more stable,
working-class incomes. (Though, in some areas, and in some states of
the job market, there may be sufficient relatively well-paid non-skilled
jobs for all the downwardly-mobile who might want them). It is not easy
for the British researcher to know how far this consideration would apply
in the United States.

There are, however, other considerations which suggest that the
formulation of the problem in terms of individual choice is defective.
We know that, among holders of a particular occupation, there is a
degree of variance in I.Q. (Tyler, 1965). It may be presumed that there
is variance too in characteristics such as health and application. We
may suppose that a boy emerging from a white-collar home has to be
somewhat defective in one or more of these characteristics before he is
in danger of slipping out of his class. There is, as it were, a certain
stickiness in the mechanism which translates potential mobility into
actual movement. We may liken the class boundary to the freezing point
of water: it was found to be necessary to introduce the concept of latent
heat to explain why a drop in temperature to freezing point or slightly
below did not immediately lead to freezing. In so far as a class boundary
exists the weaker member of the superior class, when he crosses that
boundary, will find himself in competition with the élite of the lower
class. But, it may be said, the boundary between middle and working
class in the United States appears to be fairly weak, in that 29 per cent
of middle-class sons fall below it and 37 per cent of working-class sons
rise above it (Tables 25 and 26). However, it must be observed that the
class boundary is also a functional boundary which divides highly-
skilled jobs of lower status from unskilled jobs of higher status. To put
the point crudely, a man who leaves the middle-class because he is of
poor intelligence may be incapacitated for, or precluded from obtaining,
many higher-income blue-collar jobs, (though, with the development of
process production, high-income 'manual' work is becoming more accessible to the downwardly mobile), and his failure may be due, not only to

the defects which led to his demotion, but also to characteristics, such as poor physique, which were irrelevant to success in his previous class but have become maladaptive in his new class.

It cannot be denied that some downwardly-mobile individuals will prefer status to income (though we must always ask whether an expressed status preference is a *post eventum* endorsement of the actual situation). But there are good reasons for supposing that many downwardly mobile men are not faced with a practical choice between the two.

Turning now to the empirical evidence that clerical occupations are slightly closer* to blue-collar than to white-collar occupations in their sources of recruits (even when the self-employed élite is omitted from the white-collar cluster), we can see that, if anything, it is the sons of blue-collar workers and farmers[†] who, in choosing the lowest of the white-collar categorie s, are 'preferring' status to income. But here again the preference may be dictated by absence of aptitude or qualifications for the higher-income manual jobs.

Explanatory hierarchy

In Part II of this paper we introduced the concept of a canonical hierarchy as a decomposition of the correlation matrix due to regression,

$$\mathbf{X}\mathbf{X}' = \mathbf{C}_{xy}\mathbf{C}_{yy}^{-1}\mathbf{C}_{yx}$$
$$\mathbf{Y}\mathbf{Y}' = \mathbf{C}_{yx}\mathbf{C}_{xx}^{-1}\mathbf{C}_{xy}$$

Now we introduce the analogous concept of an explanatory hierarchy. Let us write $\mathbf{D}_{xx}$ for the diagonal matrix containing the diagonal elements of $\mathbf{C}_{xx}$ and, similarly, $\mathbf{D}_{yy}$ for the matrix containing the diagonal elements of $\mathbf{C}_{yy}$. Then we define our explanatory hierarchies as

$$\mathbf{E} = \mathbf{D}_{xx}^{-\frac{1}{2}}\mathbf{V}_{xe}\,\mathbf{L}_{ee}^{\frac{1}{2}}$$
$$\mathbf{F} = \mathbf{D}_{yy}^{-\frac{1}{2}}\mathbf{V}_{yf}\,\mathbf{L}_{ff}^{\frac{1}{2}}$$

and we have

$$\mathbf{E}\mathbf{E}' = \mathbf{D}_{xx}^{-\frac{1}{2}}\mathbf{V}_{xe}\mathbf{L}_{ee}\mathbf{V}_{ex}\mathbf{D}_{xx}^{-\frac{1}{2}}$$
$$= \mathbf{C}_{xy}\mathbf{C}_{yy}^{-1}\mathbf{C}_{yx}$$

where the $\mathbf{C}$ matrices contain correlations. Similarly we have,

$$\mathbf{F}\mathbf{F}' = \mathbf{C}_{yx}\mathbf{C}_{xx}^{-1}\mathbf{C}_{xy}$$

and also

$$\mathbf{X}\mathbf{X}' = \mathbf{E}\mathbf{E}'$$
$$\mathbf{Y}\mathbf{Y}' = \mathbf{F}\mathbf{F}'$$

* The clerical category is virtually equidistant between Proprietors and Craftsmen in manufacturing but Proprietors are closer to retail salesmen than to the clerical category.

[†] 26 per cent of the clerical category are drawn from the white-collar categories (1 − 7), compared with 33 per cent of Proprietors.

We referred to a column of X, x_i, as a base of a canonical hierarchy, and we may similarly refer to the columns of E and F, e_i and f_j, as *bases of explanatory hierarchies*, the hierarchies themselves being the matrix products $e_i e_i'$ and $f_j f_j'$ which are components of EE' and FF'. Just as each element of X and Y is a correlation between a dummy variable and a canonical variate so each element of E and F is a correlation between a dummy variable and an explanatory variate. Just as we calculated tables of percentage determinations from the canonical hierarchies so we may calculate *percentage determinations in the explanatory hierarchies*. The sum of the percentage determinations for a particular dummy variable is identical in the two cases, but the sum of the percentage determinations in the first column of an explanatory analysis will almost certainly exceed, and can never be less than, the comparable sum for the canonical case. Indeed, the column sums of the two sets of percentage determinations for the explanatory case are the latent roots L_{ee} and L_{ff}. Table 27 contains the percentage determinations in the explanatory hierarchies of the English data. This may be compared with Table 13 which contains the percentage determinations in the canonical hierarchies.

PART V   DISCUSSION

Implications for future research in social mobility

The canonical analysis of a contingency table was introduced by Fisher and has occasionally been employed in biometry. In this paper the analysis has been approached by means of defining dummy variables, and the method of canonical regression has been introduced to counteract the current over-emphasis on canonical correlations and canonical vectors. It has been shown that the latter may be seriously misleading because they do not take into account the quantitative importance of the dimensions to which they relate. The two approaches are facets of one and the same larger analysis, and they make identical assumptions.

It has been observed that the correlation coefficient employed to measure the strength of association between dummy variables is the phi coefficient, which is the coefficient appropriate to point distributions. It might be objected that the social grading of occupations leads to continuous variables which ought to be treated as such. The English categories analyzed here were based on the Hall—Jones scale of occupational prestige (Hall and Jones, 1950), and the U.S. data were based on the Duncan socio-economic index (Duncan, 1961). But the relationship between the occupational categorization and the underlying social gradings is not straightforward. The American data are grouped into seventeen

TABLE 27

Percentage determinations in the explanatory hierarchies. English data (cf. Table 13).

Dimensions	1	2	3	4	5	6	Sum
1	0·65	0·15	0·12	0·00	0·00	0·00	0·93
2	0·34	0·00	0·05	0·00	0·03	0·00	0·42
3	0·24	0·10	0·04	0·00	0·00	0·01	0·38
4	0·02	0·22	0·00	0·01	0·04	0·00	0·29
5	0·77	0·11	0·05	0·01	0·02	0·00	0·96
6	0·36	0·10	0·01	0·08	0·00	0·00	0·52
7	0·31	0·15	0·02	0·04	0·02	0·00	0·55
Sum	2·67	0·83	0·29	0·15	0·11	0·01	4·05

Dimensions	1	2	3	4	5	6	Sum
1	0·47	0·11	0·13	0·00	0·00	0·00	0·71
2	0·35	0·00	0·04	0·00	0·03	0·00	0·43
3	0·35	0·02	0·01	0·00	0·00	0·01	0·39
4	0·02	0·19	0·01	0·00	0·05	0·00	0·27
5	0·51	0·33	0·04	0·00	0·02	0·00	0·89
6	0·50	0·16	0·00	0·08	0·00	0·00	0·74
7	0·34	0·15	0·02	0·08	0·00	0·00	0·59
Sum	2·55	0·96	0·25	0·16	0·10	0·01	4·03

Occupational category

census categories rather than into the nineteen intervals into which the Duncan Index was divided (Blau and Duncan, 1967, p. 485*). The categorization for England and Wales is also given in terms of named groups, rather than groups which have a mere statistical homogeneity. The authors of the Scottish table endeavoured to replicate the practice of English researchers, though the model they followed was not that used in the English mobility analysis. It thus seems probable that, in treating the British data as categorized rather than continuous, we are fairly representing at least one strand in the stratification theory of those who collected the data.

It might also be objected that nice comparisons between societies cannot be made when the various categorizations differ in their number of boxes or in the relative proportion of the population falling in each box. This is, of course, true, though it is secondary to the primary consideration of discrepancies in the way in which jobs are allotted to categories. It is quite possible that, if a farming category had been employed for the English data it would have manifested a degree of rigidity comparable to that of the American or the Scottish farming categories. Because farming does not feature as a category in the English analysis we can say nothing about it. On the other hand, we are probably justified in making tentative inferences from the contrast between the British and American top categories.

The method of analysis illustrated in this paper should indicate to the research worker the sort of questions he should ask as he is collecting and organizing his data. If he is interested in the extent of intergenerational transmission for a particular set of pre-defined classes or groups such as census categories then he will organize his data into those categories. A classification system may employ more than one principle. For example, it may allot a man to a category according to his trade while distinguishing between a tradesman 'on the tools' and a man who is a chargehand or foreman. If the sociologist or demographer wishes to take account both of a man's level of skill and of his degree of responsibility he is at liberty to introduce a supervisory category which is such that a fraction of a man is allotted to that category if he is a supervisor, the remainder being allotted to the occupational category appropriate to his skill.

If, however, the research worker is interested in relative rigidities at different levels of the social or economic scale, then he will employ a continuous variable such as occupational prestige.† If international

---

* A remark on page 121 suggests that the correlation between the ordered seventeen categories and the nineteen index-intervals is $\sqrt{0.75} = 0.87$

† More informative would be a multivariate analysis in a 'stratification space' defined by several oblique axes such as income, probable post-retirement income, span of discretion and occupational prestige. Although these variables may be quite highly correlated for both fathers and sons it is not easy to forecast the extent of intergenerational transmission at different levels of the various variables.

comparisons are to be made then a standardized distribution of prestige must be drawn up for each society and it must be analyzed into a common set of intervals (it is not necessary that a particular occupation should occupy the same position in each society's distribution). This categorization of a continuous variable is of course necessary only because we are interested in studying non-linear relations between prestige and social transmission or, in other words, because we wish to study the interaction between social level and social mobility.

If we did not mind working with a contingency table containing non-integral frequencies we might begin by splitting the distribution of sons at the median into upper and lower levels, then dichotomizing each level into two sub-sets, and so on. It would be an easy matter to compute the reduction in within-level sum of squares with each split, and to stop at a point where perhaps ninety per cent of the variance lay between levels and only ten per cent within. The distribution of fathers might be similarly treated. Alternatively, the splits might be made at the same prestige levels as for the sons. Two types of approach might then be adopted. The first would involve defining a dummy variable for each level exactly as in the analyses in this paper. The second would be to define orthogonal polynomials for linear, quadratic, cubic etc. functions. The definition of orthogonal polynomials is particularly simple when the sample has been successively dichotomized at the median.

The virtue of repeated dichotomization of the sample is that it yields equal-sized categories, and so the limitation of the phi coefficient as a measure of strength of intrinsic relation is constant for all pairings of dummy variables.

Relations with other methods

At the beginning of this paper it was stated that the proposed method of analysis is an extension both of the index of association and of Blau and Duncan's (1967) regression methods.

The relation between canonical regression and the indices of association, dissociation, inertia etc. (Mukherjee and Hall, 1954) is via the chi squared statistic. It has been argued (Maung, 1941) that a canonical correlation coefficient may be regarded as a phi coefficient since, by multiplying the canonical roots by the sample size and summing over all canonical dimensions we arrive at the ordinary chi square for the original contingency table. The elements of the contingency hierarchies (e.g. Table 14) represent partitions of the deviation from expectation which enters into the numerator of chi square.

A parallel partition of the index of association for a particular cell may be carried out. If we write o_{ij} for the observed frequency in cell i,j of the contingency table, and e_{ij} for the corresponding expected frequency, then o_{ij}/e_{ij} is the index of association for that cell. The element of the kth contingency hierarchy for the cell is given by the product $e_{ij} . t_{ijk}$ where k runs from 1 up to the number of hierarchies h. We may write $t_{ijo} = 1$ for all i and j and so reproduce the expected frequencies by the product $e_{ij} . t_{ijo}$. It has been shown that the elements of the contingency hierarchies sum to the observed deviations from expectation,

$$e_{ij} \sum_{k=1}^{h} t_{ijk} = o_{ij} - e_{ij}$$

Taking the summation from zero instead of one gives

$$e_{ij} \sum_{k=0}^{h} t_{ijk} = o_{ij}$$

$$\sum_{k=0}^{h} t_{ijk} = o_{ij} / e_{ij}$$

showing that the values of t for a particular cell are partitions of the index of association.

The relationship between canonical regression and the regression methods employed by Blau and Duncan may be grasped by a consideration of their multiple-classification analyses. A multiple-classification analysis (which is a non-orthogonal analysis of variance) quantifies the effects of two or more categorized independent variables on a continuous dependent variable. In calculating the proportion of the variance of the dependent variable which can be explained by the independent variables Blau and Duncan, in effect, assign a dummy variable to each category of each independent variable and then calculate the coefficient of determination R^2 for the regression of the dependent variable on the dummy variables. In order to avoid capitalizing on chance variations they ignore possible interactions among the independent variables. They found that father's occupational status (midpoint score in one of nineteen intervals of the Duncan index) can explain 15 per cent of the variance of son's status (actual score on the Duncan index), and they report that the non-linear multiple-classification analysis explains very little more than a simple analysis of the linear regression of son's on father's status.

Blau and Duncan's analysis differs from that reported above in that they worked with status scores and status intervals rather than with census categories. It is however possible to apply the linear regression model to the census categories by assigning natural numbers to the categories in their given order and calculating a product-moment correlation coefficient. This yields a value of 0·426, showing that 18 per cent of the variance of son's occupational category is predictable from a knowledge of father's category.* This percentage may be compared with the value

* Professor Duncan has kindly supplied the mean index score of sons in each of the seventeen census categories. When the categories are reordered in terms of these means the correlation becomes 0.401. Reordering in no way affects the canonical regression analysis.

of 2·56 per cent which is the mean predictability of son's category determined by the method of percentage determinations. The two values, and the methods from which they are derived, are in no sense contradictory since they are solutions to different problems. The purpose of both linear regression and the multiple classification approach is to predict the rung of an assumed social ladder on which a son is likely to find himself. In both cases the analysis is interested in his occupational or social mobility only in so far as he moves vertically, whether upwards or downwards. The method of percentage determinations quantifies the predictability of movement in any direction, from any source to any destination, without regard to ordering of occupations. Only at the stage of interpretation, when the relative rigidities of the destinations (and sources) have been determined, is a social ranking introduced to cast light on the sociological importance of constraints on mobility.

Finally, we may examine the relationship of canonical regression to very simple statistics. The simplest form of contingency table is a table with two rows and two columns. It is instructive to trace the steps in the application of the method to such a table. The 2×2 matrices $\mathbf{C}_{xx}$ and $\mathbf{C}_{yy}$ are singular, hence each has only one dimension. The correlation between the two row variables is therefore minus unity and so is the correlation between the two column variables. The correlation between each row variable and each column variable is ϕ, where phi may be calculated in the usual way from the 2×2 contingency table (and is, for this special case, equal to Kendall's tau). Since there are effectively only two variables in the analysis, one paternal and one filial, the one and only canonical correlation is equal to the correlation between those variables, that is it is equal to phi. The predictable proportion of the variance of each dummy variable is ϕ^2, and so the weighted mean proportion of predictable variance is ϕ^2 for both fathers and sons.

Computation

The calculations described in Part I of this paper were carried out by a method which was developed for the general case in which (a) the matrices $\mathbf{C}_{xx}$ and $\mathbf{C}_{yy}$ may be singular, (b) we may be given a partitioned correlation or covariance matrix but not the data matrix from which it was derived, and (c) the original data may have been incomplete to such an extent that the partitioned matrix is not self-consistent. The application of the method to a contingency table by the use of dummy variables was suggested by a consideration of Fisher's blood-serum analysis. The calculations are necessarily complicated by the generality of the conditions under which they are intended to work. If conditions are not so severe computation may be simplified by observing that the standardized axes which form the bases of the canonical hierarchies consist of product-moment correlations between canonical variates and the original dummy variables. Since there are two sets of variables and two sets of variates care must be taken in pairing variables with variates.

References

BARTLETT, M.S. (1951). The goodness of fit of a single hypothetical discriminant function in the case of several groups. *Ann. Eugen.*, **16**, 199–214.

BARTLETT, M.S. (1965a). R.A. Fisher and the last fifty years of statistical methodology. *J. Amer. Statist. Assoc.*, **60**, 395–409.

BARTLETT, M.S. (1965b). Multivariate analysis. In *Theoretical and mathematical biology*. (ed. T.H. Waterman and H.J. Morowitz). Blaisdell, New York.

BLAU, P.M. & DUNCAN, O.D. (1967). *The American occupational structure*. Wiley, New York.

BUCKLEY, W. (1958). Social stratification and the functional theory of social differentiation. *Amer. Sociol. Rev.*, **23**, 369–75.

BURT, C. (1938). The unit hierarchy and its properties. *Psychometrika*, **3**, 151–68.

DUNCAN, O.D. (1961). A socioeconomic index for all occupations. In A.J. Reiss, *Occupations and social status*. Free Press of Glencoe, New York.

DUNCAN, O.D. (1966). Methodological issues in the analysis of social mobility. *In Social structure and mobility in economic development* (ed. N.J. Smelser and S.M. Lipset). Aldine, Chicago.

DUNCAN, O.D. (1968). Social stratification and mobility. In *Indicators of social change* (ed. E.B. Sheldon and W.E. Moore). Russell Sage Foundation, New York.

FARBER, B. (1965). Social class and intelligence. *Social Forces*, **44**, 215–25.

FISHER, R.A. (1940). The precision of discriminant functions. *Ann. Eugen.*, **10**, 422–9.

FISHER, R.A. (1958). *Statistical methods for research workers*. (13th edn). Oliver and Boyd, Edinburgh.

GLASS, D.V. (1954). *Social mobility in Britain*. Routledge and Kegan Paul, London.

GOODMAN, L.A. (1965). On the statistical analysis of mobility tables. *Amer. J. Sociol.*, **70**, 564–85.

GOODMAN, L.A. (1969). How to ransack mobility tables and other kinds of cross-classification tables. *Amer. J. Sociol.*, **75**, 1–40.

HALL, J. and JONES, D.C. (1950). The social grading of occupations. *Brit. J. Sociol.*, **1**, 31–55.

HOPE, K. (1968). *Methods of multivariate analysis*. University of London Press.

HOPE,K. (1969). The complete analysis of a data matrix. *Brit. J. Psychiat.*, **115**, 1069–79.

HOPE, K. (1970). The complete analysis of a data matrix: Application and interpretation. *Brit. J. Psychiat.*, **116**, 657–66.

HOTELLING, H. (1936). Relations between two sets of variables. *Biometrika*, **27**, 321–77.

HSU, P.L. (1940). On the generalized correlation ratio. *Biometrika*, **31**, 221–37.

KENDALL, M.G. (1961). *A course in multivariate analysis*. (2nd edn). Griffin, London.

KENDALL, M.G. and STUART, A. (1967). *The advanced theory of statistics*, vol. 2 (2nd edn). Griffin, London.

MAUNG, K. (1941). Measurement of association in a contingency table with special reference to the pigmentation of hair and eye colours of Scottish school children. *Ann. Eugen.*, **11**, 189–223.

MAXWELL, J. (1969). *Sixteen years on*. University of London Press.

MUKHERJEE, R. (1954). A further note on the analysis of data on social mobility. In D.V. Glass, *Social mobility in Britain*. Routledge and Kegan Paul, London.

MUKHERJEE, R and HALL, J.R. (1954). A note on the analysis of data on social mobility. In D.V. Glass, *Social mobility in Britain*. Routledge and Kegan Paul, London.

PEARSON, K. (1901). On lines and planes of closest fit to systems of points. *Phil. Mag.*, **2**, 559–72.

PEARSON, K. (1904). Mathematical contribution to the theory of evolution XIII: On the theory of contingency and its relation to association and normal correlation. *Drapers Company Research Memoirs*, Biometric Series No. 1.

POREBSKI, O.R. (1966). On the interrelated nature of the multivariate statistics used in discriminant analysis. *Brit. J. Math. Statist. Psychol.*, **19**, 197–214.

PRAIS, S.J. (1955). Measuring social mobility. *J. Roy. Statist. Soc.*, A118, 56–66.

ROGOFF, N. (1953). *Recent trends in occupational mobility*. Free Press of Glencoe, New York.

THOMSON, G.H. (1947). The maximum correlation of two weighted batteries. *Brit. J. Psychol. (Statist. sec.)*, **1**, 27–34.

TYLER, L.E. (1965). *The psychology of human differences*. (3rd edn). Appleton-Century-Crofts, New York.

WHITE, H.C. (1963). Cause and effect in social mobility tables. *Behavioral Science*, **8**, 14–27.

YULE, G.U. (1912). On the methods of measuring associations between two attributes. *J. Roy. Statist. Soc.*, **75**, 579–642 .

SOCIAL MOBILITY, CANONICAL SCORING
AND OCCUPATIONAL CLASSIFICATION

by P. DUNCAN-JONES

Summary. Canonical methods of scoring occupational categories are introduced. Scores are fitted to a number of father-to-son mobility tables and canonical correlations are calculated. The method serves to highlight a number of difficulties in the analysis of mobility tables. It is concluded that no satisfactory scoring system can be derived from internal analysis of a single mobility table. Generalized scoring procedures are presented in outline. These allow more data to be used in fitting scores.

This paper was read to the International Sociological Association Research Committee on Stratification, 7th world congress of Sociology, Varna, September 1970.

Measures of mobility

'Social' mobility between generations has nearly always been presented in terms of mobility tables, showing informant's occupational category cross-classified by father's occupational category. Much effort has gone into the development of indices that would summarize the information in a mobility table or exhibit its structure more clearly. These indices serve several purposes:

(a) summarizing the degree of mobility in a particular society, or birth cohort within the society, for comparison with other societies, with the same society at another time, or with other birth cohorts.

(b) micro-analysis of mobility tables, particularly to examine hypotheses of greater 'status persistence' at the extremes of an occupational hierarchy, or of particular links between certain occupational groups.

(c) measuring individuals' degree of mobility or distance between father and son, taken as an independent variable.

(d) supporting a multivariate explanation of individuals' current location in the occupational hierarchy or stratification system.

(e) separating the effects of 'structural' and of 'circulation' or 'free' mobility.

Various methods of attack have been proposed.

1. Many workers have focussed attention on the diagonal cells of the mobility table, and calculated indices of association and dissociation for each class or stratum in turn.

2. This focus on the separate rows and/or columns of the table has recently been extended and strengthened by several workers. MacFarland (1969a) using information statistics and Goodman (1969a, 1969b), using sampling theory of cross-ratios have each shown more rigorous and exact ways of 'ransacking' mobility tables, supposing we have reason to suspect a complex structure in them. Keith Hope (see the paper 'Quantifying constraints on social mobility' in this volume) has introduced 'multivariate regression' analysis of the rows and columns of the table (taken as dummy variables) using methods closely related to those of this paper.

3. Others have attempted to summarize the relationship between father's and son's occupational grade in a correlation coefficient. Thus

Carlsson (1958, chapter 8) has attempted to estimate the correlation on the assumption that the mobility table represents a bivariate normal surface in disguise. Svalastoga (1965) fits log-normal distributions to the marginal frequencies, and uses the resulting scores to calculate correlations. Duncan calculates the correlation between his Socio-Economic Score for father and son (Reiss, 1961; Blau and Duncan, 1967; Duncan, Featherman and Duncan, 1968). I return to these approaches later. For the moment, note that they require, as the previous approaches do not, a strong ordering (at least) of the row and column categories of the mobility table. Implicitly or explicitly, they require that each category should be assigned a score. It is surprising that rank-order correlation coefficients have not been much used in this context.

4.   Since Prais (1955), several workers have treated the mobility table as a realization of a simple Markov chain. This approach has been admirably dealt with by Duncan (1966) and MacFarland (1969b), so I shall not discuss it further.

5.   Sometimes, the mobility table has been transformed, for example by row and column multiplications, to a related table which might exhibit certain structural features more clearly. Thus Levine has used the Yule—Gini transformation (Pompilj, 1950) to convert to a table with all the marginal totals equal (Levine, 1967, Mosteller, 1968). I believe this and other transformations are useful as an adjunct to the analysis given below.

There is no exact match between the objectives and the methods proposed. However, the correlational tradition is mainly associated with overall summary measures and with multivariate explanation. The work described below belongs to this tradition. If we are concerned with *social* mobility (rather than with, say, problems of labour economics) we should be concerned with movement along a dimension. It is more useful than misleading to regard this dimension as continuous. There may well be more than one relevant dimension, but they should be separable—at least in principle. Thus, we should start by seeking simple monotonic (probably linear) relationships. But in practice there may be pertubations in the data. These may arise for at least three reasons—because one has muddled several dimensions together, because there are gross systematic errors in classification procedures or because there are inherent non-linearities or heteroscedasticity in the data. One needs a method of analysis which will fit a monotonic relationship but will be insensitive to pertubations in the data. Canonical scoring methods have some claim to fulfil these requirements.

Introduction to canonical scoring

Canonical analysis of contingency tables was first proposed by

Hirschfeld (1935), who sought row and column scoring systems that would produce linear regressions. The method was developed by Fisher, Maung and Williams (among others) and more recently Lancaster has presented a fuller and more general formulation of the theory. Kendall and Stuart (1967, chapter 16) give a clear summary. A fuller treatment will be found in Lancaster's book and several papers (especially Lancaster, 1957, 1958 and 1969).

Canonical analysis of a contingency table finds a score for each row category of the table, a score for each column category and a 'canonical' correlation between the row variable and the column variable scored in this way. The row and column scores will have an exact linear relationship to each other, and the canonical correlation is the highest that could be obtained from the table by any system of scoring. No assumptions are made about the ordering of the row and column categories and we shall see that the canonical solution can contradict one's a priori notions of the ranking of the categories.

Consider a very familiar example—the British 1949 social mobility table (Glass, 1954). I use the version given by Miller (1960), with eight categories (class 5 being divided into manual and non-manual). Canonical scores for the row and column categories are given in Table 1. These scores give a canonical correlation of 0·531.

TABLE 1.

Canonical scores for Glass data

Class	Fathers		Sons	
	Score	%	Score	%
1	3·96	3·7	4·34	2·9
2	2·13	4·3	2·01	4·6
3	0·70	9·9	0·93	9·6
4	0·07	14·8	0·05	7·0
5a	−0·04	4·5	0·15	13·1
5b	−0·36	38·7	−0·39	33·9
6	−0·68	13·1	−0·61	17·0
7	−0·77	11·0	−0·73	12·1
		100·0		100·0

There is an impressive regularity about these figures; but then it is well known that this table has rather a regular pattern. If we simply score the categories 1, 2, 3, ... we obtain a product-moment correlation of 0·462. The canonical scores allow one to account for 7 per cent more of the variance. Apart from the overall regularity of the scores, it is worth noting where they are less regular. Classes 4 and 5a are very close (in the scoring system for sons they are actually reversed) and one is led to question the quality of the occupational grading scheme in this neighbourhood. Certainly the subdivision of Class 5 is strongly supported.

The mathematical method

Before studying other examples, it seems appropriate to sketch in the mathematical model and computational method used in deriving these scores. The model involves a decomposition of each cell of the observed frequency table:

$$P_{ij} = P_{i.} \cdot P_{.j} \; (1 + \sum_k R_k \, X_{ik} \, Y_{jk})$$

where P_{ij} is the observed proportion of the sample in the i,jth cell

$P_{i.}$, $P_{.j}$ are marginal proportions

R_k is the kth canonical correlation

X_{ik} is the kth canonical score for row category i, and

Y_{jk} is the kth canonical score for column category j.

Note the first term in the decomposition is simply the product of the marginal proportions, corresponding to the familiar chi-squared expectation, and that there are (as might be expected) several canonical correlations and sets of scores. To be precise, there are m components in the decomposition, where m is either the number of rows or the number or columns in the table, whichever is the lesser. They consist of the 'chi-squared' component and $m-1$ components associated with canonical correlations. Corresponding to each canonical correlation there is a set of row scores and a set of column scores. The scores associated with any one canonical correlation are orthogonal to those associated with any of the others.

The canonical solution proceeds as follows:

Let $[n_{ij}]$ be the original array of frequencies, with marginal totals $n_{i.}$ and $n_{.j}$. Adjust this array to give a new matrix

$$\mathbf{C} = [c_{ij}] = [n_{ij}/(n_{i.} \cdot n_{.j})^{\frac{1}{2}}]$$

Form the matrix product $\mathbf{CC}'$ (or $\mathbf{C'C}$ —either will give the same final results), and find its latent roots and vectors. Discard the largest root (always unity) and its associated vector. These correspond to the first, simple chi-squared component in the decomposition. The following roots are the canonical correlations, and the corresponding vectors (after dividing by the roots of the corresponding marginal proportions) are the row scoring systems (if one has solved from $\mathbf{CC}'$). The corresponding column scoring systems are obtained by multiplying the original n_{ij} matrix by the matrix of row scores, and dividing the j,kth element of the resulting matrix by R_k (the corresponding canonical correlation) and $n_{.j}$ (the corresponding marginal). That is, the score for a column is the average of the row scores for the column, scaled by the canonical correlation.

This last result (which is used later) can perhaps be clarified by considering its connection with the correlation ratio. Take the row scores as given and consider the correlation ratio expressing the proportion of variance in row scores explained by the column classification. A little algebra will show that if we wished to assign scores to the columns in such a way as to achieve a correlation equal to the correlation ratio we would assign them in precisely this way (apart from the scaling factor, which is of course irrelevant here). And since the correlation ratio is the highest correlation that could be achieved, given the row scores, it must be equal to the canonical correlation. All this of course applies equally (*mutatis mutandis*) if one solves initially for the column scores.

Corresponding to the decomposition of the cell frequencies, the method provides a decomposition of the total chi-squared for the table.

$$\phi^2 = \chi^2/N = \sum_k R_k^2$$

Thus a component of chi-squared with appropriate degrees of freedom may be associated with each canonical correlation. However, it also follows that the canonical correlation will be bounded in the same way as the phi coefficient. It is well known that in the two-by-two table phi (in this case equal to the canonical correlation) can reach $\pm 1 \cdot 0$ only if the two marginal distributions are identical. Marginal distributions must similarly restrict phi-squared, and consequently the canonical correlation, in larger tables, but the effect of this has not been investigated.

So far I have mentioned the existence of several orthogonal canonical scoring systems, but only given an example of the first. One might hope that studying several orthogonal systems could (as in multiple-factor analysis) give rather a complete picture of the structure of a complex table. However, in this paper attention is restricted to the first scoring system (i.e. the one associated with the highest canonical correlation), for two reasons. First, I have studied additional scoring systems from many tables and found nothing that seemed to have any clear meaning (though my colleague Keith Hope has been luckier). Secondly, there are theoretical reasons for expecting the higher scoring systems to be meaningless. Suppose the table to be analyzed represented a bivariate normal distribution, arbitrarily partitioned, then the second, third, ... scoring systems would be exact polynomial functions of the first one, (Lancaster, 1957).

Some more examples

The Glass table that we studied earlier is based on a classification of occupations designed specifically for stratification research. The different grades are intended to be unidimensionally ordered in a relevant way. I now consider three examples, from the United States, Australia and Britain, using more heterogeneous classifications. These come from Blau and Duncan (1967), from Broom and Jones (1969a, 1969b) and previously unpublished data from Butler and Stokes's panel study of the British electorate (reported in Butler and Stokes, 1969). The classifications used in these tables are in two cases population census schemes and in the third a scheme with rather similar intentions devised by the investigators (Broom, Jones and Zubrzycki, 1965; Broom and Jones, 1969b). This latter scheme is a grouping of the occupational categories used in the Australian census, reducing these first to one hundred categories and then to sixteen, 'using the main criterion that jobs in each category involve the same level of skill or skill type. Wherever possible meaningful industrial distinctions were maintained'.

Schemes of this kind have often been used in mobility studies. Sometimes no satisfactory unidimensional scheme was available for the society under study. Or an investigator may have thought that a division into more heterogeneous socio-economic groups might serve several different purposes, beyond those of stratification specialists. More fundamentally, it has been argued (e.g. by Carlsson, 1958) that we do not know precisely what is the most relevant dimension for mobility studies, that there are probably several relevant dimensions, and hence that one should use a classification that reflects several of the more significant dimensions. At one time I hoped that internal analysis of mobility tables could provide useful and satisfactory scores for hetero- geneous occupational classifications. Elsewhere in this volume, Kenneth Macdonald reports work with similar motivation. The results to be reported now suggest rather convincingly that no internal analysis of single mobility tables is likely to provide a scoring system that is demonstrably and uniquely appropriate for mobility research.

First, let us look at the United States. Blau and Duncan base most of their work on an occupational grading using Duncan's socio- economic status table (S.E.S.) (Reiss, 1961), but they present three appendix tables showing the cross-tabulations of informant's current occupation, his first occupation and his father's occupation, using a Census Bureau classification into 17 groups. I have made a canonical analysis of each table. The canonical correlations can be compared with those reported by Blau and Duncan, using the S.E.S.

	S.E.S.	Canonical
Father's occupation and first occupation	0·42	0·55
Father's occupation and current occupation	0·41	0·42
First occupation and current occupation	0·54	0·56

Two of the correlations are very similar, but one shows a substantial difference 'in favour' of the canonical method. *A priori*, one might have expected the S.E.S. correlations to be higher, since they use a more appropriate occupational classification, but the canonical analysis trades on ties between occupations other than those of social standing. The canonical scoring of the occupational categories is in fact not a pure status scoring. For instance, farmers, as well as farm labourers, are at the bottom of the scale.

Next, note that these three tables yield, not just one scoring system for the occupational categories, but six. It may seem reasonable that the three different items of occupational information should represent different variables for which different scoring systems might be appropriate, It is less clear intuitively that father's occupation (for instance) should be scored differently depending on whether it is related to first occupation or to current occupation. But consider the problem of optimal prediction of (say) income and of political affiliation from current occupation. Clearly different scoring schemes for occupation might be optimal for these tasks. We may calculate the correlation between two scoring schemes for the same classification. For the Blau and Duncan data we have

Father's occupation	0·92
First occupation	0·73
Current occupation	0·92

The correlation for first occupation is remarkably low, and the others are not as high as one might wish. It is clear one cannot use these scoring systems for multivariate analysis. We offer a possible solution to this problem later.

There is something unsatisfactory about a situation where variables can change their meaning in this way. In fact, whenever one fits or assigns a scoring system to a set of categories, one is restricting attention to a part of the information contained in the categories. One is focussing on a particular dimension underlying the classification. There may always be others.

One last point about this data. Blau and Duncan present multidimensional scaling analyses of this data, based on 'inflow' and 'outflow' distances between occupations. They derive two dimensions from each analysis, the first approximating to a 'status' dimension in each case. They note several apparent 'quirks' in the status ordering of their first dimension. Canonical analysis using a totally different mathematical apparatus, confirms nearly all these quirks. In particular, the high position of non-retail salesmen is fully supported. The Spearman rank correlation between canonical scores for father's occupations and the ranking from the outflow analysis is 0·98. That for the current occupation scores and the inflow analysis ranking is 0·999.

The Australian data is summarized in Table 2. It brings out very dramatically one point that we had already sensed from the United States data. In some societies the cleavage between urban and rural occupations may be so great as almost to submerge everything else. Broom and Jones' data give canonical correlations of 0·56 for father's occupation by current occupation and 0·69 for first occupation by current occupation. Each scoring system we have calculated puts Graziers and Farmers at one end, then Farm Workers, and after that all the urban occupations in various orders, but with little differentiation among them in scores. The career mobility analysis makes somewhat better sense than the father-to-son analysis, since it at least groups together at one end the Upper and Lower professional, Managerial and Clerical workers. But it puts them at the opposite pole from the Graziers, who clearly come very high on the Australian prestige (and income) scale.

TABLE 2.

Scoring of Australian occupational groups

(Data from Broom and Jones)

	Father's job		First job		Current job		
	Score	%	Score	%	Score (A)	Score (B)	%
Graziers	3·77	4·9	1·97	1·4	4·65	1·69	3·4
Farmers	0·97	14·9	1·51	5·8	1·28	1·44	7·8
Farm workers	0·00	3·3	0·88	13·0	0·92	0·86	1·8
Managerial	− 0·17	9·4	− 0·56	0·7	− 0·21	− 0·16	11·8
Operatives	− 0·26	8·0	0·14	8·7	− 0·14	0·30	9·4
Shop proprietors	− 0·30	2·8	0·23	0·4	− 0·23	0·20	1·3
Drivers	− 0·37	6·4	0·37	4·0	0·19	0·42	6·4
Labourers	− 0·39	8·4	0·18	6·3	− 0·15	0·40	5·4
Clerical workers	− 0·48	7·9	− 0·51	15·9	− 0·49	− 0·33	12·0
Armed services, police	− 0·49	1·9	− 0·34	1·4	− 0·21	0·00	1·0
Lower professional	− 0·52	1·3	− 1·52	3·3	− 0·53	− 1·09	3·8
Service workers	− 0·55	4·9	0·15	3·1	− 0·39	0·20	4·1
Craftsmen	− 0·55	18·5	− 0·03	25·8	− 0·47	0·07	22·8
Miners	− 0·58	3·1	0·23	1·3	− 0·62	0·28	1·0
Upper professional	− 0·64	3·1	− 4·29	3·2	− 0·42	− 3·35	5·7
Shop assistants	− 0·65	1·2	0·12	6·0	− 0·16	0·10	2·4
	100·0		100·0				100·0

A: Solution from analysis by father's occupation

B: Solution from analysis by first occupation

The Australian results are based on a relatively small sample (just under 2000), and some peculiarities may be nothing more than sampling fluctuations. Out next example is based on a sample of only 900 British male electors, interviewed in 1963. The occupational information was coded very scrupulously and several alternative summary classifications are available. The sample is fully described in Butler and Stokes (1969). In this paper I use the system of socio-economic groups developed for the British population census of 1961. In Britain, with its relatively small agricultural sector and high population density, one would scarcely expect such a dramatic urban/rural separation as in Australia. In fact, the results are rather similar to those for Australia. We have a correlation of 0·62 between father's and current occupation, and scoring systems which place 'Farmers: employers and managers' and 'Farmers: own account' at one extreme, with little differentiation among other occupations. The details are given in Table 3, which also exhibits a more 'reasonable' scoring system. This alternative scoring system is explained later. For the moment, note that some categories are very small. In particular, the curious results for Personal service occupations, though they may contain a grain of truth, are probably due to sampling fluctuations.

TABLE 3
Scoring of British Socio-Economic Groups
(Data from Butler and Stokes)

	Fathers			Sons		
	A	B	%	A	B	%
1. Employers and managers	0·17	2·03	7·6	−0·02	1·23	12·8
2. Professional	0·17	2·68	1·8	0·51	2·84	4·0
3. Intermediate non-manual	−0·13	0·95	2·2	−0·11	1·35	5·1
4. Junior non-manual	−0·16	0·66	5·6	0·05	0·45	11·2
5. Personal service	0·08	2·42	0·6	−0·36	−0·79	1·0
6. Foremen and supervisors: manual	−0·05	0·06	3·8	−0·15	−0·30	7·8
7. Skilled manual workers	−0·26	−0·32	28·6	−0·21	−0·56	29·9
8. Semi-skilled manual workers	−0·35	−0·86	18·3	−0·37	−0·96	12·7
9. Unskilled manual workers	−0·35	−0·91	8·8	−0·40	−1·09	5·8
10. Own account (not professional)	−0·18	0·58	5·6	0·52	0·33	0·7
11. Farmers: employers and managers	7·17	2·26	1·6	7·16	1·12	1·7
12. Farmers: own account	1·88	0·73	3·4	4·42	1·57	0·4
13. Agricultural workers	−0·28	−1·33	5·7	0·09	−1·13	2·1
14. Armed forces	−0·28	0·05	2·2	−0·32	0·60	1·4
			100·0			100·0

A: Scores from bivariate canonical solution

B: Scores from predictive solution (see below)

Occupational classification

The analysis just offered makes an important point about occupational classification in mobility studies. For the *assessment* of social mobility, and comparison of the 'openness' of different societies, heterogeneous occupational classifications are little use. Social

mobility will be confounded with effects of industry and occupational
'situs'.* The effect of urban/rural separation can be demonstrated in
several other countries (e.g. France, using the table given by Bertaux,
1969, or Sweden, using Carlsson's data). It is quite possible that other
industries may make a similar, though less marked, impact on social
mobility patterns. What is wanted, clearly, is a unidimensional index
of social stratification. An occupational classification may be the best
available proxy for this, but it must be constructed (or scored) in such
a way as to mirror whatever aspect or aspects of the social order are
held to be most relevant. Thus, occupational classifications may be
constructed to reflect occupational prestige, life chances, life styles or
all of these.

Given that one wants a unidimensional classification of occupations, practical problems may still arise in constructing it. Data from
occupational prestige studies can provide one basis. Similarly, if one
has good income data for detailed occupational categories, the problem
may be relatively straightforward. But suppose one wants to work with
some wider definition of life-chances, or with life-styles, or suppose
one's concept of social class embraces both life-style and life-chances.
Then there is little alternative to fitting some scoring system for occupations, from the data in hand. Later in this paper I propose methods of
doing this, using generalized canonical scoring procedures.

Of course, the study of social mobility has other objectives beyond
summarizing the degree of mobility in a society. If one is concerned to
diagnose the constraints upon social mobility then other kinds of occupational classification may be relevant. One dimension of constraint is
the effect of industrial location on employment opportunity. Analysis of
this dimension needs much more detailed occupational classifications,
and the methods of this paper are probably not relevant.

Evaluation of canonical scoring

How far does canonical scoring meet the objectives of mobility
measurement that I noted earlier? I will take the points out of order and
start with the question of analyzing degree of mobility, or distance
moved. The distance between father's category and informant's category
can be measured by the difference between category scores. Thus (from
Table 1) we could say the distance travelled by an informant in grade

---

* Often, a plot of the first two dimensions from a dimensional analysis of a mobility
table will show the urban occupations in a swarm that could be quite well fitted by a
straight line. It is tempting to rotate the dimensions to give a good fit to the urban
occupations, and then to declare the fitted dimension to correspond to social status.
But the rotation will involve some essentially arbitrary fitting criterion. There will be
room for dispute about the angle of rotation. And the location of the *agricultural*
occupations on the 'status' dimension will depend critically on this angle.

2 whose father was in grade 4 is 2·13−0·05, i.e. 2·08.* Similarly, the distance from a father in grade 1 to a son in grade 6 is −0·61−3·96, i.e. −4·57. The method can throw some light on structural mobility, since it provides a measure of the 'movement' of categories or grades between generations. Thus we can say that grade 3 in the Glass data has moved a distance of 0·23 over a generation, since this is the difference between its score in the fathers' and the sons' scoring system. Most of these category distances are small, suggesting that structural changes may be largely self-cancelling when mobility is modelled in terms of an underlying dimension of stratification.

The canonical method does not seem well adapted to examining hypotheses of status persistence at particular points in the status system. Nor is it suitable, in the form in which we have so far presented it, for multivariate studies in which several variables are used to explicate mobility or to develop models of the multiple determination of current status, since (as we have already seen) cross-analysis by different variables will produce different scoring systems.

I have already noted one or two specific uses of canonical scoring, and will briefly describe one more. Goodman (1969b) has advanced a hypothesis of quasi-perfect mobility. Crudely summarized, this states that the probability of a son being found in any particular occupational category is independent of his father's category, *given* that his occupational category is different from his father's. It is well known that mobility tables exhibit concentration in the diagonal cells, representing 'occupational inheritance'. Goodman proposes a method of blanking out the diagonal cells and then testing for independence over the rest of the table. He finds no evidence against the hypothesis of quasi-perfect mobility in the Glass data, when this is collapsed to a 3×3 table.

I have studied this problem myself, by a slightly different method. I 'get rid of' the diagonal by inserting dummy values in the diagonal cells that will be equal to their expected values (in the usual chi-square sense), calculated from the modified table. Analysis of a 3×3 version of the Glass table confirms that the canonical correlation vanishes after this adjustment. However, I have studied several larger tables (5×5 and 8×8) that use suitably graded occupational classifications. In every case, canonical analysis *after* adjusting the diagonal elements turned up reasonable scoring systems and canonical correlations of the order of 0·3. I conclude that the hypothesis of quasi-perfect mobility cannot readily be sustained.

An index for comparative studies?

We have seen that the canonical method can highlight peculiarities

___
* The scores are standardized to zero mean, unit variance.

in occupational classifications, that it can be used to motivate distance measures and that it can throw light on some specific hypotheses about the structure of mobility tables. But the main criterion for judging the method must be the usefulness of the canonical correlation as a summary measure for comparative studies. I shall argue (a) that the canonical correlation is about as good a measure as we shall get, (b) that it may not be good enough, and hence (c) that simple comparisons between societies or cohorts are likely to be misleading.

Several studies (e.g. Fox and Miller, 1965) have compared mobility rates in different countries, and Svalastoga and Rishøj (1965) have calculated correlation coefficients from mobility tables for a number of countries, assuming that status always has a log-normal distribution. Studies of this kind use an index of mobility for a society as a dependent variable, and seek to explain variations between societies. Correlation coefficients (or transformations of them) seem the best indices of mobility for this purpose, to the extent that they will be less affected by differences between societies in the overall occupational distribution. But any correlation coefficient will require a scoring system, and scores fitted to the data seem preferable to a distribution imposed *a priori*. If we accept that it is reasonable to expect a linear relationship then the canonical system will give an upper bound to the correlation, and the best linear fit attainable. Typically the values found are higher than Svalastoga and Rishøj obtained. (It turns out their figures are actually *covariances*, not correlations—see Svalastoga and Rishøj (1970)).

	Canonical	Svalastoga
Britain	0·53	0·38
Denmark	0·49	0·38
Sweden	0·49	0·37

The canonical solution is not constrained to symmetry, and is often asymmetric. Thus if a log-normal distribution were appropriate it could be approximated.

Calculating correlation coefficients will only make sense if the occupational classification is appropriately graded. From our earlier discussion it seems unlikely that anything will make much sense with an inappropriate occupational classification. We cannot rely on internal analysis of the mobility table to produce the correct gradation of a heterogeneous occupational classification—though both Svalastoga and Carlsson seem to have done so. Most scoring systems will assume that the occupational classification is equally 'good' throughout the range. But it may be that two categories near the middle are not correctly distinguished from each other and overlap considerably. We may, perhaps, rely on the canonical solution to allow for *minor* weaknesses in the occupational classification, provided they approximate to random error.

Suppose we have mobility tables from several countries, each based on adequate samples and using reasonable unidimensional classifications. Suppose we calculate canonical correlations from each. Shall we be misled if we compare them with each other? Probably we shall. First there will usually be differences between the studies in methods of measurement, though with co-ordination these might be overcome. Next, the classifications used may vary in their quality. They may all be intended to reflect a common definition of life-chances (say) but in some countries occupations may have been more successfully matched against the criterion than in others. But even if these difficulties are overcome other troubles of a more purely technical kind may arise. We can use the canonical method to illustrate them. The classification scheme will result in a certain number of grades. This number may be critical. We noted earlier that the 8×8 version of the Glass table gives a coefficient of $0 \cdot 53$. If this is collapsed to 5×5, the coefficient drops to $0 \cdot 50$. A 3×3 version gives $0 \cdot 36$. One must remember that collapsing a table too far (perhaps in an attempt to make occupational classifications comparable with each other) will mean that the coefficients are constrained by the marginals—probably to a different extent in different tables.

Thus indices of mobility can be affected by the size of the table, and by the marginal distribution. Let us look further at the marginals. Suppose we alter the marginal distributions of a table, using Gini's transformation, which preserves association in the sense that the cross-ratios are unaffected. The canonical correlation may nevertheless change quite sharply. Thus in some tables with fairly skew distributions (like the Glass table) transforming to a table with all marginals equal has doubled the proportion of variance accounted for by the canonical analysis.

Thus there are technical obstacles to international comparisons as well as more common-sensical ones. I would not wish to argue that any of these obstacles are necessarily insuperable. But at the moment one would be very lucky to avoid them all. And it is rather difficult to know what allowance to make for some of them. Svalastoga has remarked that the correlations from different European countries are mostly of similar size. Hence any error or bias in particular coefficients could seriously distort comparative analysis.

Generalized canonical scoring

I hinted above that the method I have outlined could be extended. The main object of this extension is to allow a set of scores to be fitted to a number of classifications simultaneously, rather than just fitting them two at a time. It turns out that this can also produce intuitively acceptable scoring procedures for some more heterogeneous occupational classifications.

First, let us make this more concrete. Suppose we wish to set up a correlation matrix and conduct a path analysis for:

Father's occupation
Informant's type of school
Whether informant had any further education
Informant's occupation
Informant's self-assessed social class.

All of these are categorical, non-quantitative variables. But suppose one could fit a score for each category in each classification in some 'optimal' way. Then one could form a correlation matrix for the five 'variables', and set up a path diagram. I leave for another occasion discussion of the logical status of these variables, but give examples of fitted scores shortly. Cattell (1962) has an interesting discussion of the philosophy of linearization.

There are two main methods of solution for the 'optimum' scores, and one variation seems worth mentioning. The original solution is due to Guttman, and he has given a very clear exposition of it (Guttman, 1941—similar methods have been developed by Hayashi e.g. Hayashi, 1954). Very briefly, consider a sample of people each classified in each of several ways (by father's occupation, by type of school, and so on). Assume scores are to be assigned for each category of each classification. Then the total score for an *individual* is the sum of the scores assigned to the different categories in which he falls (thus he will have a score for his 'father's occupation' category, a score for his type of school, and so on). Guttman considers the maximization of two correlation ratios. The first approach is to minimize the variability of the scores for different categories within persons, which amounts to maximizing the correlation ratio for scores between persons. The second approach is to consider the assignment of an individuals' *total* score to each category in which he falls, and then maximize the variability of these total scores, between categories. It turns out that the two problems have the same solution, and the scores that will maximize one correlation ratio also maximize the other.

Lingoes has developed a computer program for this method, MAC-1 i.e. Multivariate Analysis of Contingencies (Lingoes, 1963)— and he has also developed an alternative method, christened MAC-3 (Lingoes, private communication). The latter is more tractable with large numbers of classifications. In MAC-3 each classification is taken in turn. It is cross-tabulated by each of the other classifications included in the analysis, and this array of cross-tabulations is then matrix-multiplied by its transpose to give a product matrix. From here the solution proceeds as in the bivariate case, providing a score solution for the classification.

It occurred to me that when one is principally interested in prediction, or in analysis of the determinants of a single independent variable, one might simply carry out the MAC-3 solution for that one variable, and then solve for scoring systems for the other variables by the same 'back solution' used in the bivariate analysis. It follows from our earlier remarks about scoring in such a way as to equate the correlation coefficient to the correlation ratio that, given the solution for scores for the criterion classification, this procedure will maximize the correlation of each predictor with the classification. This 'predictive' scoring procedure is relatively very economical in computer time, and from limited experience seems to give similar results to the other methods. I now give an example.

Predictive canonical scores.   An example.

I use Butler and Stokes' data again, to fit scores to the informant's socio-economic group, in terms of a variety of other variables linked to social status. A back solution gives scores for each of the other variables. The scores for the actual socio-economic categories have already been given in Table 3 above. Table 4 lists the variables used as 'predictors' in this analysis and their correlations with informant's socio-economic status, using the fitted scores.

TABLE 4
Variables used in predictive canonical analysis

	Correlation
Socio-economic group, father	0·42
Income, head of household	0·54
Age of leaving school	0·48
Type of secondary school	0·48
Whether any further education or training	0·39
Informant's self-assessed social class	0·51
Informant's assessment of his family's social class, when he was young	0·39
Father's political party	0·20
Mother's political party	0·19
Whether informant's home is owned or rented	0·34
Type of daily newspaper read by informant	0·40

This is a mixed list, including indicators of parental background, life-style and life-chances. It might be quite an appropriate list if one wished to fit scores to occupations that would reflect a broad concept of social class.

As one now has a set of consistent scores for the set of variables one can calculate a complete correlation matrix and (if one is so minded) produce path models. But this goes beyond the scope of the present paper. My immediate object is merely to show that the technique produces reasonable results. We have already seen that it produces a 'sensible' scoring of occupations. I now give two examples of the scores fitted to other classifications.

Type of school:

'Public' (i.e. private) school	1·38	2·0%
Grammar	0·77	13·9%
Technical college	1·53	1·6%
Elementary, secondary modern	− 0·23	79·7%
Private commercial schools	0·96	1·2%
Other and unclassified	0·93	1·6%
		100·0

Tenure of home:

Rents council house/flat	− 0·43	28·6%
Rents house/flat (not council)	− 0·14	23·4%
Owns/is buying	0·37	42·9%
Other/no information	− 0·11	5·1%
		100·0

To anyone with a knowledge of British society, these scores will seem plausible. It is likely that one could get almost equally good results by dichotomizing school into 'Elementary, secondary modern' and 'All others'. But if one dichotomized home tenure one would clearly be throwing away useful information.

Acknowledgements—I am grateful to Professor Alan Stuart for first bringing the bivariate canonical method to my attention about ten years ago. My colleague Keith Hope kindly showed me his own paper on canonical scoring. He has been working on this topic at the same time as myself, but from a different point of view. Professors Broom and Lancaster Jones supplied me with the original frequencies for their mobility tables. I am particularly grateful to David Butler and Donald Stokes for access to their data.

References

BERTAUX, D. (1969). Sur l'analyse des tables de mobilité sociale. *Revue Francaise de Sociologie*, **10**, 448–90.

BLAU, P.M. and DUNCAN, O.D. (1967). *The American occupational structure*. Wiley, New York.

BROOM, L.J. and JONES, F. LANCASTER (1969a). Father-to-son mobility: Australia in comparative perspective. *Amer. J. Sociol.*, **74**, 333–42.

BROOM, L.J. and JONES, F. LANCASTER (1969b). Career mobility in three societies: Australia, Italy and the United States. *Amer. Sociol. Rev.*, **34**, 650–58.

BROOM, L.J., JONES, F. LANCASTER and ZUBRZYCKI, J. (1965). An occupational classification of the Australian workforce. *Australian and New Zealand Journal of Sociology*, **1**, Supplement.

BUTLER, D.E. and STOKES, D.E. (1969). *Political change in Britain*. Macmillan, London.

CARLSSON, G. (1958). *Social mobility and class structure*. Gleerup, Lund.

CATTELL, R.B. (1962). The relational simplex theory of equal interval and absolute scaling. *Acta Psychologica*, **20**, 139–59.

DUNCAN, O.D. (1966). Methodological issues in the analysis of social mobility. In *Social structure and mobility in economic development* (ed. N.J. Smelser and S.M. Lipset). Aldine, Chicago.

DUNCAN, O.D., FEATHERMAN, D.L. and DUNCAN, B. (1968). *Socioeconomic background and occupational achievement: extensions of a basic model*. U.S. Department of Health, Education and Welfare.

FOX, T.G. and MILLER, S.M. (1965). Economic, political and social determinants of mobility: an international cross-sectional study. *Acta Sociologica*, **9**, 76–93.

GLASS, D.V. (1954). *Social mobility in Britain*. Routledge and Kegan Paul, London.

GOODMAN, L.A. (1969a). How to ransack mobility tables and other kinds of cross-classification tables. *Amer. J. Sociol.*, **75**, 1–40.

GOODMAN, L.A. (1969b). On the measurement of social mobility: an index of status persistence. *Amer. Sociol. Rev.*, **34**, 831–50.

GUTTMAN, L.L. (1941). The quantification of a class of attributes. In *The prediction of personal adjustment* (ed. P. Horst). Social Science Research Council, New York.

HAYASHI, C. (1954). Multidimensional quantification with the applications to analysis of social phenomena. *Annals of the Inst. of Statist. Mathematics*, **5**, 121–43.

HIRSCHFELD, H.O. (1935). A connection between correlation and contingency. *Proc. Camb. Philos. Soc.*, **31**, 520–4.

KENDALL, M.G. and STUART, A. (1967). *The advanced theory of statistics*, vol. 2, (2nd edn.). Griffin, London.

LANCASTER, H.O. (1957). Some properties of the bivariate normal distribution considered in the form of a contingency table. *Biometrika*, **44**, 289–92.

LANCASTER, H.O. (1958). The structure of bivariate distributions. *Ann. Math. Statist.*, **29**, 719–36.

LANCASTER, H.O. (1969). *The chi-squared distribution*. Wiley, New York.

LEVINE, J.H. (1967). *Measurement in the study of intergenerational status mobility*. Ph.D. Thesis, Department of Social Relations, Harvard University.

LINGOES, J.C. (1963). *Multivariate Analysis of Contingencies: An IBM program for analysing metric/non-metric or linear/non-linear data*. Computation report; University of Michigan Computing Centre.

McFARLAND, D.D. (1969a). Measuring the permeability of occupational structures: an information-theoretic approach. *Amer. J. Sociol.*, **75**, 41–61.

McFARLAND, D.D. (1969b). *Intra-generational social mobility as a Markov process: a case study in model development*. Paper written for the annual meeting of the American Sociological Association.

MILLER, S.M. (1960). Comparative social mobility. *Current Sociology*, **9**, 1–89.

MOSTELLER, F. (1968). Association and estimation in contingency tables. *J. Amer. Statist. Assoc.*, **63**, 1–28.

POMPILJ, G. (1950). Osservazioni sull'omogamia: La trasformazione di Yule e il limite della trasformazione ricorrente di Gini. *Rendiconti di Matematica e delle sue Applicazioni*. Ser. V, **9**, 367–88.

PRAIS, J. (1955). The formal theory of social mobility. *Population studies*, **9**, 72–81.

REISS, A.J. (1961). *Occupations and social status*. Free Press of Glencoe, New York.

SVALASTOGA, K. and RISHØJ, T. (1965). Social mobility: the Western European model. *Acta Sociologica*, **9**, 175–82.

SVALASTOGA, K. and RISHØJ, T. (1970). Western European mobility. *Amer. J. Sociol.*, **76**, 520–23.

MDSCAL AND DISTANCES BETWEEN
SOCIO-ECONOMIC GROUPS

by K.I. MACDONALD

Summary.   Results obtained from the application of a multidimensional scaling technique to a neglected 1951 occupational interchange tabl e are used to support the claim that some users of the technique have been insufficiently sceptical.

The data to be considered come from an elegant but oddly neglected paper by Benjamin (1958) giving, for 2600 occupied males in a systematic sample of 1951 census schedules, subject's occupation from the schedule by father's occupation from the subject's birth cirtificate. The mode of summarization* to be employed (recovery of the space underlying a dissimilarity matrix) has been applied to such data by Blau and Duncan (1967, pp. 67 ff.). In the present case the resulting spatial configuration is unsurprising. This piece of unoriginal analysis is nevertheless worth undertaking to emphasize that, while such techniques help recover the space in which the objects lie, they are (expectedly) little help in identifying appropriate dimensions by which to *describe* that space; statements such as 'Evidently socioeconomic status is a fundamental dimension of the social distance between occupational groups' (Blau and Duncan, 1967, p. 74) transcend the evidence.

The occupations in the table considered (Benjamin 1958, p. 266) are categorized in the thirteen socio-economic groups of the 1951 Census. Benjamin stresses that this categorization is based more on the concept of skill and associated material rewards than on notions of 'status' or social value: 'There is therefore no intention of entering upon an examination of what has been termed social mobility' (p. 267). This qualification should be borne in mind. Further, if the verbal formulations which follow appear unaware that we lack generations (Duncan 1966), the lapse is for convenience of exposition only.

A measure of similarity between occupation A and occupation B can be constructed by forming the percentaged outflow distributions (from these two occupations into all other available occupations) then summing the positive differences between these outflows. The measure varies from the case where the sons of A and B have identical occupational destinies (A and B on this measure identical) to the case where their occupational destinies do not overlap at all (A and B maximally different). The measure can be interpreted as the percentage of the sons of A (or B) that would have to be reallocated jobwise for the sons of

* I am grateful to L. Erbring for introducing me to this area, and to R. Carr-Hill, P. Doreian and J.M. Ridge for (to me) profitable disputations on the problem of this paper. The Editor has rescued me from some of my errors of sense and expression. Without that friendliest of computers, KDF9, programming and computation would have been tedious; and, as always, Oxford University Computing Laboratory has been generous of time and facilities.

A (or B) to match the sons of B (or A). This does make some intuitive sense as a measure of distance, for it places close together occupations yielding similar occupational outcomes for the next generation. Further, the measure has the advantage of not presupposing an occupational ranking*. A complementary measure can be derived from inflow distributions.

There are qualifications to be made. A ranking is not presupposed, but a categorization certainly is. We cannot look at similarity of occupations, only of occupational groups; any grouping requires criteria, and may involve the agglomeration of entities distinct from the viewpoint of social distance.† Moreover the measure of distance is a measure of social distance in the sense stated only. While empirically it is probable that occupational categories close on the measure are also close in the sense that outflow (or inflow) from one to the other is easy, there is nothing in the logic of the measure to require this.** Two comparatively small occupational categories having a low degree of self-recruitment could be very similar on this measure though the probability of a son of one landing in the other were zero.

To the impurity of the occupational categories we return later. On the problem of the interpretability of the dissimilarity measure as a measure of social distance, it is perhaps sufficient to remark that as defined it does have some direct meaning, and the user who reads in more does so at his own risk.‡

The two dissimilarity matrices thus obtainable from the interchange table given by Benjamin are presented in Table 1. These matrices were analyzed using J.B. Kruskal's program MDSCAL4. The reader interested in the details of the technique is referred to Kruskal's lucid exposition (1964a, b). The program attempts to recover a spatial configuration in a given dimensionality which will satisfy the given dissimilarity matrix. The configuration is returned with an associated stress coefficient,

* For an attempt to use this measure and MDSCAL to discriminate between occupational rankings see Macdonald and Ridge (1971).

† The Registrar General's three-digit occupational coding is the finest determinate grouping available, but even it provides odd mixtures. Cross-classification by status can sort out categories such as 267 (e.g. attending at baths and wash-houses, owning cinemas). But it is not much help with, say, 078 ('other metal working; jewellery and electrical process workers') which includes persons assembling motor-car bodies, persons employed as process workers, fitters' and electricians' mates, maintenance hands (vehicles), riveters—categories which are well documented in the sociological literature as being not similar.

**Other measures might be constructed. Analysis of a similarity matrix based on 'indices of association' might be more interpretable. I have chosen to leave this notion in a footnote, partly because 'indices of association' generate their own puzzles, discussion of which would tangle the present purpose, and partly because I am unclear as to the nature of a similarity matrix involving such indices.

‡ Admittedly the term 'social distance' has been adopted as a semi-technical usage in another context (Bogardus, 1925). But a fresh given definition can take precedence over custom.

which can be read as a measure of the discrepancy between spatial configuration and original dissimilarity matrix. Trying solutions in spaces
of differing dimensionality provides some indication of the lowest order
space needed to account for the data. A helpful and often used, though
imprecise, physical analogy is given by a set of wooden blocks each con-
nected to every other by pieces of string of varied length. The task is
to arrange the blocks such that all the lengths of string are taut. This
may be possible by placing the blocks in a straight line. It may require
the blocks spread out on a plane surface. Or some of the blocks may
have to be moved above the plane to form a three-dimensional configuration. And at three dimensions the analogy must rest. Some measure of
the amount of slack and stretch present in the strings is the analogical
parallel to the stress coefficient.

The analogy is importantly imprecise. The technique deals with
dissimilarity measures, not with (as the pieces of string would be)
proper distance measures, and the constraint on the final configuration
is that the attained distances be monotonic with the dissimilarities
(which is not to require each string to be taut). Suppose our dissimilarity matrix contains the elements D_1, D_2, D_3 with $D_1 > D_2 > D_3$, then
their relative magnitudes (other than inequality) are not considered, and
a corresponding set of distances d_1, d_2, d_3 with $d_1 \geqslant d_2 \geqslant d_3$ in the
achieved configuration would be taken as satisfactory. It might be felt
that in the present case we do have strict distance measures, so the
analysis is discarding information, and a tighter regression of the d_i on
the D_i would have been appropriate. The matter may be argued. Our
analysis treats the matrices as dissimilarity matrices merely. The resulting inter-point distances from the two dimensional solution were, however, plotted against the difference measures treated as distances
(Figures 1 and 2). The relationship is pleasingly linear, apart from an
intercept and slope shift for the longer distances in the inflow case.
Someone, therefore, insisting upon the strict distance interpretation of
the matrix, though he may claim that precision has been lost, should
not be tempted to reject the analysis as yielding a configuration incompatible with his premises.

The MDSCAL analysis was tried in spaces of one, two and three
dimensions. From the outflow matrix the resulting stress coefficients
were 0·165, 0·056, and 0·025; for inflow 0·086, 0·027 and 0·013.*
Criteria for evaluating the stress and deciding what constitutes a
'good' stress coefficient are ill-defined. From the work of Klahr (1969)
it would seem that Kruskal's own statements are over-optimistic. But
Klahr's findings are themselves too general for our present purpose.

* The stress coefficients reported throughout this note were checked not to be local
minima by the procedures described below, and were checked to be minima by over-
running, with a high ceiling on the number of iterations as the only stopping rule.

TABLE 1

Socio-economic group dissimilarity matrices. Summed positive differences between percentage inflow or outflow distributions derived from the table in Benjamin 1958, p. 265.

Note: The figures summing to 100·0 are the percentage of fathers (case A) or sons (case B) in the sample's socio-economic groups.

A. OUTFLOW

	(100·0)	1	2	3	4	5	6	7	8	9	10	11	12	13
1. Farmers	3·4	—												
2. Agricultural workers	6·8	51·1	—											
3. Higher admin. etc.	2·5	71·4	75·8	—										
4. Other admin. etc.	5·0	63·0	52·7	36·9	—									
5. Shopkeepers	4·7	58·6	57·7	40·8	32·3	—								
6. Clerical workers	3·2	67·0	55·6	38·6	17·7	38·2	—							
7. Shop assistants	3·2	63·4	52·3	39·4	13·4	27·8	27·3	—						
8. Personal service	2·0	54·5	43·3	55·5	29·3	41·1	35·0	23·5	—					
9. Foremen	2·1	71·2	47·5	56·5	26·2	41·0	35·6	21·1	36·1	—				
10. Skilled workers	38·3	65·2	44·3	62·3	33·0	45·1	42·1	27·4	32·0	14·7	—			
11. Semi-skilled workers	12·4	65·7	43·0	68·2	39·0	50·8	47·3	33·3	36·0	15·7	8·4	—		
12. Unskilled workers	14·6	60·1	34·2	69·4	39·8	51·9	47·2	35·5	30·4	23·9	21·1	19·3	—	
13. Armed forces (OR)	1·8	66·7	41·9	62·7	36·1	44·6	42·7	29·0	35·9	21·2	20·7	18·4	18·9	—

B. INFLOW

	1	2	3	4	5	6	7	8	9	10	11	12	13
1. Farmers	2·3	—											
2. Agricultural workers	6·5	58·1	—										
3. Higher admin. etc.	3·4	75·5	65·7	—									
4. Other admin. etc.	8·5	72·9	63·1	20·0	—								
5. Shopkeepers	5·3	65·7	55·1	35·7	25·2	—							
6. Clerical workers	6·0	71·4	59·1	27·7	14·0	26·4	—						
7. Shop assistants	3·3	69·8	54·1	30·6	23·3	22·1	23·2	—					
8. Personal service	1·9	65·8	43·1	39·8	28·5	30·8	20·9	27·9	—				
9. Foremen	3·2	74·4	58·5	47·6	34·6	39·6	28·7	34·7	30·4	—			
10. Skilled workers	37·7	71·2	51·8	45·7	33·9	36·5	26·3	32·0	23·5	9·6	—		
11. Semi-skilled workers	10·2	75·3	52·3	50·1	38·9	42·3	32·1	35·5	26·2	9·4	10·7	—	
12. Unskilled workers	10·9	68·5	45·4	50·8	39·3	41·9	33·8	36·5	21·1	25·1	19·5	—	
13. Armed forces (OR)	0·8	68·3	47·1	49·6	41·4	40·0	37·7	36·2	29·6	28·3	24·0	19·2	—
	(100·0)												

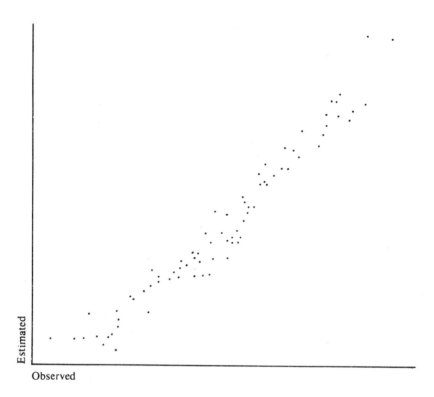

Observed

FIG. 1. Outflow. Taking the dissimilarity matrix as a distance matrix, plotting estimated against observed in the two-dimensional solution.

He examines the distribution of the coefficient, for a given dimensionality and number of points, over random dissimilarity matrices. We are more concerned with the, as far as I am aware unexplored, distribution for given dimensionality and number of points over random configurations in some determinate higher dimensionality. In the absence of criteria, and in the light of popular wisdom, the two-dimensional solutions were adjudged satisfactory. The three-dimensional solution for outflow is considered briefly later, and does yield a comforting interpretation. But part argument of this note is that interpretation is variable, and in the absence of adequate on-line computer graphics with which to explore three-dimensional configurations it is perhaps best to stick at two. Besides Occam is in favour.

The axes returned by the program are arbitrary in their orientation. Clearly comparison between outflow and inflow coordinates on such axes is unilluminating. The simplest determinate location criterion, principal components, was chosen*, and Table 2 presents the configurations

* The configuration reported by Blau and Duncan (1967, p. 70) if rotated to its principal axes gives a main axis yielding an occupational ranking further from socio-economic status than the axis which they discuss and for which they report no selection criteria.

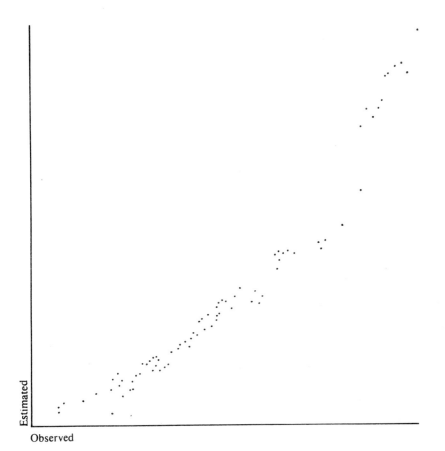

Estimated

Observed

FIG. 2. Inflow. Taking the dissimilarity matrix as a distance matrix, plotting estimated against observed in the two-dimensional solution.

rotated to their principal axes. On the assumption that we have 'true' configurations, the main axis accounts for 81% of the variation in the inflow, 57% of the variation in the outflow space. It is tempting to see the inflow space as simpler, more dominated by one dimension. Inflow, one might suggest, and this makes some substantive sense, is more directly determined by prestige than is outflow. It is not, however, clear what the dimensions are, nor does there appear to be much comparability between inflow and outflow configurations. Coordinates are not easy reading; a picture is required.

But first, since we are talking as much about the doing as the thing done, some comments on the behaviour of the program MDSCAL4 are in order. The technique is of the family of 'hill-climbing' algorithms—the program starts with a trial configuration, wishes to minimize stress, calculates in which direction stress is least, moves the configuration

TABLE 2

Outflow and inflow two-dimensional solutions in terms of their principal axes.

Dimension (variance)	Outflow (stress 0·056)		Inflow (stress 0·027)	
	1 (0·565)	2 (0·435)	1 (0·810)	2 (0·190)
1. Farmers	−0·496	−1·944	2·694	0·306
2. Agricultural workers	−1·213	−0·453	1·108	−0·298
3. Higher admin. etc.	1·708	0·117	−0·856	0·717
4. Other admin. etc.	0·508	0·235	−0·580	0·394
5. Shopkeepers	0·766	−0·516	−0·040	0·593
6. Clerical workers	0·761	0·276	−0·053	0·208
7. Shop assistants	0·297	0·220	−0·256	0·403
8. Personal service	−0·120	−0·270	−0·123	−0·052
9. Foremen	−0·115	0·519	−0·531	−0·397
10. Skilled workers	−0·352	0·550	−0·422	−0·333
11. Semi-skilled workers	−0·592	0·547	−0·411	−0·533
12. Unskilled workers	−0·691	0·283	−0·092	−0·469
13. Armed forces (OR)	−0·461	0·534	0·013	−0·539

a step in that direction, and repeats. It varies the step size according to its reckoning of proximity to the minimum, and has various stopping rules to force report when a minimum is reached. In using this program on occupational transition matrix data (not only the current matrices) a local minimum close to the 'true' minimum occurred more frequently than a reading of the literature might suggest: metaphorically, there usually exists a well-defined valley but its floor has at least one bump. Kruskal suggests (1964b, p. 122) recomputing the configuration with a very large step size (to give effectively a fresh starting point) and recommencing the iteration as a way of evading local minima. This modification, when programmed into our copy of MDSCAL4, was found unrewarding and computationally expensive, though occasionally reassuring. We did, however, discover one useful modification. MDSCAL4 as written started in a high dimensioned space, found a solution, dropped one dimension of that solution and took the truncated configuration as its starting point in the space of next lowest dimensionality.* It was felt intuitively that a better solution in k dimensions could be obtained by expanding the $k-1$ dimensioned solution than by contracting the $k+1$ dimensioned solution. Accordingly MDSCAL4 was modified to 'bounce'—ascend from low to high after descending—and consistently yielded improved fit.

The two-dimensional solutions reported in Table 2 are plotted in Figure 3. Looking at this more interpretable presentation, comments

* As a move towards increasing the efficiency of this operation, we extended the program to rotate its configuration to a principal components representation and discard the component accounting for least variance.

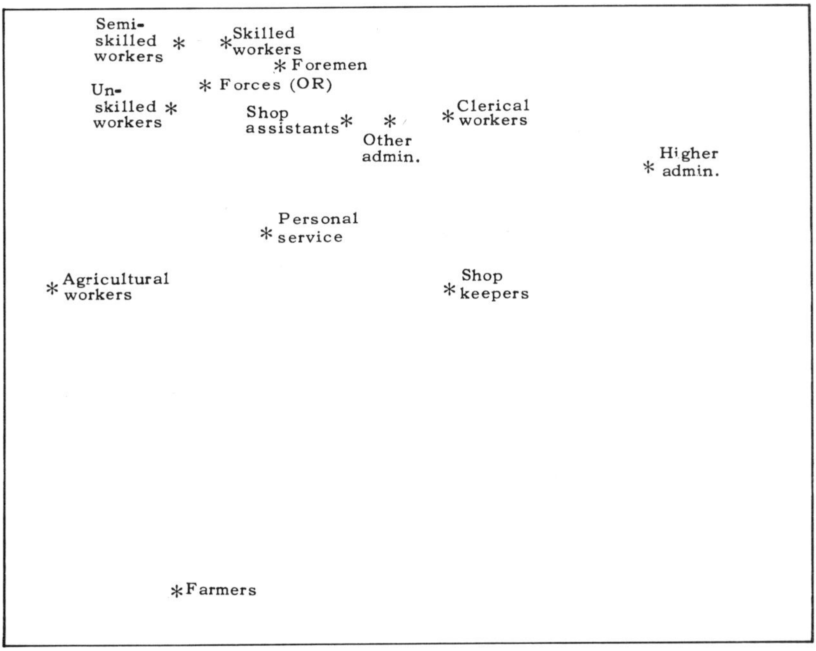

Outflow. Stress 0·0564

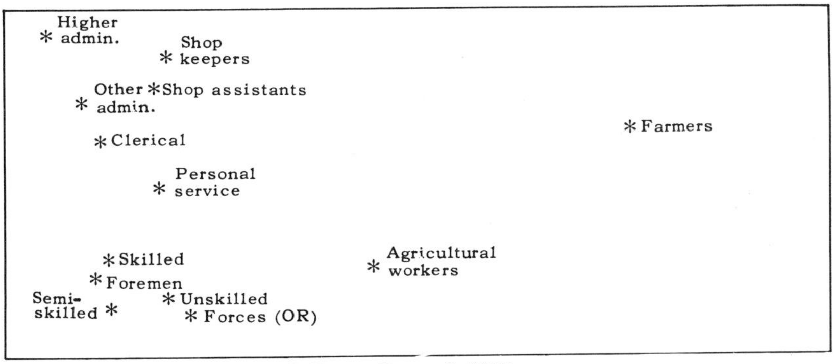

Inflow.   Stress 0·0274

FIG. 3. Two-dimensional solution rotated to principal axes.

seem obvious. It might, in passing, be noted that the MDSCAL configuration is not implausible, and there are pleasing clusterings of agricultural, manual and non-manual groups. (It is comforting when numeric techniques return a simulacrum of the real world). In terms of outflow, what one might see as a skill or education dimension is more important; whereas for inflow the 'rural' aspect predominates. Initially it had been hoped to compare the ranking along the various axes with the educational distribution of the socio-economic groups (SEGs). This might have helped tighten the claim that the main outflow dimension is an education one. Unfortunately, for the 1951 Census no SEG/Education table exists, nor can such a grouping be recovered from the most detailed education table printed (Census 1951, General tables, table 46) since the breakdown of the occupational sub-orders is not sufficiently fine to map onto the SEGs (Census 1951, Occupation tables, table 1). Nevertheless, the suggested reading does make sense. For outflow, the educational base which an occupation provides its sons is the main factor. For inflow, situational aspects, particularly the urban/rural, predominate. As part support for this, note that the distance between shop assistants and shopkeepers in the outflow is reduced in the inflow configuration. Shopkeepers' sons have a better start than those of shop assistants; but the recruitment patterns of both occupations one might expect to be more alike.

Tidy though this may be, and tidy though it is to fix on principal axes as determinate, we have little justification for taking 'percentage of variation accounted for' as the criterion of importance of a dimension. Further, these axes do not appear helpful in comparing the two configurations. Eyeballing Figure 3 suggests that inflow and outflow configurations are more similar than their presentation indicates. This line of thought leads naturally to Figure 4, where the outflow configuration has been stood on its side, and the inflow configuration turned by eye to a visually similar orientation; this involves a rotation of $-19.3°$ around the centroid. Although the axes have been moved the configurations are, of course, unaltered. And the apparently different spaces of Figure 3 now reveal marked similarities in structure.

Although these rotations have 'reduced' the isolation of the agricultural sector apparent in Figure 3, this deserves comment before interpreting Figure 4. That sector, as always, displays a certain individuality; indeed there is apparent in the quantitative literature a tendency to drop agricultural categories from analyses. It might be argued that in the present case 'Farmers' and 'Agricultural workers' are distorting the space—once the dissimilarity measures are computed each category exerts the same weight irrespective of size and an oddball category can force inappropriate solutions. Accordingly, the MDSCAL program was rerun dropping these two categories, and, for good measure, the 'Military'.

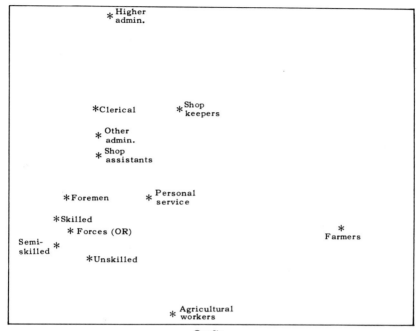

Outflow

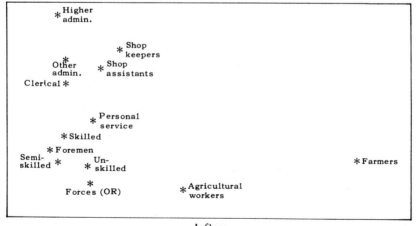

Inflow

FIG. 4. Two-dimensional solution with outflow rotated so that principal axis is vertical, inflow rotated −19·3° from its principal axis.

The resulting configurations, allowing for rotation and reflection were very similar to those illustrated in the relevant areas of Figure 3. This stability supports the retention of the agricultural categories. Besides, they are part of the 'real world'. (It might be noted that the reduced outflow matrix yielded three similar but not identical configurations of identical stress. These ten points do not provide sufficient information for a determinate two-dimensional solution.)

In Figure 4 there is, in each space, a readily identifiable and similar 'main' axis. This axis appeals as a better, more 'real' descriptor of the data than do the principal axes. Admittedly, the direction of variance shifts somewhat between the inflow and outflow configurations of Figure 4; but this does not quite engender the statements made from looking solely at Figure 3. On a vertical comparison, which is the more interesting, given that the urban/rural split so dominates the horizontal, there are several interpretable shifts. While for outflow, 'Foremen' and 'Personal service' rank equally, for inflow 'Personal service' is left alone as a bridging category between manual and non-manual groups. The 'Semi-skilled'—'Unskilled' gap virtually disappears in inflow. There, despite increased horizontal separation, 'Agricultural workers' seem closer on the 'main' axis to the manual group. And in inflow 'Shop-keepers' and 'Shop assistants' seem to form their own dyad. For all of this one can concoct sociological explanations; particularly if the horizontal axis is labelled 'prestige'.

If, however, the dissimilarity matrix is to be taken as essentially a distance matrix, a qualification must be made. In the inflow solution farmers are more isolated than in the outflow case. But as we have noted from Figure 2, on that assumption some twelve inter-point distances are overestimated. These turn out to be the distances from 'Farmer' to the other categories. Faced with this disturbing information, there are at least two possible responses. One may decide that the solution is unsatisfactory. MDSCAL has only been able to accommodate 'Farmers' by removing them to a distance where they no longer affect the solution (this is compatible with the absence of effect, noted above, on removing the agricultural sector from the analysis). On the other hand one may claim that the measures in the observed matrix do, in the case of 'Farmers', experience a 'ceiling' effect. In some sense farmers actually are at the distance represented in the diagram, though the dissimilarity matrix cannot attain the requisite values. Despite some unhappiness at the difficulty of cashing 'in some sense' this response preserves a plausible substantive interpretation (rural occupations are more unlike urban in recruitment than in outflow). And, by way of slight backing, it may be noted that the three-dimensional solution, which is an even tighter fit (stress 0·013), maintains the kink in the observed/expected scattergram. Which thus looks less like a two-dimensional miss-fit. A third conceivable response, that MDSCAL simply distorts a distance matrix, is not plausible. Were this so we would expect some curvilinear scattergram, not this appearance of a faulted coalseam.

There is a more important, and less evadable, qualification to be made. It comes through realizing that we preferentially make comparisons horizontally and vertically, and through realizing that the rotation of Figure 4 was by eye and others are possible. We can concoct various criteria for best fit rotation. Figure 5 presents an obvious one. The inflow configuration has been rotated around its centroid so as to minimize the sum of squared inter-object distances—that is, if $\mathbf{A}(1:n, 1:2)$ represents one configuration and $\mathbf{B}(1:n, 1:2)$ the other, we have minimized $\Sigma[(a_{i_1} - b_{i_1})^2 + (a_{i_2} - b_{i_2})^2]^{\frac{1}{2}}$ with respect to the b_{ij}. Again the spaces are unchanged, but the two configurations now appear even more alike. Further, the inflow/outflow differences noted in Figure 4 are no longer striking. Instead, the marked downward movement of the 'Farmers' in inflow requires comment (the eye paid more attention to their orientation than did the formula). A small shift in presentation has largely tangled interpretation.

But there is no good reason to rest here. The three figures so far considered are orientated on the principal components solution of the outflow table, and this has determined our horizontal and vertical comparisons. Why not rotate both configurations? A possible criterion would be to rotate inflow and outflow to give a maximally cross-configuration correlated pair of axes. One might verbalize this by saying that an axis which is 'steady' over both inflow and outflow does in some sense provide a good description of the world. Or one could perform a principal components analysis of the combined spaces. And there are other possibilities.*

But enough has been said to show that MDSCAL, however useful for recovery of spaces gets only partway to a destination. For axes to which a space is referred are important, not just when considered as scales in isolation, but in any attempt to compare configurations qua configurations. This last may be obvious. Certainly obvious, I trust, in retrospect. But the literature tends to bury the fluidity of much quantitative analysis. A reading of the orthodox references had led me to expect that the present exercise could be tidly and determinately completed within one diagram and a couple of pages. Yet who would have thought the old man to have

* Lest it be thought that I am here perversely feigning (or avowing) ignorance of an extensive literature on the analytic rotation of axes, it may be noted that such literature is not directly pertinent. Admittedly a factor analysis model with each variable owning an individual error variance might be more apt. Admittedly various rotation criteria, on orthogonal or non-orthogonal rotations in 'person space', are available. But to discuss these in the present context is to sweep the problem under a carpet of parameters. Given the (argued for) extreme sensitivity of interpretation to the location of axes, and given our uncertainty as to how the space should be described (hence the exercise), then the case against *any* axes holds, whether or not we introduce the full paraphernalia of factor analysis.

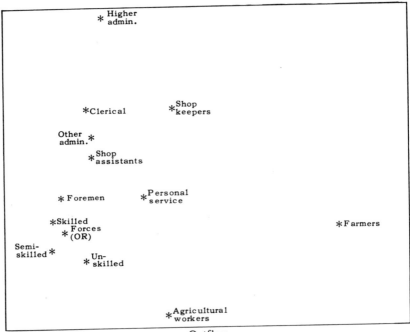

Outflow

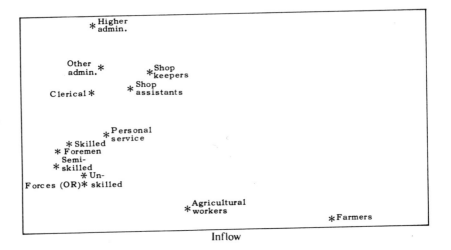

Inflow

FIG. 5. Two-dimensional solution, outflow with principal axis vertical, inflow rotated around centroid so that sum of squared differences between it and outflow is minimum. (Variance of horizontal axes: Outflow 0·435, Inflow 0·651).

had so much blood in him? Perhaps the mess should be made more public as a guide to future operators.

I wish to end this note with a small substantive finding. But first a point directed against an as yet unused straw man, but one incipient in the temptation, occasionally succumbed to above, to identify one dimension with 'prestige'. Reading Blau and Duncan's presentation (1967, pp. 67 ff.) and noting the (misleading) identification of a socio-economic status (SES) axis as the main axis of the space, it is tempting, were one interested in SES and social mobility, to run the following argument.

Being engaged on the study of social mobility, we wish, for various reasons to assign some SES rating to British occupations, and lack the resources for a separate prestige study. Nor is neat replication of the Duncan strategy available since our Census omits income information. But we note that the main dimension from a smallest space analysis of Blau and Duncan's interchange table virtually reproduces an SES scale. So what we shall do is collect social mobility data, group the occupations into some set of plausible categories, form and analyse the interchange table, and assign to the categories their values on the main axis as their SES score. We shall then have a scale which can be used in calculations leading to international comparisons.

This is nonsense, though this note was begun with that aim. It is nonsense in part because of the indeterminacy of any axis. But independently because of the impurity of the categories. A heterogeneous category (heterogeneous from an SES standpoint) with a given SES score is under no obligation whatever to behave, in pertinent situations, similarly to another category with identical SES score. (This heterogeneity may also undermine my next point.)

To suggest that it is possible to avoid, in MDSCAL analysis, misleading emphasis on axes, I wish to look briefly at the outflow three-dimensional configuration qua configuration (this emphasis is closer to Kruskal's original formulation than many subsequent uses).*

---

* An elegant and imaginative use of MDSCAL is a recent application (Kendall, 1971) to the recovery of maps from inadequate contiguity data, recovering a space the structure of which has (appears to have) independent reality. Part indeed of the worry of this paper may be around the dubiousness of any usage of 'dimension' in social science data analysis. Despite the verbal similarity, this is not the physicists debate on dimensional analysis, more an invocation of a point made by Dempster:

'[a second] attitude says that it is difficult to contemplate any space of variables without at least some indefinite hints of Euclidean structure present. For example, a plot ... presumes related scales of measurement in different directions, so as to yield a picture comprehensible to the eye. Likewise, the visual impact of such a picture depends on the initial angle between the coordinate axes v_1 and v_2.

'The user of a principal components analysis adopts the second of these two attitudes. In fact, he must promote vague feelings about scales and angles among $v_1, v_2, \ldots v_p$ into a precise inner product. This inner product is not determined wholly by the sample data ...

'In practice, the reference inner product has usually been chosen in one of two ways. In both of these ways, the directly observed set of variables $V_1 \, V_2, \ldots V_p$ is regarded as an orthogonal set ...'

(Dempster, 1969, pp. 136–7)

Cont. on p. 228|

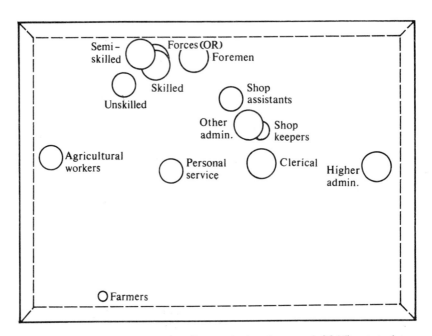

FIG. 6. Three-dimensional outflow solution (stress 0·0245) rotated to principal axes (cf. Fig. 3). The axis with least variance (0·151) is perpendicular to the plane of the paper.

Figure 6 represents an attempted perspective drawing of this space; we are looking in the top of a box containing the occupations, the areas of the circles being proportional to their distances from the reader. The stress (0·0245) is an improvement on the two-dimensional fit, but the improvement is not so marked as to lead us, on these grounds alone, to reject the lower space. In the drawing the configuration is pictured in terms of its principal axes. True, this is arbitrary. And crystallographers, who have most experience with suchlike points in space, tell cautionary tales of researchers who failed to locate the symmetry of structures by viewing them from the 'wrong' angles. But this configuration does seem happy in its principal components stance. We have a fair approximation to a plane, two of the axes lying in it, with two points off the plane. Comparing Figure 6 with Figure 3, the most marked feature is the accommodation of the two 'ownership' groups ('Shopkeepers', 'Farmers') by this third dimension. The remaining occupations lie roughly on the one

Footnote continued from p.227

And this particular mode of representation, which is not commonly argued for, determines interpretation; we are accustomed, with no good reason other than convenience, to ignore and drop the clause 'relative to the chosen reference inner product', But worry over this leads beyond MDSCAL.

plane, and their arrangement on this plane may be held more meaningful than in the two-dimensional solution. These occupations fall neatly into two straight line groups—that from 'Agricultural' to 'Foreman', and that from 'Shop assistant' to 'Clerical' (though 'Foreman' as pivot might claim dual status). 'Personal service', being an odd category, and the horizontal straight line, being not group-like, we can for the moment ignore. There are, then, two angled straight lines thus, ∧   . If this description is not the 'three bricks make a wall' of archaeological fame, then there is an elegant interpretation for the zigzag. We have two strictly ordered social groups, manual and non-manual. The distance from 'Shop assistant' to 'Clerical' is the sum of the distances from 'Shop assistant' to 'Other administrative etc.' and from 'Other administrative etc.' to 'Clerical'. Similarly within the manual. But these two systems are not laid end to end. The distance from 'Unskilled' to 'Shop assistant' is *less* than the sum of the distances from 'Unskilled' to 'Skilled' and from 'Skilled' to 'Shop assistant'. 'Higher administrative etc.' could be taken as a one-member third system. To read this as saying, 'if you are unskilled and wish to become a shop assistant the direct route is shortest' makes doubtful sense. Better to say that we have three groups within which occupational distance is one-dimensional, but which do not form an overall one-dimensional system. This interpretation is dependent for its bite upon prior identification of manual and non-manual groups, but it is to say more than that there are manual and non-manual groups. Intuitively we could as well have foreseen groups separated upon a fuzzy but continuous line (the picture suggested by the two-dimensional space). MDSCAL by returning these angled straight lines has given a non-trivial solution. And to say that we have three groups which do not form an overall one-dimensional system is, paradoxically, not to say that we should describe the configuration in terms of two, or three 'dimensions'.

Appendix:
Multidimensional scaling and explanatory variate analysis

The Editor suggests that the above could with benefit be related to his method of analysis applied to the same data. He writes,

'[your paper is] of particular interest to me because I had already applied my method of explanatory variate analysis (see the paper 'Quantifying constraints on social mobility') to Benjamin's data. As you will see from the enclosed table and diagrams (reproduced as Table 3 and Figures 7 and 8) the results are substantially in agreement with yours. This is the more reassuring in that I derive the distance matrix quite differently, and I employ an interval metric rather than a ranking method.

'I find that knowledge of son's occupational group enables us to retrodict 5.56% of the variance of father's occupation, and knowledge of father's group enables us to predict 5.47% of the variance of son's occupation. Explanatory

variates have the property of successively explaining as much as possible
of one or other of these percentages subject to the constraint that the variates form an orthogonal set. In fact the components of the percentages which
are explained by the first six variates are:

Variate	Fathers	Sons
1	2·68	2·40
2	1·37	1·64
3	0·74	0·58
4	0·34	0·34
5	0·24	0·28
6	0·10	0·13
.		
.		
.		
Total	5·56	5·47

'There is no clear break in either column. On the other hand the proportion of the variance of a particular variate which is explicable from the opposite set of arrays does show a break after the third variate (these proportions are analogous to the squared canonical correlations associated with
canonical variates but, unlike their analogues, they are not necessarily in
descending order of size):

TABLE 3

*Means of occupational groups on the first two explanatory variates
(Hope's analysis), arranged to correspond as closely as possible with
Table 2 above. Note the inversion of the order of the variates for fathers.*

	Fathers (outflow)		Sons (inflow)	
Group	Second variate	First variate	First variate	Second variate
1	−0·62	1·01	1·58	0·45
2	−1·15	0·53	1·00	−0·81
3	1·16	0·82	0·22	0·94
4	0·72	0·21	0·06	0·66
5	0·66	0·58	0·24	0·68
6	0·87	0·37	−0·04	0·46
7	0·54	0·11	0·16	0·46
8	0·05	0·16	0·12	−0·06
9	0·29	−0·13	−0·31	−0·07
10	0·03	−0·26	−0·26	−0·11
11	−0·06	−0·29	−0·27	−0·22
12	−0·34	−0·06	0·02	−0·48
13	−0·01	−0·03	0·10	−0·28
Percentage of variance of other array accounted for	1·64	2·40	2·68	1·37

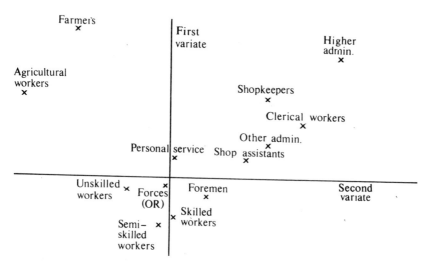

FIG. 7. Positions of occupational groups of fathers on the first two
explanatory variates, Hope's analysis.

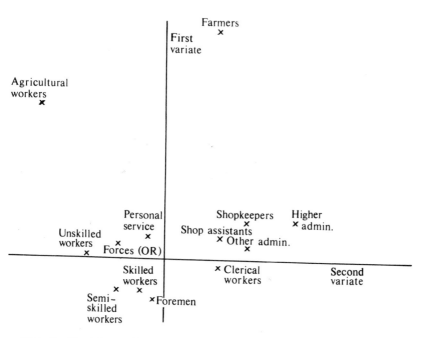

FIG. 8. Positions of occupational groups of sons on the first two
explanatory variates, Hope's analysis.

Variate	Fathers	Sons
1	0·14	0·12
2	0·16	0·19
3	0·11	0·09
4	0·02	0·02
5	0·05	0·04
6	0·02	0·02'

The reader may, according to temperament and orientation, find the congruence between results derived from diverse analyses reassuring or disturbing.

Having been requested to comment I have only two points to make. Firstly, the argument above against treating particular axes seriously, should, if it holds, hold against Keith Hope's presentation also. Secondly (and this, though not directly pertinent to the present discussion, meshes with its sceptical orientation) a note of caution may be in order on the interpretation of the results from his method of 'percentage determinations'. The method involves generating dummy variables (Suits 1957) both for the independent and for the dependent (Boyle 1970) variables, and interpreting the resulting R^2 as a 'precise quantification of the relative concentration of constraints on intergenerational mobility' (see above, p. 129). Since the regression coefficients are not under direct consideration conventional cautions on inefficiency from the resulting heteroscedasticity (Goldberger 1964, p. 249) are unimportant.

But consider the model,

$$y_i = x_i + e_i$$

where the x and e are independent drawings from an $N(0, 1)$ variable. That is, cashing, a son's occupational level is an additive function of his father's occupational level and a random disturbance term. If further (possessing only the Hall—Jones scale) we categorize these continuous variables x and y into seven categories so as to give for fathers and sons the marginal distributions observable in the 1949 table, then we have a very simple model of a possible underlying continuous but categorized process, with seeming equality of rigidity. Applying regression with dummy variables to data generated according to this model* yields the striking patterning of column B of Table 4; Keith Hope's figures for 1949 are presented for comparison. The sharp 'end-point' predictability in the artificial data is describable either as the greater efficiency in prediction of a linear over a curvilinear relationship (even using dummies), or as ceiling and floor effects, and these are unfortunately not separable. But the figures for the 1949 data should at least be read against this marked structuring returned from a relatively unstructured model. The two sets of figures for categories one and two are virtually identical. And although the first category is uniquely underestimated, the explanatory concern then shifts from the high to the low occupational groups.

The claim of this section—that we should be alert to the behaviour of analysis techniques in simple situations lest we misperceive the meaning of their structures—can be applied against the substantive conclusion of my note above. Rather than bemoan the lack of blanket sampling experiments, it might have made more sense to generate simplistic artificial data, as in this example, and seen what MDSCAL made of that.

* The results reported are averaged from only four experiments, samples of 1300, since the program used (Macdonald, 1971) lacked, at the time of writing, the simulation facilities which had been incorporated in the KDF9 version. The results were, however, stable over the four experiments.

TABLE 4

'The extent of intergenerational constraints on mobility associated with each occupational category.'

A.   *1949 data, from paper 'Quantifying constraints on social mobility', Table 4, p.130.*

B.   *Results from artificial data, average of 4 experiments, $N = 1300$. The figures are the R^2 ($\times$ 100) from the regressions of*

$$y_j = \Sigma b_i x_i + C$$

where the subscripts identify dummy variables representing category membership, and i ranges over 6 categories.

C.   *'Observed' minus 'Expected'.*

	A	B	C
1	18·8	16·7	2·1
2	7·6	8·4	−0·8
3	3·5	9·5	−6·0
4	1·8	4·3	−2·5
5	2·8	8·8	−6·0
6	4·0	7·6	−3·6
7	4·2	22·8	−18·6

References

BENJAMIN, B. (1958). Inter-generation differences in occupation. *Population studies*, 11, 262–8.

BLAU, P.M. and DUNCAN, O.D. (1967). *The American occupational structure.* Wiley, New York.

BOGARDUS, E.S. (1925). Measuring social distance. *J. Appl. Sociol.*, 9, 299–308.

BOYLE, R.P. (1970). Path analysis and ordinal data. *Amer. J. Sociol.*, 75, 461–80.

DEMPSTER, A.P. (1969). *Elements of continuous multivariate analysis.* Addison–Wesley, Reading, Mass.

DUNCAN, O.D. (1966). Methodological issues in the analysis of social mobility. In *Social structure and mobility in economic development* (ed. N.J. Smelser and S.M. Lipset). Aldine, Chicago.

GOLDBERGER, A.S. (1964). *Econometric theory.* Wiley, New York.

KENDALL, D.G. (1971). Construction of maps from 'odd bits of information'. *Nature*, 231, 158–9.

KLAHR, D. (1969). A Monte-Carlo investigation of the significance of Kruskal's nonmetric scaling procedure. *Psychometrika*, 34, 319–50.

KRUSKAL, J.B. (1964a). Multidimensional scaling by optimizing goodness of fit to a nonmetric hypothesis. *Psychometrika*, 29, 1–27.

KRUSKAL, J.B. (1964b). Nonmetric multidimensional scaling: a numerical method. *Psychometrika*, 29, 115–29.

MACDONALD, K.I. (1971). FAKAD: an interactive general purpose regression program for use on the Essex University PDP10. Mimeograph, Department of Government, University of Essex.

MACDONALD, K.I. and RIDGE, J.M. (1971). Social mobility. In *Trends in British society since 1900* (ed. A.H. Halsey). Macmillan, London.

SUITS, D.B. (1957). Use of dummy variables in regression equations. *J. Amer. Statist. Assoc.*, **25**, 458–51.

PATH ANALYSIS: SUPPLEMENTARY PROCEDURES

by K. HOPE

Summary. The first purpose of this paper is to indicate the circumstances in which path coefficients may be accepted as adequate guides to the relative importance of anterior (causal) variables in a path analysis. It is shown that weights in a regression equation may be regarded as indicators of importance, in the sense of determinants of proportions of variance, if the (projection of the) variate defined by the equation coincides with a principal component of the anterior variables.

The second purpose of the paper is to illustrate the usefulness of employing analysis by canonical correlations as an aid in the interpretation of a path diagram.

The discussion is illustrated by reference to the path analysis which appears in 'Ability and achievement' by Professor O. Dudley Duncan.

This paper appeared in *Sociology*, 1971, vol. 5, and is reproduced here by courtesy of the Editor and the British Sociological Association.

The method

A path analysis is summarized in a path diagram, such as Figure 1 of Professor Duncan's article 'Ability and achievement'.* A path diagram consists of a set of points, each point representing a variable, and a set of lines, to each of which a numerical quantity has been assigned. In the simplest case, that of a recursive system, the lines are of three sorts, and to each sort there is an appropriate kind of coefficient. The analyst decides where lines shall be drawn in the diagram, and in drawing each line he indicates its status by the form which he gives to it. If a line joins two points and has an arrow head at one end it indicates that the anterior variable is considered as a possible determinant of the posterior (target) variable, and the path coefficient assigned to the line is a standard partial regression coefficient, sometimes called a net regression coefficient. If a line has an arrow head impinging on a posterior variable but has no anterior variable at its back, it stands for the influence of all possible unspecified determinants of the posterior variable, and the path coefficient assigned to it is a residual. More particularly, it is $\sqrt{(1 - R^2)}$ where R is the multiple correlation between the posterior variable and its set of anterior variables. If a line joins two variables but has no arrow head (or, in some diagrams, if it has a head at either end), it indicates the presence of a possible correlation between the two variables, and its associated coefficient is a product-moment correlation coefficient. These three are the only sorts of line which appear in a simple path diagram. The analyst's task is to see that the configuration of his diagram conforms to the logic of the sociological situation which he is picturing, while at the same time ensuring that his data, which are, typically, correlations among the variables in the analysis, are sufficient for the solution of the equations from which the coefficients are to be derived.

An artificial example

The partial regression coefficients and residual coefficients of a path diagram are derived from regression equations. Elsewhere (Hope, 1968) I have illustrated the method of multiple regression by an artificial example which lends itself to representation in a path diagram. This diagram, which stands for a simple psychic economy, is given in

* *Eugen, Q.* (1968), 15, 1–11.

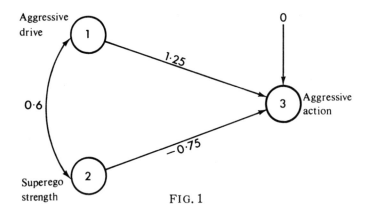

FIG. 1

Table 1

Correlations amond the Three Variables of Figure 1

		1	2	3
1	Aggressive drive	1·0		
2	Superego strength	0·6	1·0	
3	Aggressive action	0·8	0·0	1·0

Figure 1. The correlation matrix from which the coefficients of Figure 1 are derived is shown in Table 1.

The residual coefficient for the posterior variable of Aggressive action is zero because the multiple correlation R is unity. Because the multiple correlation is perfect, a geometrical representation of the relations among the three variables may be drawn on the two-dimensional surface of a sheet of paper (Figure 2). At first sight Figure 2 looks very different from Figure 1, and yet the quantitative information contained in the one is contained, at least implicitly, in the other. The correlation between Superego strength and Aggressive drive is represented by the cosine 0·6 in the path diagram and by the corresponding angle 53° in the vector diagram. The zero residual coefficient of Figure 1 reveals itself in Figure 2 by the fact that the vector of Aggressive action lies in the plane of the other two variables. The path diagram gives regression coefficients explicitly, whereas the vector diagram incorporates the corresponding angles, but either set of coefficients is derivable from the other, given the remaining information in the diagram. The only additional information displayed in the path diagram is the assumed nature of the relationships among the variables.

The contrast between the two diagrams serves to point up the nature of a path diagram. The regression coefficients which are printed on the paths of such a diagram are weights which must be applied to

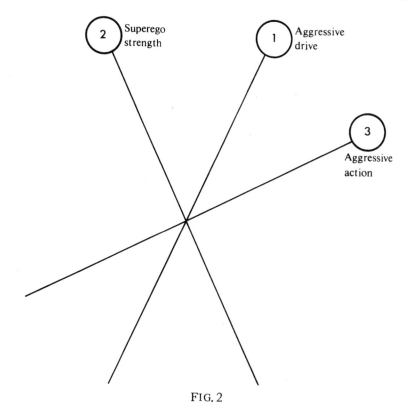

FIG. 2

the standardized values of the anterior variables in deriving an estimated value of the posterior variable. They do not represent strength of
determination in the sence of association or correlation. The weight of
Superego strength in predicting strength of Aggressive action is -0.75,
but the two vectors are at an angle of $90°$, indicating zero correlation
between them.

The difference between a path coefficient and a correlational
measure of association between two variables is that the latter is invariant under change of all other variables whereas the former is not.
Suppose, for example that, instead of Aggressive drive, we were to
measure some other variable which has an angle of $120°$ with Superego
strength and $30°$ with Aggressive action. The path coefficient for
Superego strength would then be $+0.577$, and that for the new variable
would be 1.155. If we think of the analysis as being defined by the geometrical space in which the variables lie then the analysis remains in
all essentials unchanged if, as happens in the example, the substitute
variable lies in the same space as the original variable. The relation
between Superego strength and Aggressive action in the vector diagram

is unchanged by substitution of a new variable for Aggressive drive. Thus a vector diagram has the property of representing the constancies in the relations between variables, whereas the path diagram represents the relativities.

It should not be supposed that these relations between the two types of diagram are dependent on the presence of perfect multiple correlation. If the posterior variable does not itself lie in the space of the anterior variables we may consider the relations between its *projection* in that space and the anterior variables. If we imagine the two anterior variables as diameters of the surface of a circular sundial, the gnomon of the dial represents the posterior variable. When the sun is directly overhead the gnomon casts a shadow on the dial, and this shadow is equivalent to the projection of the posterior variable. The cosine of the angle between the gnomon and its shadow is the multiple correlation coefficient, and it remains unchanged no matter how the anterior variables are rotated in the plane of the dial. So long as there are two non-identical anterior variables, and so long as they lie on the surface of the dial (i.e. so long as the relation between their plane and the posterior variable is constant), the space of the analysis remains constant.

If, in the hypothetical example, Aggressive drive were to rotate out of the plane of the paper until it came to rest at 90° to that plane then, in the course of rotation, the value of the multiple correlation would drop to zero. The angle between Superego strength and Aggressive action would be in no way affected, though the regression weights of both anterior variables would fall to zero. A similar rotation of Superego strength (with Aggressive drive in its original position) would reduce the multiple correlation to the correlation for Aggressive drive alone, and the regression coefficient for that variable would also be 0·8, while that for Superego strength would be zero.

A sociological example

Let us now examine a regression analysis which provides one of the elements of Professor Duncan's path analysis in 'Ability and achievement'. This is the regression of (4) a subject's educational grade on (5) his early intelligence, (6) his number of siblings, (7) his father's education, and (8) his father's occupational status. The path (net regression) coefficients are,

		Path coefficient
5	Early intelligence	0·40
6	Number of siblings	−0·15
7	Father's education	0·16
8	Father's occupation	0·20

The residual coefficient $\sqrt{(1 - R^2)}$ is 0·76. The value of the squared multiple regression coefficient R^2 is 0·42, which tells us that the four anterior variables, acting separately or jointly, account for 42 per cent of the variance of educational grade.

Table 1 of 'Ability and achievement' contains the correlations between variables, and from these it is possible to perform the calculations necessary to the construction of a vector diagram. With four anterior variables the calculations appear more complicated than in the simple two-variable case of the hypothetical example but they are in principle the same.

The four anterior variables lie in a four-dimensional space. By means of principal component analysis (Table 2) it is possible to collapse these four dimensions into three in such a way that 87 per cent

Table 2

Latent Roots and Vectors of Four Background Variables

	Component			
	1	2	3	4
Early Intelligence	0·61	0·53	0·59	−0·03
Number of Siblings	−0·62	−0·46	0·64	−0·04
Father's Education	0·77	−0·39	−0·02	−0·51
Father's Occupation	0·76	−0·40	0·06	0·50
Latent root	1·94	0·80	0·75	0·51
Percentage of variance	48	20	19	13

of the variance is retained. In fact more than 99 per cent of the variance of early intelligence and number of siblings is represented in the reduced space, and about 75 per cent of the variance of each of the other two variables. This three-dimensional space may be pictured on the plane of a sheet of paper by means of a spherical coordinate projection (Figure 3). In this diagram each variable is conceived as a diameter of a sphere like the globe of the earth, and the point where a variable-diameter meets the surface is marked in degrees of longitude and latitude. A minus sign is placed against number of siblings because it is the negative end of this variable which lies on the hemisphere shown in Figure 3. In other words, the correlations between number of siblings and the other three variables are such that those who score high on the other variables tend to have few brothers and sisters.

The projection of the positive end of the posterior variable in this space is also marked in the figure. Like the anterior variables, it projects to some extent into the fourth dimension of the space, but the extent of this projection happens to be negligible. Virtually the whole

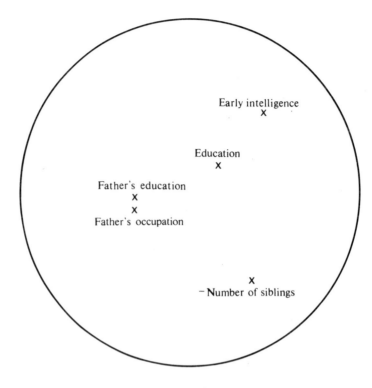

FIG. 3

of the predictable 42 per cent of the variance of educational grade lies in the sphere represented by Figure 3.

The projection of the posterior variable is also to be thought of as a diameter of the three-dimensional sphere of the diagram. As such it makes an angle with each of the four anterior variables at the centre of the sphere. The cosines of these four angles are roughly proportional to the correlations between the four anterior variables and educational grade. The proportionality is strict if all four dimensions are retained.

The sphere may be thought of as having three axes, each axis being a diameter at right angles to the other two. These axes may be identified with the first three principal components of the set of four anterior variables. The first is the diameter which emerges in the very centre of the diagram, where an imaginary Greenwich line crosses an imaginary equator. The second is also on the equator but touches the surface at the extreme easterly horizon, and the third emerges at the North Pole.

The proximity of educational grade to the centre of the diagram shows that the first component is of over-riding importance in predicting educational level. Of the squared multiple correlation of 0·42, 0·38 is due to the first component, and 0·02 to each of components two and three. These values are independent and additive because the components are at right angles to one another. They are, in fact, coefficients of separate determination. The nature of this coefficient is discussed below.

Comparison of the two analyses

A comparison of Figure 3 with Figure 2 reveals an important difference. In Figure 3 the posterior variable lies within a cluster of anterior variables, that is, it is closely associated with one of their principal components (the first). In Figure 2 the first component of the two anterior variables is equidistant from Superego strength and Aggressive drive and runs North-South on the page. The second component is similarly equidistant from both variables and runs East-West. Aggressive action lies at a distinct angle to both these components.

A principal component, whether or not it is the first component, may be regarded as related to the variables from which it is derived as the stock of an umbrella is related to the ribs. But, in general, variables do not form so neat a pattern as do the ribs of an umbrella. Nevertheless, a component has the property of being at a point of equilibrium, such that the pulls exerted upon it by the variables cancel out. In matrix terms it may be defined as a vector $\mathbf{x}$ such that

$$\mathbf{A}x = \lambda\mathbf{x}$$

where $\mathbf{A}$ is the matrix of which it is a latent vector and λ is a scalar constant, This equation does not determine an absolute value for elements of x but only their relative values.

We are now in a position to appreciate the differences between our artificial example and the analysis taken from 'Ability and achievement'. In the latter analysis 90 per cent of the predictable variance of educational grade is attributable to a single component. In the artificial example 20 per cent of the predictable variance of Aggressive action is attributable to the first component and 80 per cent to the second. If the vector, $\mathbf{k}$ say, which consists of correlations between the anterior variables and the posterior variables happens to be identical with a latent vector (any latent vector) of the correlation matrix $\mathbf{A}$ for the anterior variables then we have

$$\mathbf{A}k = \mu\mathbf{k}$$

where μ is a constant. When we calculate path coefficients we invert $\mathbf{A}$ and calculate

$$\mathbf{p} = \mathbf{A}^{-1}\mathbf{k}$$

where $\mathbf{p}$ is a vector of path coefficients (standard partial regression coefficients).

However, it can be shown that the set of latent vectors of $\mathbf{A}$ is identical with the set of latent vectors of $\mathbf{A}^{-1}$. Thus we may write

$$\mathbf{p} = \mathbf{A}^{-1}\mathbf{k} = \nu\mathbf{k}$$

In performing a multiple regression analysis it is customary to calculate the squared multiple correlation as

$$R = \mathbf{k}'\mathbf{p}$$

In the special case we are considering this amounts to calculating a sum of squared correlation coefficients divided by a constant. The elements of the inner product of $\mathbf{k}$ and $\mathbf{p}$ are known as coefficients of separate determination,* and they purport to show how much of the variance of the posterior variable is attributable to each anterior variable. If the anterior variables are uncorrelated with one another then the coefficients are unambiguous. In the analysis in terms of uncorrelated components reported above the value of $R^2 = 0.42$ was broken down into coefficients 0.38, 0.02 and 0.02 for three components, with a coefficient of practically zero for the fourth. If however the anterior variables are correlated with one another then the coefficients of separate determination display some odd properties. It frequently happens, for example, that some coefficients are negative, suggesting that certain variables are detracting from the efficiency of prediction, although we know that this cannot be so.

Path analysis and determination

It is our purpose here to point out, first, that the deficiencies of the coefficient of separate determination are always paralleled by deficiencies of the corresponding path coefficients, and second, that a supplementary method of analysis, accompanied by a modified form of path diagram, may be employed to detect the presence of such deficiencies.

Readers who are not familiar with the method of multiple regression may have been surprised by the occurrence of a regression coefficient exceeding unity in the artificial example. They may also be surprised to see that a variable with a path coefficient of -0.75 can have a coefficient of separate determination of zero. The vectors $\mathbf{k}$, $\mathbf{p}$ and $\mathbf{d}$ (where the elements of $\mathbf{d}$ are coefficients of separate determination) for the example are

	k	p	d
Aggressive drive	0·8	1·25	1·0
Superego strength	0·0	−0·75	0·0
			R^2 1·0

*The nature of these coefficients, and their generalization to the case of several posterior variables, are discussed in chapter 10 of Hope, *Methods of multivariate analysis*.

The vector diagram (Figure 2) makes it clear that the coefficient for Superego strength is zero because Superego strength is at right-angles to Aggressive action.

If **k** and **p** are identical, apart from a constant, then it may be shown (see Appendix A) (a) that no element of **p** can exceed unity, and (b) that each element of **p** has the same sign as the corresponding element of **k**, and so the associated element of **d**, which is the product of the two former elements, cannot be negative. Thus the oddities of path coefficients and coefficients of separate determination disappear when the posterior variable projects into the space of the anterior variables along the line of a principal component of the latter.

In practice, the oddities of coefficients of separate determination are more evident than those of path coefficients because a path coefficient cannot exceed unity unless R^2 is high, whereas a coefficient of separate determination may be negative whatever the value of R^2. When we impugn the behaviour of **p** and **d** we do so from the standpoint of sociologists or demographers who wish to quantify the strength of the relations between several independent variables and a dependent variable. If we consider them purely as regression equations, rather than as guides to the relative importance of variables, we have no reason to prefer a **p** which is proportional to **k** to one which is not.

Path analysts sometimes speak as if the square of a path coefficient were the proportion of the variance of the posterior variable which is attributable to the anterior variable acting alone. This manner of speaking can be very puzzling to the sociologist who is not thoroughly familiar with regression methods, since he may easily find that the sum of squared regression coefficients exceeds R^2, which is the total explicable variance of the posterior variable. It seems probable that this misleading turn of phrase derives from the analysis of a coefficient of separate determination into additive components, one component representing determination by the anterior variable alone, and the other components representing determination which the anterior variable in question shares with other anterior variables.

The analysis of a **d** coefficient into its components may be simply expressed in matrix terms (Hope, 1968). The elements of **p** may be written as the diagonal elements of a diagonal matrix **B**. The matrix **BAB** (where **A** is the correlation matrix of the anterior variables) is a symmetric matrix whose typical element is $p_i p_j r_{ij}$ where r is a correlation between the anterior variables. If $i = j$ we have $p_i p_j r_{ij} = p_i^2$. It is well known (Ezekiel, 1941) that a coefficient of separate determination is the sum of a set of such elements over i or j. Thus the row or column totals of the symmetric matrix **BAB** are coefficients of separate determination, and the diagonal elements p_i^2 may be thought of as the determination which a variable does not share with other variables. This is not by any means the same as saying that $p_i{}^2$ is the proportion of the variance of the posterior variable which is due to i acting alone. $p_i{}^2$ is necessarily positive, but the remaining components of d_i may be positive or negative.

Criterion of interpretation

Having shown the circumstances in which a regression analysis yields unambiguous quantities for insertion in a path diagram we now turn to the modifications in the practice of path analysis which our discussion suggests. Clearly, we need some way of expressing the extent to which, in a particular analysis, the posterior variable is related to the principal components of the anterior variables. The coefficients of separate determination of components* are unambiguous values because the components are uncorrelated with one another. The omission of a component reduces R^2 by the amount of the coefficient of separate determination of the omitted component.

In order to illustrate the proposed modification, Duncan's path diagram has been redrawn in a new form (Figure 4). It is suggested that a diagram of this kind is a useful supplement to the ordinary path diagram, telling us how much credence we should give to the path coefficients of the latter when they are considered as guides to the relative importance (as opposed to the relative weights) of the anterior variables. The paths in Figure 4, which might be called a conjoint path diagram, are identical with those of Duncan's analysis except that the paths from a set of anterior variables always converge and merge before reaching their posterior variable. This proposed convention is intended to imply that we are now considering determination by weighted sums of the anterior variables. These weighted sums are principal components, and the weights for a particular component are elements of a latent vector.

Two numbers appear on each path after the point of juncture. The first is the largest coefficient of separate determination for any of the components of the anterior variables. The second number, which is in brackets, is the sum of the coefficients of separate determination of

---

* It is to be hoped that no confusion will arise from the use of 'component' to stand for an additive part of a d coefficient and its use in the sense of principal component. A principal component may be regarded simply as a variable. The correlations among a set of such variables are all zero, and so the correlation matrix for principal components is the unit matrix. Hence the standard partial regression coefficients for the principal components are equal to the correlations between the components and the posterior variable, and the coefficients of separate determination are the squares of these correlations.

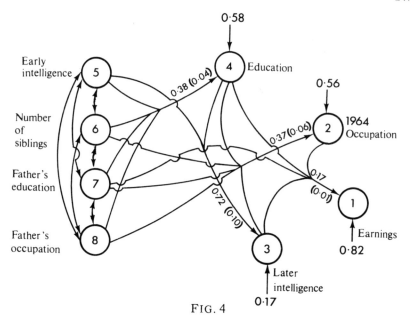

FIG. 4

the remaining components. The residual coefficient of a posterior variable may, as in an ordinary path diagram, be given as $\sqrt{(1 - R^2)}$, or as $1 - R^2$. The latter values have been inserted in the conjoint diagram because it may then be seen that the three numbers on the two paths converging on any posterior variable always sum to unity. In comparing the two sorts of diagram it should be borne in mind that the quantities in the conjoint diagram are numbers taken to the second power. It would, of course, be possible to report the square roots of these quantities. The important thing to note is that, in a conjoint diagram, unlike an ordinary path diagram, the quantities assigned to paths converging onto a variable are proportions of variance, and have the property of summing to unity (apart from rounding errors).

Figure 4 gives a pretty clear indication that the regression analyses of the original path diagram may be taken at their face value, because in every case the posterior variable is almost exclusively associated with a single component of the anterior variables.

The conjoint path diagram has been kept as simple as possible for purposes of exposition. It may, however, be elaborated further if, as happens in this case, a single component prevails over its rivals. The contribution of a variable to the dominant component may be inserted on the path for that variable before it reaches the point of juncture. For example, the squared weights of variables 5, 6, 7 and 8 in the component which links them to education are respectively, $0 \cdot 07$, $-0 \cdot 08$, $0 \cdot 12$, $0 \cdot 11$. These weights are derived from the first latent vector of the four anterior variables (Table 2) by squaring each element of the vector and then adjusting the sum of squares until it equals the coefficient of separate determination for the first component. It is convenient to retain negative signs for squared values. This adjustment has the effect of preserving additivity in the diagram. It can be seen that educational grade is primarily related to a dimension which is virtually a simple sum or average of the four background variables.

Canonical analysis

In this section we suggest a further form of analysis which may help in the interpretation of a path diagram and which is a natural extension of the employment of multiple regression analysis.

In 'Ability and achievement' both occupational status and earnings are posterior to both educational grade and later intelligence. It is possible to envisage several ways in which the two pairs of variables might be related. The correlation between education and intelligence is 0·59, and that between occupation and earnings is 0·39. We might take each pair, analyse its variance into that which is due to the sum of the variables and that which is due to their difference, and ask how the pairs of sums and differences are related.

When there are only two variables on either side of the analysis the relations can be expressed very simply. The first principal component of two positively correlated standardized variables is necessarily their unweighted sum, and the second is an unweighted difference. Two independent dimensions of relationship between the pairs of variables may be isolated by means of a canonical analysis (Appendix B). The first dimension exhibits a sizable canonical correlation of 0·66, and the second yields a negligible correlation of 0·08. The empirical relations between the anterior and the posterior variables appear to be particularly simple. The coefficients of separate determination for the first dimension are 0·39 for the sum of education and intelligence and 0·37 for the sum of occupational prestige and earnings. These two values come close to accounting for all the variance of the dimension which is common to the two sets of variables. The common variance is the square of the canonical correlation, $0·66^2 = 0·43$. The shared dimension accounts for 0·30 of the correlation of 0·59 between education and intelligence, and it accounts for 0·24 of the correlation of 0·39 between occupation and earnings.

Although canonical analyses are often complicated and uninterpretable, this particular analysis is quite straightforward: mean status and pay are determined by mean education and intelligence. The fact that some jobs have low status relative to pay, while others are poorly paid relative to their status, is not explicable in terms of education, intelligence, or discrepancies between the two. Nor, on the other hand, do discrepancies between education and ability serve to explain aspects of occupational level or pay.

This last finding is the more interesting in that the discrepancy between (later) intelligence and education does occur as one of the two dimensions relating these variables to the four background variables. The first canonical correlation of this latter analysis is 0·90 and represents little more than the high correlation between early and later intelligence. The second canonical correlation is 0·41, giving a shared variance (canonical root) of 0·17. The component contributes 0·14 to the common variance. The correlations **k**, path coefficient **p** (elements of the second canonical vector), and coefficients of separate determination **d** for the four background variables in this dimension are,

	k	p	d
Early Intelligence	0·03	0·19	0·01
Number of Siblings	0·23	0·16	0·04
Father's Education	−0·29	−0·18	0·05
Father's Occupation	−0·31	−0·23	0·07
			0·17

The coefficients for the two components of the posterior variables are:

	k	p	d
Later Intelligence + Education	−0·17	−0·17	0·03
Later Intelligence − Education	0·37	0·37	0·14
			0·17

It is evident that the path coefficients of the background variables are not proportional to their correlations with the canonical dimension. This indicates that the relation between the two sets of variables is not identical with any principal component of the background variables. It is therefore inadvisable to attempt to employ the path coefficients as guides to the relative importance of variables in explaining the deviations of education from intellectual ability.

If early intelligence is omitted from the analysis the two canonical roots take the values 0·28 and 0·001, and the component which contrasts later intelligence with education plays virtually no part in the analysis. The second component of any pair of standardized variables necessarily has a variance of $1-r$ where r is the (positive) correlation between them. Thus the variance of the contrast between education and intelligence is $1-0·59 = 0·41$. Whereas all four background variables can explain 0·11, or about one quarter, of this variance, the reduced set (with early intelligence omitted) can explain only 0·01.

The first canonical dimension of the reduced analysis, that is the dimension which has a canonical root of 0·28, is a straightforward association between the first component of the three background variables and the first component of education and later intelligence. The ordinary product-moment correlation between these two first components is in fact 0·50. Here again, about one quarter of the variance of the posterior dimension is explicable by an anterior dimension.

To sum up, socio-economic origin, as measured by three variables, can predict later intellectual level (education plus intelligence) to the extent of about one quarter, and socio-economic origin and intelligence can, to about the same extent, predict divergences between later intelligence and education.

The two canonical analyses which have been reported here for illustrative purposes show that early social factors determine to a modest extent the use which a boy of a given level of intelligence makes of the educational system. But differential usage, over and above that associated with differences in ability, is not a determinant of future occupational level, earnings, or any discrepancy between the two.

Summary

The complexities of regression analyses and polar coordinate projections may, for some readers, have obscured the argument of the first part of this paper, so it will be restated here as baldly as possible.

A path coefficient cannot, in a straightforward sense, be regarded as yielding the square root of the proportion of the variance of a posterior variable explained by an anterior variable. On the contrary, a path coefficient may exceed unity, which would render such an interpretation absurd. The temptation to interpret path coefficients in this way is reinforced by the fact that path coefficients are likely to exceed unity only when the multiple correlation R is high, and this is rarely the case in sociological studies.

The interpretation of the squares of path coefficients in these terms is derivative from the analysis of the coefficient of separate determination into components of the posterior variable's variance accounted for (a) by a single anterior variable (the square of the path coefficient) and (b) jointly by the anterior variable in question and the remaining anterior variables. The coefficient of separate determination is generally regarded with suspicion because it can yield negative results, even though its components purport to be proportions of variance. However, the circumstances in which the coefficient of separate determination tends to be negative are also, and in the same degree, the circumstances in which the regression coefficient can, if R^2 is large enough, exceed unity. These circumstances occur when the projection of the posterior variable in the space of the anterior variables is not identical with any principal axis of that space. When the projection of the posterior variable is identical with an axis of the anterior space then the correlations k and the path coefficients p are proportional to one another, and the coefficients of separate determination d are necessarily non-negative. In these circumstances the zero-order correlation and the partial regression coefficient are both, as it were, telling the same story, and the coefficients of separate determination are a fair representation of the proportions of R^2 attributable to the anterior variables severally. One way of making a quantified statement of the extent to which such a situation prevails is to draw a conjoint path diagram which reports the part of R^2 attributable to the most influential single component in each regression analysis. A reanalysis of Duncan's 'Ability and achievement' diagram shows that it passes this test extremly well.

Three objections might be levelled against the argument of this paper. One is that it is not sensible to accept the conclusions of an analysis simply because two reciprocally-dependent sets of figures tell the same story. A second is that the criterion of interpretability appears to be arbitrary. And a third is that the whole point of resorting to multiple regression is to get away from zero-order correlation in order to arrive at regression weights which may differ from the correlations.

The reply to the last objection has already been hinted at. A vector of weights is unexceptionable for its purpose, but it can be a misleading guide to the dimension which it produces, whereas a zero-order correlation between two variables is invariant because it lies in the space of those two variables and is unaffected by addition or subtraction of other variables. The second objection—that identification of the posterior variable with a principal component is arbitrary—is at first sight cogent. But there appears to be an intuitive parallel between the meaningfulness of quantifying a set of paths in a path diagram and the identification of that set of paths with a principal dimension of the variables at the anterior ends of the paths. Figure I is a path diagram which purports to represent the determination of human action by mental characteristics. The fact that one path coefficient is positive and the other is negative suggests that aggressive action is determined by the balance, rather than by the sum, of aggressive drive and superego strength. But both the image of balance and the concept of summation are inaccurate and misleading. The correlations which are expressed in terms of angles in Figure 2 show that superego strength (or rather its opposite, superego weakness) is not balancing aggressive drive so much as straining it nearer to the posterior variable as if it were a crooked gate-post. The re-analysis of Duncan's data shows that such lines of strain are not present and his path diagram may be taken at its face value.

The reply to the second objection implicitly counters the first. The parallelism between the correlations and the partial regression coefficients is a consequence of the identity between the projection of the posterior variable and a component of the anterior variables. We do not accept the evidence of the two vectors simply because they agree, but because their agreement is a sign that the path diagram is representing a situation in which lines of strain do not occur.

A sociologist has to be extraordinarily skilled and knowledgeable in his field to light upon arrangements of variables which do not exhibit strain.

Appendix A

Proof that if the projection of the posterior variable in the space of the anterior variables is identical with (any) principal component of that space, then no path coefficient can exceed unity unless there is negative overlap among the predictor variables.

If k is a latent vector of A, the correlation matrix of the anterior variables, then we may write $Ak = \lambda k$, where λ is the associated latent root, and also $A^{-1}k = \lambda^{-1}k$. If the vector k consists of correlations between the anterior variables and the posterior variable we write $p = A^{-1}k = \lambda^{-1}k$ for the vector of standard partial regression coefficients.

An element of p can exceed unity only if $\lambda < k_i$ where k_i is the corresponding element of k. The identity $p = \lambda^{-1}k$ shows that elements of p are proportional to, and have the same signs as, elements of k. Thus, writing p_m for the largest element of p, we have $\lambda < k_m$ if $p_m > 1$.

$R^2 = p'k = \lambda^{-1}k'k$, therefore $\lambda = R^2 k'k$. Since $R^2 \leq 1$, λ is less than unity (and hence possibly less than k_m) only if $k'k < R^2$.

We have shown that, if k is a latent vector of A, a path coefficient can exceed unity only if (a) the latent root associated with k is less than unity and, indeed, is less than the element of k corresponding to the path coefficient, and (b) the square of the multiple correlation exceeds the sum of squared correlations between the anterior variables and the posterior variable.

The term 'negative overlap' is sometimes used in reference to an analysis in which $k'k < R^2$. From this inequality, taken together with the equality $R^2 = \lambda^{-1}k'k$ we may deduce that the presence of negative overlap implies that λ is less than unity. The two inequalities are therefore equivalent because either implies the other. We may, therefore, for the special case considered, define negative overlap as association between the posterior variable and a component of the anterior variables which has a latent root less than unity. Whereas the inequality $k'k < R^2$ provides a criterion for detecting the presence of negative overlap, the proposed definition refers explicitly to the relations among the anterior variables which constitute negative overlap.

It may be seen that the occurrence of large path coefficients is a particular case of the general rule that, other things being equal, a dimension with a small variance will be assigned a large regression weight. It has been pointed out elsewhere (Hope, 1968, p. 127n) that one of the advantages of the coefficient of separate determination is that it is unaffected by stretching or contracting the variance of the dimension to which it refers.

Appendix B:

Canonical analysis

For the purposes of this paper multiple regression has been considered as a particular case of canonical analysis in which one of the two sets of variables has only a single member. Furthermore the variables entering into an analysis are sometimes the original variables and sometimes the components of the original variables. In addition, enterprising sociologists may define linear combinations of the original variables which are of interest to them, and explore the relations between these artificial variables and some other set of variables. In the example in the text in which occupation and earnings are related to education and intelligence the principal components of either set happen to be identical with the dimensions which a sociologist would most probably wish to define. When there are more than two variables in a set this happy identity of principal components with dimensions of theoretical interest will not so readily occur.

The posterior variables of a canonical analysis need not be of the same type as the anterior variables. In one of the analyses in the text relations were explored between two components and four original variables.

The data furnished by Professor Duncan consist of a matrix of correlations given to two decimal places. All the calculations of this paper were performed by applying matrix transformations to this correlation matrix. The operations are rather complex and are not particularly illuminating. Their rationale is best explained by reference to columns of 'scores' of persons on components or canonical variates, rather than by a bare recital of operations with weighting vectors. The former type of explanation has been attempted to some extent in Hope 1968.

A canonical variate, like a principal component, may be regarded simply as an artificial variable. Thus it is possible to correlate variables with a canonical variate, considered as an artificial posterior variable, and to express the correlations as elements of a vector k. Indeed, it is the writer's opinion that such correlations should always be examined, since they have the property of invariance which is illustrated in Figure 2. Any canonical variate may be treated simply as a dependent variable in a multiple regression equation and interpreted accordingly. The alleged uninterpretability of many canonical analyses is a consequence of exclusive attention to canonical vectors by workers who have grown accustomed to the interpretation of factor analyses by examination of latent vectors.

It may not be out of place here to pass on a practical hint derived from experience with several types of canonical analysis. In performing an analysis, it is the writer's practice to transform both sets of variables into their principal components, to carry out the canonical analysis in terms of the principal components associated with non-zero latent roots, to report a considerable amount of interpretative material for the components, and then to transform the canonical vectors for components back into canonical vectors for the original variables, and to report interpretative material for the variables. This practice has several advantages: (a) it detects the presence of singularity or near-singularity, (b) it avoids the obstacles arising from singularity by the obvious device of reducing the dimensionality of the space, (c) it enables the user to attempt an interpretation of the particularly simple case of uncorrelated anterior variables (i.e. components), and (d) it enables him to assess the weight which may be placed on the path coefficients. Since both principal components and canonical variates constitute orthogonal sets of variables it is possible to print out geometrical (spherical coordinate) analyses with alternative sets of axes. The Atlas Autocode programme PATH has been written for the production of path analyses.

Consideration of multiple regression as a special case of analysis by canonical correlation leads naturally to a reciprocal analysis in which the variance and covariance of both sets of variables is analysed into that part which is attributable to each of the canonical dimensions in turn, and that part which represents deviation from regression. In a canonical analysis, the proportion of the variance of a particular variable which is explained by all the canonical dimensions is equal to the squared multiple correlation of that variable with the variables of the other set. Thus, in looking at the parts of a variable's variance accounted for by the several dimensions, we are, in effect, allocating proportions of R^2 to the various dimensions. The covariances or correlations between variables may be similarly allocated (as in the example in the text), though it is quite possible for the sum of the explained parts of a correlation to exceed the original correlation

References

DUNCAN, O.D. (1968). Ability and achievement. *Eugen. Q.*, **15**, 1–11.
EZEKIEL, M. (1941). *Methods of correlation analysis*. (2nd edn). Wiley, New York.
HOPE, K. (1968). *Methods of multivariate analysis*. University of London Press.